Criminal Justice

Recent Scholarship

Edited by
Marilyn McShane and Frank P. Williams III

A Series from LFB Scholarly

Violent Youth in Adult Court
The Decertification of Transferred Offenders

Kareem L. Jordan

LFB Scholarly Publishing LLC
New York 2006

Library of Congress Cataloging-in-Publication Data

Jordan, Kareem L., 1978-
Violent youth in adult court : the decertification of transferred offenders / Kareem L. Jordan.
p. cm. -- (Criminal justice recent scholarship)
Includes bibliographical references and index.
ISBN 1-59332-143-0 (alk. paper)
1. Juvenile courts--Pennsylvania. 2. Transfer of cause--Pennsylvania. 3. Juvenile delinquents--Legal status, laws, etc.--Pennsylvania. 4. Violent offenders--Legal status, laws, etc.--Pennsylvania. 5. Violence in children--Pennsylvania. I. Title. II. Series: Criminal justice (LFB Scholarly Publishing LLC)
KFP596.J67 2006
345.748'081--dc22

2005031133

ISBN 1-59332-143-0

Printed on acid-free 250-year-life paper.

Manufactured in the United States of America.

Table of Contents

List of Tables

Acknowledgements

There are several people who I would like to acknowledge for contributing to this book. First, I would like to thank Dave Myers for his help and assistance. He read several drafts of this book, and without him, this final work would not have come to fruition. I would also like to thank Dan Lee, Jamie Martin, and Dennis Giever for their insightful input to this work. It was truly appreciated.

I would also like to thank the Pennsylvania agencies that granted me access to data and the criminal justice professionals who made themselves available for interviews, because without their cooperation, this book would not have been possible. Next, I would like to thank Leo (LFB) for examining several versions of this book and helping me with the much needed formatting. I really appreciate his assistance. Finally, I would like thank my friends and family for their support and patience while this book was being completed; I truly value all of you.

CHAPTER 1

Introduction

At some point during their teenage years, virtually all young people become involved in law violating behavior. Societal reactions to this behavior can vary dramatically, often based on characteristics of the offense and the offender. To illustrate, from the late 1980s through the mid 1990s, American youth violence became a major public concern (Zimring, 1998). Aggregate juvenile violent crime arrest rates increased by more than 60% from 1988 to 1994 (Snyder, 1998), and the murder arrest rate for juveniles rose by more than 100% over this time period (Cook & Laub, 1998; Zimring, 1998). In addition to surges in violent youthful offending, violent victimization of adolescents also increased substantially. It appeared that juveniles not only were becoming more involved in violent acts, but they also were suffering at the hands of their peers. In this context, serious and violent delinquents started to be branded as "super-predators" (Dilulio, 1995, 1996) who were thought to be more dangerous than previous generations of youth, as well as younger when they started exhibiting their violent behavior.

As a result of growing public concern about youth violence, legislatures and juvenile courts responded with a number of "get tough" policies and strategies (Taylor, Fritsch, & Caeti, 2002). For example, more juvenile offenders were sent to detention and correctional facilities, and for lengthier periods of time. The most popular approach, though, was for states to make it easier to "transfer" or "waive" certain youth to adult criminal court (Torbet, Gable, Hurst, Montgomery, and Szymanski, 1996). Although juvenile transfer actually has been in existence since the early 1800s (though unofficially then, as the first juvenile court was not established until 1899), its use traditionally was reserved for small numbers of the most serious and violent offenders. In general, modern waiver laws sought to change and increase the use of this practice, by reducing judicial discretion in juvenile court, enhancing prosecutorial power to file charges directly in adult court, and statutorily excluding certain offenses and offenders from juvenile court jurisdiction. The underlying rationale was that greater use of juvenile transfer, particularly for violent offenders, would boost accountability and punishment, and this would have a beneficial impact on juvenile crime.

Since 1994, violent juvenile crime arrest rates have declined steadily, essentially returning to levels representative of the mid 1980s (Snyder, 2002). Although some policymakers have claimed that these decreases are a result of tougher policies and sanctions, a variety of explanatory factors may have contributed to the drop in youth violence, and in some cases declines in juvenile arrest rates began to occur prior to the implementation of the most highly touted strategies. Despite the questionable impact of harsher laws and penalties on adolescent offending, providing more severe punishments for serious and violent juvenile offenders continues to receive political and public support, and transfer laws enacted during the 1990s remain in place.

All states (and the District of Columbia) now have at least one legal mechanism that allows for youth to be transferred to the adult criminal justice system (Griffin, Torbet, & Szymanski, 1998). The general criteria and procedures for transfer vary across states, but usually a combination of determining factors is considered (e.g., age, prior record, offense seriousness, and amenability to treatment). Contemporary transfer laws have tended to focus on offense seriousness (specifically violent offenses) and prior record, while also lowering the age at which a youth can be waived. With this in mind, prior to the youth violence surge that began in the mid 1980s, property offenders comprised the largest percentage of those waived to criminal court (Bishop & Frazier, 1991; Bishop, Frazier, & Henretta, 1989; Bortner, 1986; Champion, 1989; Gillespie & Norman, 1984). However, with the more recent change in transfer focus, violent offenders now make up the largest group of waived youth (Clarke, 1996; Fritsch, Caeti, & Hemmens, 1996; Kinder, Veneziano, Fichter, & Azuma, 1995; Sickmund, Snyder, & Poe-Yamagata, 1997).

PAST EMPIRICAL RESEARCH

During the past 20 years, as transferring juveniles to adult court grew in popularity, an increasing number of empirical studies also were conducted on this topic. In general, past research can be grouped into three categories. First, a number of studies have examined the factors that potentially determine or predict waiver to the adult system. This body of research has considered the influence of both legal variables (e.g., offense seriousness and prior record) and extralegal factors (e.g., age and race) in the transfer process. Second, a fair amount of research has focused on the case outcomes (e.g., conviction and sentencing) of transferred youth. Third, a relatively small number of studies have assessed the impact of expanded waiver laws on aggregate juvenile crime (i.e., general deterrence) and the effect of transfer on the future criminal behavior of waived youth (i.e., specific deterrence).

Overall, research that has examined the characteristics of waived offenders generally indicates that offense seriousness and prior record are the strongest predictors of the decision to transfer (Barnes & Franz, 1989; Clarke, 1996; Clement, 1997; Fritsch et al., 1996; Houghtalin & Mays, 1991; Keiter, 1973; Kinder et al., 1995; Myers, 2003b). However, extralegal variables also may play a role. Older youths, for example, consistently are found more likely to be waived than younger offenders (Fagan & Deschenes, 1990; Myers, 2003b; Podkopacz & Feld, 1996; Poulos & Orchowsky, 1994). In contrast, the effect of race is widely debated. Most descriptive research finds that nonwhites make up a majority of those who are transferred to adult court (Clarke, 1996; Clement, 1997; Keiter, 1973; Thomas & Bilchik, 1985). However, other multivariate studies have found no direct race effect, while controlling for other explanatory factors (Fagan, 1990; Fagan, Forst, & Vivona, 1987; Podkopacz & Feld, 1996). Some researchers believe that the effect of race on transfer is indirect, affecting court outcomes earlier in the process (e.g., pre-dispositional custody), which in turn may have a subsequent effect on transfer.

In terms of case outcomes, it is generally expected that juvenile transfer will result in harsher sanctions than those typically imposed in the juvenile system. The case outcomes usually addressed by researchers include pre-dispositional custody, conviction, incarceration, incarceration length, and case processing time. There has only been one known study, however, that examined the effect of transfer on pre-dispositional custody (Myers, 2001b; Myers & Kiehl, 2001). The main finding was that transferred offenders were more likely to be released prior to disposition, as compared to similar youth retained in juvenile court. This research suggested an initial "custody gap" resulting from waiver, perhaps due to the bail rights and practices commonly utilized in the adult system. Furthermore, of the released offenders in this study, those who were transferred exhibited greater recidivism than their juvenile court counterparts.

A number of descriptive studies have shown that transferred offenders generally experience high conviction rates (between 60% and 96%) in adult court (Champion, 1989; Gillespie & Norman, 1984; Houghtalin & Mays, 1991; Thomas & Bilchik, 1985). However, because only waived offenders were examined in these studies, there was no way of determining whether the conviction rates were higher than those of similar youth retained in juvenile court. When comparison groups have been used in other research, the findings have been more equivocal. Some research indicates that transferred offenders have a higher rate of conviction than similar retained youth (Eigen, 1981a; Myers, 2003a), while others show that retained offenders have a higher conviction rate (Rudman, Hartstone, Fagan, & Moore, 1986), or that the conviction rate depends upon the offense (i.e., violent versus nonviolent) committed (Fagan, 1995).

Concerning incarceration, much of the descriptive research found that a fairly large percentage (60% to 70%) of the transferred and convicted offenders subsequently were imprisoned (Bishop & Frazier, 1991; Bishop et al., 1989; Houghtalin & Mays, 1991; Thomas & Bilchik, 1985). Comparative studies usually have produced supportive results, suggesting that transferred offenders (particularly those committing violent acts) are more likely to be sentenced to incarceration than are similar retained youth (Fagan, 1995; Myers, 2003a; Podkopacz & Feld, 1996; Rudman et al., 1986). However, some research has indicated that although transferred offenders are more likely to be incarcerated, many of those waived to criminal court end up receiving probation as a sentence. One early descriptive study, for example, found that more transferred offenders were sentenced to probation than were incarcerated (Bortner, 1986).

In addition to a higher likelihood of incarceration, the length of incarceration is normally expected to be greater for transferred youth, as compared to those in the juvenile system. Past research generally supports this finding, with some exceptions. Although some descriptive research has found that a majority of transferred offenders are sentenced to 4 years or less of incarceration (Bishop & Frazier, 1991; Bishop et al., 1989; Clement, 1997; Thomas & Bilchik, 1985), comparative studies (especially those focusing on violent offenders) usually find that transferred youth are sentenced to longer periods of incarceration than are retained offenders (Myers, 2003a; Rudman et al., 1986). Still, other research suggests that there is little difference in sentence lengths imposed by either court (Fagan, 1995). It must also be noted that the research just discussed usually examined the sentences imposed by courts, not actual time served. When actual time served was taken into consideration, one study found that transferred youth served only a small portion of their sentence, also suggesting that waived youth may be incarcerated for equal or shorter lengths of time as compared to similar retained offenders (Fritsch, Caeti, & Hemmens, 1996).

Another aspect of juvenile transfer pertains to case processing time, or the length of time it takes to move a case through the system. This is an issue in both juvenile and adult courts, as it relates to such things as speedy trial rights, the swiftness of punishment imposed, and efficient placement in appropriate treatment and rehabilitation programs. Although relatively few studies have considered case processing time, past research does indicate that transferred offenders experience longer periods of case processing than do similar youth retained in juvenile court (Fagan, 1995; Myers, 2003a; Rudman et al., 1986).

The last major area of transfer research has to do with deterrence. Supporters of this practice often argue that by providing harsher punishment in the adult system, waiver should subsequently deter those who were sanctioned from committing future illegal acts (i.e., specific deterrence). Also, stronger juvenile transfer laws should prevent other potential offenders from committing crime, due to a fear of receiving adult court sanctions (i.e., general deterrence). Somewhat surprisingly, only a small number of studies have examined the effect of transfer on the future offending behavior of waived and retained youth (Bishop, Frazier, Lanza-Kaduce, & Winner, 1996; Fagan, 1995; Myers, 2003b; Podkopacz & Feld, 1996; Winner, Lanza-Kaduce, Bishop, & Frazier, 1997). To date, the findings consistently show that transferred offenders exhibit greater and more serious recidivism, and do so more quickly, than similar youth retained by the juvenile court. Contrary to popular expectations, these results suggest that waiving offenders can increase, rather than decrease, subsequent criminal behavior.

Finally, there only have been a few studies that examined the effect of transfer on aggregate juvenile crime (Jensen & Metsger, 1994; Risler, Sweatman, & Nakerud, 1998; Singer & McDowall, 1988). In general, these researchers attempted to determine if juvenile crime decreased as a result of the implementation or expansion of transfer laws. Again, contrary to popular thought, the findings indicated that the introduction of transfer laws had little or no effect on juvenile crime rates.

The research discussed above suggests that the overall effect and effectiveness of juvenile transfer is debatable. Legal factors tend to be a strong predictor of transfer, but it is not as clear as to whether extralegal factors (e.g., race) also are determinants of the transfer decision. The research also has shown that transferred youth may not always be treated more harshly in the adult system, and sanctioning may be delayed by pre-dispositional release on bail and longer case processing times. Finally, a smaller number of studies have suggested that expanded use of juvenile transfer laws produces little or no general deterrent effect, and that waiver to the adult system actually can amplify (rather than deter) the future illegal behavior of transferred youth.

LIMITATIONS OF PAST RESEARCH

While past empirical research on juvenile transfer has provided quite a few important findings, this body of literature also is limited in several ways. First, a large majority of waiver studies have examined juveniles transferred through judicial waiver, which occurs when a juvenile court judge makes the decision to send a case to adult court (DeFrances & Strom, 1997; Griffin et al., 1998). Much less research has been done on prosecutorial waiver, which in certain cases grants prosecutors the authority to file charges directly in adult court, and hardly any studies have investigated legislative waiver, whereby certain offenses or offenders are statutorily excluded from juvenile court jurisdiction (Howell, 1996; Myers, 2001a). The lack of research on legislative waiver is particularly striking, since this approach became very popular as a response to the increase in juvenile violence from the mid 1980s to the mid 1990s.

Within many legislative waiver laws are provisions for decertification, which allows youth initially transferred to adult court to be "reverse waived" back to juvenile court. To date, there has been only one multivariate study that examined the predictors of decertification, and this research used data from the late 1970s and early 1980s (Singer, 1996). Another study described the characteristics of decertified youth, using data from 1996, but the determinants of decertification were not assessed while controlling for the effects of other possible explanatory factors (Snyder, Sickmund, & Poe-Yamagata, 2000). Therefore, while much empirical research has examined the predictors of transfer to adult court, mainly through judicial waiver, the lack of research on decertification presents a gap in the literature.

Another issue is that most of the earlier research on juvenile transfer produced only descriptive findings concerning waived youth, as comparison groups of similar offenders retained in juvenile court were not employed (see, e.g., Bishop & Frazier, 1991; Bishop et al., 1989; Bortner, 1986; Champion, 1989; Keiter, 1973; Thomas & Bilchik, 1985). Though these studies provided information on the characteristics of transferred offenders and their case outcomes, the lack of comparison groups and multivariate analyses limited the conclusions that could be made. Although more recent research has started to overcome these weaknesses, further comparative studies utilizing appropriate statistical techniques and multiple research methods are needed.

Last, considering that deterrence is a cornerstone of transfer policies, more research is required that examines the impact of waiver on both overall juvenile crime and the future criminal behavior of youths sent to the adult system. Concerning the latter issue, few studies have attempted to determine the effect of juvenile transfer on recidivism (Bishop et al., 1996; Fagan, 1995; Myers, 2001, 2003b; Podkopacz & Feld, 1996; Winner et al., 1997), but the findings to date are not supportive of a specific deterrent effect from waiver. One limitation with most of this research is that short follow-periods were used, meaning that future studies should consider recidivism over a longer term.

PURPOSE OF THE STUDY

The current research sought to add to the existing body of transfer literature in three main ways. First, the decertification process and the predictors of decertification were examined. As mentioned above, much of the existing empirical research focused on factors that potentially impact on transfer to adult court, but very little is known about reverse waiver to juvenile court. Second, decertified youth and offenders retained in adult court were compared in terms of their case outcomes (i.e., conviction, incarceration, incarceration length, and case processing time). Finally, the two groups were compared with regard to their recidivism. This comparative research built on a limited number of previous comparison studies on this topic, and provided further evidence of the effectiveness of juvenile transfer to adult court.

CHAPTER 2

Juvenile Justice and Youth Violence

While transferring juvenile offenders to adult court continues to be a current "hot topic," it is difficult to understand how this strategy has developed without first understanding the history of the juvenile court. The inception of the juvenile court about 100 years ago did not mark the beginning of youth being treated differently from adults. Differences in treatment can be traced back almost four centuries prior to the juvenile court being established. In fact, the treatment of juveniles, as compared to adults, appears to have moved in a cyclical fashion. Juveniles once were treated similarly to adults; they later were treated differently. Based on current policies in addressing juvenile crime, it seems that many juveniles are treated similarly to adults again. Therefore, for many youth, it looks as though society's views of juveniles have come "full circle."

In this chapter, the history of the juvenile court will be discussed. More specifically, the development of the concept of "childhood" will be examined, as children were not always thought of as being different from adults. Following the discussion of "childhood," the next section will examine the process of how the juvenile court came into existence. As a result of the nature of juvenile court operations and procedures during the first half of the 20th century, a series of U.S. Supreme Court cases subsequently influenced the future direction of juvenile courts, including the practice of transferring offenders to adult court. The remainder of the chapter then will examine the increase in violent juvenile crime from the mid 1980s to the mid 1990s, along with society's response. In particular, various juvenile transfer methods will be discussed, and specific practices in the state of Pennsylvania will be considered.

THE DEVELOPMENT OF "CHILDHOOD"

Prior to the 15th century, there was little or no concept of childhood (Bernard, 1992). Although youth were present, their existence generally was not recognized. Young children (under age 6) were given little special attention, mainly due to the high infant mortality rate of the time (Bernard, 1992; Empey, Stafford, & Hay, 1999). Parents often did not get emotionally attached to their children, because they felt as though the likelihood of death at a young age was high. Once children became older and the chance of death decreased, they essentially were treated the same as adults.

Bernard (1992) discussed the onset of two "ideas" of childhood. The first idea emerged near the year 1400. As infant mortality started to decrease, parents began to emotionally bond with their children while they were babies. However, although the likelihood of childhood death was not as high as before, parents continued to be fairly pessimistic about children growing into adulthood. Therefore, they did not make great attempts to "mold" their children, or parent with a goal of allowing them to one day become productive adults.

The second idea of childhood emerged around the year 1600. As infant mortality continued to decrease, teachers and moralists suggested that although children were hedonistic by nature (as were adults), they could be influenced to lead proper lives, if early interventions were used. In other words, it was believed that once children reached adulthood, it would be too late to alter their "evil" tendencies. Therefore, in order to save them from becoming self-serving adults, children should be given direction and discipline (Empey et al., 1999).

Following this second idea of childhood, children were viewed not only as innocent and fragile, but also as potentially corrupt and arrogant (Empey et al., 1999). In order for them to become productive adults, it was thought, they must be physically and morally protected, along with receiving a structured education. At the source of these changes were schoolteachers, moralists, and the church (i.e., Catholics and Protestant reformers). In general, during this time, youth under age 7 were not considered capable of being guilty of crimes. Children between age 7 and 14 were presumed innocent of crimes, but could be punished if juries thought they recognized the nature of their sins. Finally, youth over the age of 14 typically were considered and treated as adults.

ORIGINS OF JUVENILE JUSTICE

By the early 1800s, the Industrial Revolution also started to change the way children were viewed (Taylor et al., 2002). During this era, as people began to move into urban areas to work in factories, children were recruited as employees. As a result of juveniles working long hours alongside adults, reform groups began to take note and question the treatment of the children. Members of these reform groups proposed a new "social conception of law," which meant that the law must change in order to address societal conditions caused by large scale industrialization, urban growth, and mass immigration (Tanenhaus, 2000). From this perspective, societal conditions, not just individual choice, began to be viewed as potential causes of criminal behavior. This view was consistent with the development of positive criminology during the 1800s, which sought to determine the impact of forces (other than free will) on individual behavior (Vold, Bernard, & Snipes, 1998). These developments all contributed to the belief that in order to reduce crime, the law must grant states the necessary powers to address societal conditions (Tanenhaus, 2000).

As a result of this new focus, juveniles began to be viewed as needing "protection," and reforms emerged in an effort to address the new "needs" of youth. In the mid 1820s, Houses of Refuge were implemented in New York, Pennsylvania, and Boston (Howell, 1997). These facilities were designed to take in and care for dependent, neglected, and delinquent children. Supporters of these programs generally believed that needy children could be saved through hard work, education, and religion. Only juveniles who could be "rescued" were to be sent to these institutions, which most often turned out to be poor children of immigrants. The goal was to prevent them from growing up and being like their parents, who were known as "paupers" (Empey et al., 1999). The offenders who were believed to be "unsalvageable" remained in the adult criminal system. Therefore, although juvenile transfer was not officially operating during this time, an unofficial system was in place to keep more serious youthful offenders in the adult system, while less serious cases and poor, non-delinquent children would be housed in a juvenile facility.

Interventions such as the Houses of Refuge were implemented under the doctrine of *parens patriae*, or "state as parent" (Taylor et al., 2002). If adults were found to be either unable or unwilling to properly raise their children, this legal doctrine was used to allow the state to remove children from their households and raise them in place of their parents. Parens patriae originally was used during the 1500s in England (Bernard, 1992). During that time, when a child's parents died, a special court would control the deceased parents' estate until the child could take over at age 21. In essence, the state would act as a "parent" until the age the law specified that children were old enough to take care of themselves.

The doctrine of parens patriae was tested before the Pennsylvania Supreme Court in 1839, in *Ex Parte Crouse* (Bernard, 1992). In this case, Crouse, a poor child who was feared would eventually grow up and become a pauper, was petitioned by her mother to be committed to the Philadelphia House of Refuge. The father attempted to have his daughter released, claiming the commitment was unconstitutional, because no crime occurred and there was no trial. However, the Pennsylvania Supreme Court eventually upheld the doctrine, stating that when a parent cannot properly raise a child, the state has the right to take the place of the parents because they are, in essence, saving the child.

The court raised a number of points in this case (Bernard, 1992). First, the court claimed that Crouse was being helped in the House of Refuge, not punished. Because the House of Refuge was designed to salvage Crouse from pauperism, there was no punishment involved. Second, the court concentrated on the "good intentions" of the House of Refuge and compared them to the "actual performance" of the parents. Because those who worked in the institution were believed to be working in Crouse's best interests, this was viewed more positively than the actual performance of Crouse's parents. Third, the court claimed that the state legally could intervene under the doctrine of parens patriae. Finally, because Crouse was being helped and not punished, the court stated that she did not need the formal procedural safeguards that are granted to those in the adult criminal justice system.

As a result of the Crouse ruling, many more Houses of Refuge emerged throughout the country. However, in the later case of O'Connell v. Turner (1870), the Illinois Supreme Court seemed to reach the opposite opinion than that expressed in Pennsylvania about three decades earlier (Bernard, 1992). In this case, Daniel O'Connell was committed to the Chicago Reform School, because he was in danger of becoming a future pauper as an adult. The Illinois Supreme Court released O'Connell on the grounds that children could not be committed to reform schools in the absence of substantiated criminal conduct. In other words, in the *Crouse* decision, the Court upheld parens patriae in committing a youth who committed no crime, while the *O'Connell* decision rejected the same practice.

There were a number of reasons why the two state courts reached opposite decisions in cases with almost identical circumstances (Bernard, 1992). First, while the *Crouse* court stated that the child was being helped, not punished, the *O'Connell* court claimed that the child was being punished, not helped. By this time, Houses of Refuge were not seen in the positive light they once were. The institutions were becoming overcrowded, children were being sent back home more quickly to their parents, and the number of violent incidents in the facilities was increasing steadily. Second, the *Crouse* court focused on the good intentions of the Houses of Refuge, and compared them to the actual performance of the parents, while the *O'Connell* court took the opposite perspective. The actual performance of the Chicago institution was questionable, given the negative aspects previously mentioned. However, the good intentions of O'Connell's parents were more heavily weighted. Finally, the *O'Connell* court rejected the doctrine of parens patriae as a method for handling juveniles. Because O'Connell was being punished, this doctrine was deemed irrelevant, as he was being denied due process rights.

Despite the O'Connell decision, states continued to intervene in the lives of juveniles. A progressive reform movement soon began in response to the Houses of Refuge and the O'Connell ruling (Platt, 1969). A group of "prominent" women, known as "child savers," began to lobby politicians in Chicago in order to establish a separate system for juveniles; they eventually were successful. This group of women had different views than those who recently worked in the Houses of Refuge, as they appeared more optimistic about reforming youth. They also believed that juvenile facilities often were "training schools" for learning criminal behavior, and that the key to addressing young offenders was to emphasize discipline, hard work, and segregation from adults. Other examples of issues this new movement sought to address were child labor laws, child abuse, poor immigrant children, and runaways. To try to deal with these issues, the child savers initially established centers in urban areas, distributing food, clothing, and providing shelter to homeless juveniles.

An additional explanation for the child savers wanting to establish a separate juvenile system was to protect their own lifestyle (Platt, 1969). The child savers generally were anti-immigrant, not trusting of those who lived in poverty, and wanted others to accept their way of life. They believed that immigrants must assimilate into their culture in order to be productive members of society. Women were allowed to become involved in the child saving movement, due to it being an "extension" of their roles as housewives and mothers. It was as though they were taking an active part in socializing needy children.

With the legal doctrine of parens patriae again guiding the treatment of juveniles, the natural progression was for states to begin setting up separate systems of justice for youth. In the late 1800s, juveniles began to be tried separately from adults in states such as Massachusetts, New York, Indiana, Pennsylvania, and Rhode Island (Taylor et al., 2002). Although juveniles were tried separately in these states, a separate court system for juveniles did not emerge until 1899 in Cook County, Illinois, with the passage of the Illinois Juvenile Court Act. The passage of this act established the first juvenile court in the United States and specified the types of cases for which the new court would have jurisdiction. Specifically, the new act established such things as the age at which a juvenile would be considered an adult (initially set at age 16); the definitions of neglected, delinquent, and dependent children; the utilization of a separate courtroom to handle youth; and different procedures for legally handling these juveniles, as compared to those used in the adult criminal justice system.

Following the passage of the Illinois Juvenile Court Act, similar acts began to emerge in other states (Siegel, Welsh, & Senna, 2003; Taylor et al., 2002). By the mid 1900s, all states had juvenile courts. In general, the juvenile court was to act in a different capacity than the adult criminal court; it was to provide treatment in an attempt to rehabilitate youth, in contrast to the criminal justice system's focus on punishment and incapacitation. In order to rehabilitate juveniles, the court was given wide discretion in methods to be used in addressing these young people.

Although the juvenile court had jurisdiction in cases involving minors, they did not always exercise this jurisdiction (Tanenhaus, 2000). Because early juvenile court judges feared that higher courts might declare the statutes establishing juvenile courts unconstitutional, juvenile court officials sometimes did not assert their jurisdiction in cases in which prosecutors sought to try youths charged with serious offenses in adult court. The juvenile court also did not exercise jurisdictional claims in cases where older children committed crimes while on probation. The rationale was that if probation (while under juvenile court supervision) was not effective when the youth was young, it was not likely to be effective when older. Therefore, the juvenile court's decision not to claim jurisdiction in cases involving both serious offenders and recidivists allowed for "passive transfer." By the juvenile court not aggressively seeking to keep these offenders under its jurisdiction, it basically allowed for them to be transferred to criminal court.

THE DUE PROCESS ERA

By the 1950s, people began to question whether the juvenile court could successfully rehabilitate youth (Snyder & Sickmund, 1999). Although the purpose of rehabilitation was not necessarily in question, many believed that too many youth were being institutionalized in the name of treatment. For instance, many juveniles were committed to facilities for indefinite periods of time for minor offenses. Also, the growing belief during this time was that the juvenile court was not only over-stepping its bounds, but also was denying juveniles their basic legal rights. The court was accused of not giving youth enough procedural safeguards, a practice that had been justified on the basis of parens patriae. In other words, because juvenile courts were implemented to do what was in the "best interests" of the child, it was thought that courts needed to have wide latitude in addressing the "needs" of youth. In response to growing criticisms, however, a series of landmark United States Supreme Court cases originating in the late 1960's sought to change juvenile court practices and procedures.

The first of these cases was *Kent v. United States* (383 U.S. 541, 86 S.Ct. 1045, 1966). Morris Kent (16 years old) was charged with rape and robbery, while he was on probation from a previous case. He confessed to the crimes, as well as other offenses he committed. Kent's attorney, assuming that the District of Columbia's juvenile court would transfer the case to criminal court, requested a hearing on the issue of which court should have jurisdiction. The juvenile court judge did not rule on Kent's motion, but later waived the case to criminal court, stating that a "full investigation" had occurred. Kent later was found guilty in criminal court and sentenced to 30 to 90 years in prison. Kent appealed, and the U.S. Supreme Court eventually ruled the waiver invalid, stating that Kent should have received a hearing that equated to the essentials of due process and fair treatment. In addition, the Court held that Kent's attorney should have had full access to the records involved in the waiver hearing, and that the juvenile court judge needed to provide written reasons to justify transferring the case to criminal court.

The *Kent* case was very significant with regard to juvenile waiver, as the Court required due process in judicial waiver proceedings (Howell, 1997; Vito & Wilson, 1985). Based on this case, hearings must now be held in judicial waiver situations, and youth have a right to counsel at this time. In addition, the juvenile's attorney must be given access to all materials used by the juvenile court judge in making the waiver decision, and a written statement of reasons justifying the transfer must be provided by the judge.

The next landmark case, *In re Gault* (387 U.S. 1, 87 S.Ct. 1428, 1967), was ruled on by the U.S. Supreme Court a year later. This case resulted in juveniles being granted more due process rights when the case outcome could result in incarceration. These rights include the right to notice of the charges, the right to counsel, the right to question witnesses, and protection against self-incrimination. In this case, Gerald Gault (15 years old), while on probation, made a prank phone call to an adult neighbor. During his court hearing, the victim did not attend, and the court actually did not resolve the issue of whether or not Gault made any "obscene" comments. Gault then was sentenced to a training school until age 21. For a similar offense by an adult, the maximum sentence would have been 2 months in jail or a $50 fine. After the hearing, Gault obtained an attorney, stating his constitutional rights were denied.

The Court agreed with Gault, stating that he was being punished (not helped) by the juvenile court, and the doctrine of parens patriae was rejected. The majority opinion held that "juvenile court history has again demonstrated that unbridled discretion, however benevolently motivated, is frequently a poor substitute for principle and procedure" (Snyder & Sickmund, p. 90). The *Gault* case, along with the *Kent* decision, greatly expanded the procedural rights for juveniles that originally were granted only to adults.

The Supreme Court ruled on the next major juvenile case, *In re Winship*, in 1970 (397 U.S. 358, 90 S.Ct. 1068). At that time, many juvenile courts used "by a preponderance of evidence" as the standard for burden of proof. When appealed to the U.S. Supreme Court, the Court found that although juvenile courts were implemented to save (rather than punish) children, they could not use that rationale to require a lesser burden of proof. The Court stated that "reasonable doubt" should be the standard of proof in all adjudicatory hearings. Two years following this case, the Court made its ruling retroactive, meaning all youth who were convicted by a preponderance of the evidence either had to be released from custody or adjudicated again using "beyond a reasonable doubt" as the burden of proof (Bernard, 1992). However, since juveniles had no right to a jury trial, the juvenile court judge alone would make the subjective determination of whether the stronger burden of proof had been met.

The last salient due process case was *Breed v. Jones* (421 U.S. 519, 95 S.Ct. 1779, 1975). In this case, Jones was arrested for an armed robbery in California (Snyder & Sickmund, 1999). He later was adjudicated delinquent in juvenile court on that charge, along with two other robbery charges. At the disposition hearing, the judge decided to waive Jones to adult court. Jones' attorney appealed the case, stating that because Jones already was "tried" in juvenile court for the offense, subsequently trying him for the same crime in adult court would constitute double jeopardy. On appeal, the U.S. Supreme Court agreed with Jones, stating that an adjudication hearing is equivalent to a trial in criminal court, meaning jeopardy attaches at the hearing when evidence is first presented. If a youth is to be transferred to adult court, it must be done prior to evidence being presented at the adjudicatory stage in juvenile court.

Although these cases granted juveniles many of the due process rights given to adults, not all procedural rights were granted. In McKiever v. Pennsylvania (403 U.S. 528, 91 S.Ct. 1976, 1971), the Court stated that juveniles were not constitutionally entitled to a jury trial. Also, in Schall v. Martin (467 U.S. 253, 104 S.Ct. 2403, 1984), the Court maintained that juveniles were not entitled to bail, meaning preventive detention was permissible. However, aside from these two cases, the Supreme Court's decisions appeared to change the original purpose of the juvenile court, by focusing more on formal procedures.

CONTEMPORARY YOUTH VIOLENCE AND SOCIETY'S RESPONSE

The due process cases of the late 1960s and early 1970s coincided with a substantial increase in juvenile crime (Tanenhaus, 2000). This increase can be at least partially explained by the number of adolescents in the general population at this time. Following World War II, there was a large increase in the number of babies born (Myers, 2001b). It also has been shown empirically that the most crime prone years occur during mid to late adolescence, after which offending declines (Blumstein, 1995). Therefore, during the late 1960s and early 1970s, the "baby-boomers" were approaching and in their peak years of involvement in delinquent and criminal behavior, which undoubtedly contributed to the overall increase in juvenile crime.

In addition, by this time many people were losing faith in rehabilitation, and calls were being made for "just deserts" for juvenile offenders. The traditional belief in rehabilitation was challenged based on research suggesting that "nothing works" (Lipton, Martinson, & Wilks, 1975; Martinson, 1974). Consequently, due to the increase in juvenile crime and the loss of faith in rehabilitation, it was believed by some that the juvenile court no longer was able to handle many youthful offenders. In order to remain consistent with the new focus of "just deserts," the juvenile court began to stiffen the penalties for offenders, including mandatory minimums and determinant sentencing, as well as transferring more offenders to criminal court (Taylor et al., 2002).

From the mid 1970s through the mid 1980s, juvenile crime rates remained relatively stable (Cook & Laub, 1998). However, beginning in 1985 and lasting until 1994, juvenile arrests for violent offenses increased dramatically (Snyder & Sickmund, 1999; Torbet & Szymanski, 1998). The overall rate of juveniles arrested for violent crimes rose by over 70% during the span of a decade. By 1994, juveniles constituted approximately one in six arrests for homicide, rape, and aggravated assault. Juveniles also made up about one-third of the robbery arrests in the country.

When examining these trends as a whole, it appears that there was a tremendous increase in overall violent juvenile offending. However, most noteworthy was the increase in criminal homicides committed by youth (Cook & Laub, 1998; Zimring, 1998). Until this time, the percentage of juvenile arrests for all homicides committed was approximately 10%. However, beginning in the mid 1980s, this percentage started to increase, peaking in 1994 at 17%. Also, the increase in juvenile arrests for homicide far exceeded a slight rise in arrest rates for homicide committed by adults.

In contrast to the increase in violent juvenile crime, juvenile property crime arrest rates remained steady or decreased during the same time period (Cook & Laub, 1998). Although more juveniles still were being arrested for property crime as compared to violent crime, property crime arrest rates did not follow the same upward trend. However, due to the increase in juvenile violent crime, and media sensationalism of violent events committed by young people, many juveniles were thought to be extremely dangerous and generally were branded as "super-predators" (Cook & Laub, 1998).

There are two major explanations that have been presented to explain the surge in youth violence. The first focuses on a corresponding increase in the availability of handguns (Cook & Laub, 1998). Due to the popularity of crack cocaine during this time period, many of those working in drug markets carried handguns for protection from others in the "business." In addition, even juveniles who were not involved in drug dealing were more likely to carry handguns in public, due to a fear of violence. In effect, there were simply more young people carrying guns in society. As a reflection of this phenomenon, Cook & Laub (1998) discussed how non-gun homicides committed by male juveniles and young adults (aged 13 to 17 and 18-24) remained stable from 1976 to 1994. However, gun homicides committed by male youth increased dramatically. Therefore, it is likely that the increase in juvenile violence was related to handgun prevalence and usage.

A second explanation used to explain the increase in violent juvenile arrests concerns the children of the baby-boomers (Myers, 2001b). As previously discussed, following World War II, there was a large increase in the number of babies born. Also, as previously mentioned, the most crime prone years occur during mid to late adolescence, after which offending decreases (Blumstein, 1995). During the mid 1980s, children of the baby-boomers were starting to enter adolescence, meaning they were approaching their peak years of criminal involvement. This increase in the adolescent population likely contributed to the increase in arrests for violent behavior.

Regardless of whether the increase in violent juvenile crime was due to the availability of handguns, the children of baby-boomers, or other factors, society reacted harshly by "cracking down" and "getting tough" on juvenile crime through a variety of legislative responses (Zimring, 1998). The new approach was reflected in legislation passed by Congress in 1996, known as the Balanced Juvenile Justice and Crime Prevention Act (Taylor et al., 2002). This law embraced the changing assumptions about juvenile crime and sought to increase accountability on the part of offenders. The Act mentioned such issues as the increase in the frequency and severity of violent juvenile crime; that penalties imposed by the juvenile court had not succeeded in reducing violent crime; and that prosecutors should be allowed to handle serious and violent juvenile offenders as adults. Although the Act addressed a variety of issues, the purpose of the law was quite clear: juvenile crime should be addressed in a more punitive manner than done previously.

Many states subsequently passed legislation consistent with the Balanced Juvenile Justice and Crime Prevention Act of 1996 (Taylor et al., 2002). More juvenile offenders began to be sent to detention centers, correctional facilities, and training schools. The most dramatic response many states took was to pass legislation that made it easier to transfer serious and violent juvenile offenders to adult court. As discussed in this chapter, juvenile transfer has been around since even before the juvenile court's inception. However, as a result of state legislatures responding punitively to the youth violence epidemic of the mid 1980s to mid 1990s, all but six states either expanded or implemented laws that sought to increase the number of juvenile offenders waived to adult criminal court (Snyder & Sickmund, 1999). This was done in an effort to increase accountability for juveniles, along with a focus on deterrence and incapacitation.

TRANSFER METHODS AND PROCEDURES

Overall, there are three basic methods that allow for youth to be waived to adult criminal court: judicial waiver, prosecutorial waiver, and legislative waiver (Myers, 2001b). All states have at least one of these mechanisms in place, and there also are variations of these methods that various states employ. Through these strategies, it generally is believed that serious and violent offenders will be removed from the jurisdiction of the juvenile court and tried in adult criminal court. In addition, two additional provisions that are associated with juvenile waiver in some states will be examined in this section: reverse waiver and "once and adult, always an adult." Finally, considering Pennsylvania is the site for this research, this section will describe not only the current transfer practices in the state, but also how they have changed in recent times.

Judicial Waiver

Under judicial waiver, the juvenile court judge makes the decision to transfer a case to adult court (Myers, 2001b). Historically, this method has been the most commonly used. Although this is one basic type of transfer, there are three categories of procedures that fall under this method: discretionary, presumptive, and mandatory waiver (Griffin et al., 1998). When using discretionary waiver, a juvenile court judge alone makes the decision on whether a case should be tried in juvenile court or whether it should be transferred to criminal court. Forty-six states, along with the District of Columbia, allow for discretionary waivers as a method of transfer. Theoretically, in order for a judge to transfer a case to adult court, the youth must be deemed to be no longer amenable to the treatment provided in the juvenile system. Some of the basic transfer criteria to be considered by judges include age, prior record, and offense seriousness, which were identified as a result of the previously discussed *Kent* case.

The next two variations of judicial waiver are relatively recent techniques and were designed to reduce the discretion associated with judicial waiver. To begin, 15 states currently have presumptive waiver provisions (Griffin et al., 1998). Under this procedure, state law classifies a certain category of cases (based on criteria such as age of offender and current offense) as being appropriate for transfer. As opposed to discretionary waiver, in which the state has the burden of proof to show that the case should be transferred to adult court, the burden for presumptive waiver cases rests with the juvenile and defense counsel. If the youth and counsel fail to show that the case belongs in juvenile court, the juvenile court judge is directed to transfer the case to the adult system.

The last type of judicial waiver is mandatory waiver. This method specifies that juvenile offenders who meet certain criteria (e.g., age and current offense) are to be transferred automatically to adult court by a juvenile judge (Griffin et al., 1998). Currently, 14 states have provisions for mandatory waiver. Although court proceedings in these cases are initiated in the juvenile justice system, the role of the judge is simply to confirm that the waiver criteria are met, and then transfer the case to criminal court. In other words, mandatory waiver attempts to remove all discretion from the juvenile court judge in the transfer process.

During the surge in juvenile violence from the mid 1980s until the mid 1990s, offenders judicially waived to adult court also increased (Bishop, 2000). From 1985 to 1994, the number of cases judicially waived nationwide rose from 7,200 to 12,300. However, this increase in transferred cases also coincided with an overall increase in cases processed by the juvenile court. Therefore, although more offenders were being judicially waived to adult court, the rate at which cases were being judicially waived did not grow substantially. In 1986 (around the time when the youth violence epidemic began), the percentage of cases judicially waived to criminal court was 1.3% (Bishop, 2000; Bishop & Frazier, 2000). Similarly, in 1994, the percentage of cases judicially waived was 1.4%.

The type of offender being judicially waived to adult court did change as a result of the increase in youth violence. Prior to the juvenile violence epidemic, more offenders were transferred for property offenses than person offenses (Bishop, 2000). However, since 1993, the reverse has occurred, as more offenders have been transferred for person offenses than property offenses. As violent offenses increased, most notably aggravated assault, robbery, and murder, and as society wanted to "get tough" on these offenders, the result was transfer becoming a more likely outcome. At the same time youth violence was increasing, juvenile property crime was decreasing or holding steady, resulting in property offenders being transferred at a lower rate.

Prosecutorial Waiver

The second method of transfer is prosecutorial waiver, also referred to as concurrent jurisdiction (Feld, 1998; Myers, 2001b). Under this method, both the juvenile court and the criminal justice system initially have jurisdiction over the case. The district attorney makes the key decision as to in which court to prosecute the case, within the boundaries set by state law.

Currently, 15 states allow for prosecutorial waivers (Griffin et al., 1998). There is wide variation among states regarding the criteria used by prosecutors as a basis for filing charges directly in adult court. Some of the criteria again include age of the offender, offense seriousness, and prior record. Although there is not much literature available on the use of this particular procedure, the data that are available suggest that an increase in cases waived through this method occurred during the 1980s. In Florida, during the early 1980s, about 1% of all juvenile cases were transferred by prosecutors, but that percentage rose to 7.35% in 1987 (Bishop & Frazier, 1991). Over half of the offenders transferred were charged with property offenses, while less than one-third were charged with person offenses. This finding is consistent with the offense characteristics of judicially waived offenders during the same time period.

This method is the least used of the three, but nevertheless the most controversial. Historically, state legislatures have defined which offenses are not "worthy" of juvenile court jurisdiction, or they left the decision to the "expertise" of a juvenile court judge. Moreover, prosecutorial waiver is susceptible to several criticisms. Because of their status as elected "crime control' officials, some believe that prosecutors may transfer too many offenders who are likely to "age out" of criminal behavior, and others who actually are amenable to the treatment of the juvenile court (Bishop & Frazier, 1991). In turn, this may lead to these youth having negative experiences in the adult system (including a lack of rehabilitation), resulting in an increased likelihood of future offending. Others believe that prosecutorial waiver greatly contradicts the original philosophy of the juvenile court (based on parens patriae), and that prosecutors may be too concerned with retribution, rather than rehabilitation. The use of this type of waiver does reflect the shift in views from rehabilitation to retribution and deterrence, and to some, it endangers the existence of the juvenile justice system.

Legislative Waiver

The last major method of transferring juveniles to criminal court is legislative waiver, also know as statutory exclusion (Feld, 1998; Myers, 2001b). Here, state legislation automatically excludes certain youthful offenders from the jurisdiction of the juvenile court. Typically, juveniles of a certain age, who commit a certain type of crime, are excluded from juvenile court jurisdiction and are sent automatically to the adult criminal justice system.

Currently, 36 states and the District of Columbia have legislative waiver statutes in place (Feld, 1998; Feld, 2000). Because state legislatures create juvenile courts, they also can pass laws that set the criteria to determine what offenses fall under the jurisdiction of those courts. It then follows that legislatures can determine the offenses that cannot come under the juvenile court's jurisdiction, which would result in cases being automatically transferred to adult court.

This method of waiver appears to challenge most directly the original goal of the juvenile court, which was to protect and rehabilitate youth. In its early days, transfer was used on a limited basis, via judicial waiver. The juvenile court was to focus on the offender, not the offense. In modern times, by excluding certain offenders from the jurisdiction of the juvenile court (based on such attributes as age and offense seriousness) the focus is more on retribution and less on rehabilitation (Feld, 1998; Feld, 2000). Traditionally, most of the offenses that excluded mainly older offenders from juvenile court were very serious crimes, such as murder, rape, and armed robbery. However, beginning in the early 1990s, many states expanded the list of excluded offenses to include less serious crimes, and these states also lowered the minimum age for offenders to be automatically waived. This shift was consistent with the panic of those in society who believed that many youth were exhibiting dangerous behaviors at younger ages.

Reverse Waiver

Reverse waiver is a provision that can be used with each of the three basic methods of transfer, particularly those other than discretionary judicial waiver (DeFrances & Strom, 1997; Griffin et al., 1998).

Twenty-three states currently have mechanisms in place whereby juveniles who initially are waived to criminal court can have their cases transferred back to juvenile court, a process also known as decertification. The decision to transfer a case back to juvenile court normally is made by a criminal court judge because, at that time, the case is in adult court. When decertification hearings are held, criminal court judges generally are guided by similar criteria used by juvenile court judges when they decide whether to transfer a case to criminal court (e.g., amenability to treatment, age, offense seriousness, and prior record). If the criminal court judge decides that the offender is better served by, or the case is more appropriate for, juvenile court processing, the case likely will be decertified to juvenile court. Conversely, if the offender appears beyond benefiting from the treatment of the juvenile court, the judge is not likely to decertify the case, resulting in the offender being retained in adult court. In addition, in some states, offenders can be found guilty in adult court, and then transferred to the juvenile system for disposition and sanctioning.

Once an Adult, Always an Adult

Finally, 31 states have provisions that automatically transfer juvenile offenders to the adult system if they previously were convicted of an offense in criminal court (Griffin et al., 1998). Ordinarily, juveniles would have to be transferred through one of the three basic methods discussed above, but "once an adult, always an adult" provisions sidestep these provisions altogether. In other words, if a youth is convicted in adult court, every crime prosecuted thereafter will be tried automatically in criminal court, regardless of such factors as age and offense type.

There are variations in this practice across jurisdictions. Most states (but not all), do require a conviction in adult court in order for the "once an adult, always an adult" procedure to take place (Griffin et al., 1998). If juvenile offenders are not convicted in adult court, this provision would not apply, and they would have to be transferred subsequently through other waiver processes. However, a small number of states consider juveniles an "adult" if they already were declared not to be amenable to the treatment of the juvenile court, by either a juvenile court judge or a criminal court judge (in reverse waiver hearings). Therefore, in these states, conviction in criminal court is not required for "once an adult, always an adult" to apply. The rationale is that since these offenders were already deemed to be unfit for the treatment provided by the juvenile system, they no longer are afforded the opportunity to benefit from that treatment, resulting in automatic transfer to the adult system.

Last, there is one other variation of this procedure. Three states require subsequent crimes to be a felony in order for this provision to be applicable (Griffin et al., 1998). If the future crime is anything less than a felony, the case would have to be transferred through one of the three basic methods previously discussed. However, if the new offense is a felony, the case automatically will be tried in adult court.

JUVENILE TRANSFER IN PENNSYLVANIA

Although general juvenile transfer practices were just discussed, no reference was made to specific states. This is due to the wide variation in state procedures regarding juvenile waiver. With regard to the present study, though, three counties in Pennsylvania will be used as research sites. This being the case, Pennsylvania's transfer policies now will be examined, including both the current practices and how the process has changed in recent times.

Prior to 1996 in Pennsylvania, virtually all transfer cases originated from juvenile court (Lemmon, Sontheimer, & Saylor, 1991; Snyder et al., 2000). The only exception was for the charge of murder, which was excluded from the jurisdiction of the juvenile court and automatically sent to adult court. At this time, judicial waiver was the main mechanism for transfer. For the vast majority of cases, the juvenile court judge had discretion in deciding which cases to waive to criminal court, based on certain specified criteria.

The minimum criteria that had to be met were specified in accordance with the standards set forth in the *Kent* case (Lemmon et al., 1991; Snyder et al., 2000). First, the juvenile had to be at least 14 years old when the offense was committed. Second, the crime must have been a felony. Third, a *prima facie* case had to be made, meaning that there was sufficient evidence that the defendant committed the alleged offense. Fourth, the court needed to determine that the youth was not mentally ill. Finally, the youth had to be reasonably viewed as not amenable to treatment in the juvenile justice system. In determining amenability to treatment, many factors could be considered, including age, prior record, criminal sophistication, mental illness, and circumstances surrounding the current offense. In addition, transfer also could occur through the request of the juvenile.

During the mid-1990s, a major change occurred regarding Pennsylvania's handling of juvenile offenders. Similar to other states, Pennsylvania "cracked down" as a result of the dramatic increase in youth violence that spanned almost a decade (Torbet et al., 1996). In doing so, Pennsylvania redefined the purpose of juvenile justice interventions in its Juvenile Act. Prior to 1996, the focus was on a youth's condition, not on the behavior or offense. The court was to focus on treating and rehabilitating offenders, because that would be in their best interests. As part of the overall "redefinition," the purpose of the juvenile court became the following:

> Consistent with the protection of the public interest, to provide for children committing delinquent acts programs of supervision, care and rehabilitation which provide balanced attention to the protection of the community, the imposition of accountability for offenses committed and the development of competencies to enable children to become responsible and productive members of the community. (Pennsylvania Juvenile Court Judges' Commission, 1996, p. 1)

Although this definition mentions rehabilitation, it cannot be ignored that it also stresses "protection of the community" and "accountability for offenses." As a result of this new focus, many changes occurred regarding the handling of juvenile offenders, including the dissemination of fingerprints by law enforcement agencies and public court proceedings for certain felony cases (Torbet et al., 1996). The most controversial and high profile change came from Act 33, which was state legislation passed that automatically excluded certain violent youthful offenders from the jurisdiction of the juvenile court, resulting in them being transferred to adult court (Merlo, Benekos, & Cook, 1997; Snyder et al., 2000).

As mentioned above, prior to 1996, only youth charged with murder were automatically excluded from juvenile court. Act 33, which went into effect in March 1996, excluded many more offenses (in combination with other criteria) from the category of "delinquent acts." Those committing the specified offenses and meeting certain other criteria essentially bypass the juvenile justice system (since no delinquent act was committed) and are transferred automatically to the adult criminal system (Pennsylvania Juvenile Court Judges'

Commission, 1996; Snyder et al., 2000). First, except in the case of murder, the juvenile must be at least age 15 at the time of the offense. Second, the offender must be charged with a violent crime (i.e., rape, involuntary deviant sexual intercourse, aggravated assault, aggravated indecent assault, robbery, robbery of a motor vehicle, voluntary manslaughter, kidnapping, or an attempt, conspiracy, or solicitation to commit any of these crimes). Third, the youth must have either used a deadly weapon in the offense, or must have been previously adjudicated for an excluded offense (the offense of aggravated assault was not included in the repeat offender clause).

While previously only juveniles charged with murder were automatically transferred, Act 33 statutorily waived many more youth, based largely on the nature of the offense committed. Whereas juvenile court judges once had discretion regarding almost all transfer cases, based to a great extent on the issue of amenability to treatment, the new state law eliminated amenability to treatment as a consideration in sending an offender to adult court. Discretionary judicial waiver is still allowed, however, for cases that fall outside Act 33.

Finally, there is a mechanism in place for offenders who initially are waived under Act 33 to be transferred back (i.e., reverse waived or decertified) to juvenile court (Snyder et al., 2000). A juvenile can request a hearing, through a petition, to have the case considered for decertification. The burden is on the juvenile to establish, by a preponderance of the evidence, that decertification will serve the "public interest" (Pennsylvania Juvenile Court Judges' Commission, 1996). In considering this issue, criminal court judges generally can use similar criteria that juvenile court judges utilize in making a judicial waiver decision (e.g., age and amenability to treatment). If the case is decertified, it is then processed in juvenile court. If the case is not decertified, it remains in adult court. Therefore, although Act 33 greatly increases the offenses excluded from juvenile court in Pennsylvania, offenders still have the opportunity to have their cases tried in juvenile court as a result of the decertification process.

CONCLUSION

The juvenile court has been marked with many changes in its history. Its beginning focus was to be on the treatment and rehabilitation of young offenders. However, due to a number of factors, the focus of the juvenile court has shifted at least somewhat from treatment and rehabilitation to retribution, deterrence, and incapacitation. Contributing factors in this movement have been the unfair treatment of youth in the juvenile justice system, U.S. Supreme Court decisions, a lack of faith in rehabilitation, and an increase in violent juvenile crime. Although a variety of reforms occurred as a result of this shift, the most popular contemporary change involved transferring young offenders to adult court.

The practice of juveniles being placed into the adult system can be traced to prior to the creation of the juvenile court. However, since the juvenile court's inception, and due to the factors discussed in this chapter, juvenile waiver became a popular approach to handling youth charged with serious and violent offenses. Although there are different methods of transferring offenders to criminal court, the method that is most associated with the punitive response to violent juvenile crime is legislative waiver, due to the exclusion of more violent offenses from the jurisdiction of the juvenile court and the expectation of harsher punishment in the adult system.

By the mid 1990s, virtually all states made it easier to transfer juvenile offenders to adult court, in response to the increase in violent juvenile crime. In general, it was believed that these types of laws would have a deterrent effect on juvenile offending. In addition to deterrence, transfer laws were expanded because of a shift in perspective from rehabilitation to accountability and incapacitation.

CHAPTER 3

Analyzing Juvenile Transfer

Transferring juvenile offenders to adult court generally is thought to be done in an effort to provide harsher treatment than is available in the juvenile justice system. As discussed in the previous chapter, juvenile waiver became popular as a result of society believing that the juvenile court was not "equipped" to handle serious youthful offenders (Bishop, 2000). Although the practice of transferring these offenders has been in existence for some time, it gained momentum as a result of the sharp increase in violent juvenile crime that began in the mid-1980s. Transfer laws then were expanded, making it easier to waive juvenile offenders to adult court.

The purpose of this chapter is to review the research that has examined juvenile transfer, in order to consider if these laws are effective in meeting their goals. Specifically, the predictors of transfer are discussed, to identify the factors that determine which cases get transferred to criminal court. Also, the impact of transfer on pre-dispositional custody is examined. Because juveniles in adult court are entitled to bail, they actually may be more likely to be released from pre-dispositional custody, as compared to similar retained offenders. This chapter also discusses such issues as the likelihood of conviction for transferred offenders, along with the likelihood of incarceration and sentence lengths commonly imposed by the criminal court. When possible, comparisons are made with similar offenders in juvenile court, in order to determine if waived offenders are treated more harshly than retained youth. The effect of transfer on case processing time is also considered. Finally, this chapter assesses the deterrent effects of transfer. Here, the impact of transfer on recidivism (i.e., specific deterrence) and whether transferring juveniles to adult court reduces overall juvenile crime (i.e., general deterrence) is explored.

PREDICTORS OF TRANSFER

In transferring juveniles to adult court, legal factors (i.e., offense seriousness and prior record) would seem most important in guiding the transfer decision. As discussed in Chapter 2, when the juvenile court first emerged in 1899, juvenile court judges often did not contest jurisdiction in cases in which the juvenile could be charged as an adult (Tanenhaus, 2000). These judges sometimes "passively" allowed juvenile offenders who were charged with serious crimes to be tried in the adult criminal justice system. The juvenile court usually exercised jurisdiction over cases in which less serious acts were committed. Modern transfer laws also suggest that the more serious the offense and the offender, the greater the likelihood of transfer should be.

However, other factors in the transfer decision also have been empirically assessed. When extra-legal factors (e.g., race) are considered, many people have questioned whether discrimination is involved in the decision to waive offenders to criminal court. This section, then, will discuss the research that has attempted to determine the impact of both legal and extra-legal factors on the transfer decision.

Descriptive Studies

In examining the following descriptive studies, it must be remembered that they focus on only one group: transferred offenders. These studies simply describe the characteristics of offenders who are waived to adult court; there is no comparison group of youth retained by the juvenile court employed. Therefore, it actually is not possible to conclude which factors are having an impact on the transfer decision, because only transferred offenders are considered. Even though some of these studies attempt to draw various conclusions about which factors seem to predict transfer, the lack of comparison groups and appropriate multivariate analyses allows for the possibility that other factors could explain away any presumed relationships.

To begin, in Keiter's (1973) early study of cases transferred to criminal court in Illinois during 1970 (n=64), 69% of all waived cases involved homicide charges. Furthermore, 95% of the transferred cases were for murder and other violent offenses (i.e., rape, aggravated assault, armed robbery, and attempted murder). Along with offense seriousness, gender also seemed to play a role, as all of those who were waived were male. Finally, those transferred were virtually all nonwhite. Of the 64 offenders transferred, 59 were black, 3 were Puerto Rican, and 2 were white.

At face value, the finding regarding the race of offenders hints at racial discrimination. Furthermore, the only two offenders who were white also had more serious prior records than did those who were nonwhite. This could suggest that for white offenders to be transferred, it takes a more serious prior record than it does for nonwhite offenders.

In a subsequent study of juveniles transferred to adult court in Utah from 1967 to 1980 (n = 132), contrasting results were found regarding offense seriousness (Gillespie & Norman, 1984). The findings were that property offenders represented 38% of those transferred, while person offenses represented only 25%. Offenders who committed crimes against both persons and property comprised another 22% of the cases. Crimes against public order made up 5% of the cases, and the remaining offenders (10%) committed "other" crimes. These findings indicate that property and other nonviolent offenders were transferred more frequently than those charged with person offenses.

The results regarding offense seriousness in this study are consistent with trends in transfer during the time period. Although it currently would be expected that the more serious the offense committed, the greater the likelihood of transfer, prior to the increase in youth violence from the mid 1980s to the mid 1990s, property offenders were transferred at a higher rate than those who committed person offenses (Bishop, 2000). Therefore, it is likely that individual studies that used data from prior to the youth violence surge would find that many (or most) of those transferred committed property and other nonviolent crimes.

Another descriptive study from the 1980s examined juvenile transfer in Dade County, Florida (Thomas & Bilchik, 1985). All cases that were transferred to adult court and processed by the Felony Division in 1981 were included in the research (n = 844). Most of those transferred were either 16 or 17 years old (no numerical breakdowns were given), indicating that older juveniles were more likely to be transferred than younger offenders. Another finding was that most of those transferred were nonwhite (68%). This again could lead one to believe that minority offenders are more likely to be transferred than whites, suggesting some form of discrimination.

In addition, a majority of the youths were charged with either burglary or some form of robbery. Most of the offenders (approximately 60%) had a record of prior offenses, suggesting that those with a prior record were more likely to be waived than those with no offending history. These adolescents may have been seen as less amenable to the treatment of the juvenile court, making them more likely to be transferred.

Other research findings from this time period are consistent regarding the apparent relationship between certain factors (e.g., age and offense type) and transfer. Bortner's (1986) study examined 214 juveniles who were waived to criminal court in a western metropolitan county during 1980 and 1981. The results indicated that 85.5% of those transferred were 17 years old, again suggesting that older offenders are more likely to be transferred than younger offenders. In addition, this research found that 62% of the transferred juveniles were charged with property felonies. This supports the notion that transfer practices at this time actually were capturing many nonviolent offenders, which is opposite of the intent of most modern laws.

Champion (1989) found similar results in examining the use of juvenile transfer from 1980 to 1988 in four states: Tennessee, Virginia, Mississippi, and Georgia (n = 2,818 total waivers). The results actually showed a trend toward an increase in transfer use for less serious property offenders, while there was a decrease for violent offenders. For instance, 42% of those transferred in 1980 were charged with homicide, while the same charge characterized only 31% of those waived in 1988. Offenders who committed robbery in 1980 comprised 20% of the transferred cases, but these offenders comprised only 8% in 1988. Conversely, juveniles who committed vehicular theft characterized 6% of the transferred youth in 1980, while the same type of offenders represented 17% of those transferred in 1988.

Another study examined all cases (n = 583) from 1981-1984 in two Florida counties, for which prosecutors initiated transfer proceedings against juvenile offenders (Bishop & Frazier, 1991; Bishop et al., 1989). The results indicated that two variables could be related to transfer: age and offense type. Most of the juveniles who had transfer proceedings initiated against them were 17 years old, with the next largest group being 16 years old, followed by those being aged 15 or younger. In addition, this research found that while only 29% of the juveniles were transferred for violent felonies, 55% were transferred for property felonies.

Shortly thereafter, Houghtalin & Mays (1991) examined the waiver process in New Mexico, also to consider which factors play a role in the waiver decision. In this study, all available juvenile probation files for transferred offenders from 1981 to 1990 were examined (n = 49). Prior record and offense seriousness appeared to play a role. Not only did most of the juveniles have at least one prior offense, but they also were likely to be charged with a serious crime (measured as Uniform Crime Report Part I Index offenses, either personal or property, and Part II person offenses)

In addition to legal variables, age also seemed to have an effect, as most of those transferred were older offenders. Nearly 60% were 17 years old, while close to 30% were 16 years old, and the rest were 15 years old. The main limitation with this study, however, was that even though the researchers utilized all available cases, those examined might not have been representative of all the transferred cases in New Mexico, because state law required probation files to be destroyed after offenders reached their 22nd birthday. This undoubtedly contributed to the very small sample size of 49.

More recently, Fritsch and his colleagues (1996) also considered the offense characteristics of transferred youth. In this research, correctional data were collected on youth who were transferred to criminal court from 1981-1993 and later were sent to prison (n = 946). Data were obtained from the Department of Criminal Justice-Institutional Division in Texas. One finding was that 76% of those transferred were convicted of a violent offense, while 24% were convicted of property or other felony crimes. In contrast to most of the previous research (Bishop & Frazier, 1991; Bishop et al., 1989; Bortner, 1986; Champion, 1989; Gillespie & Norman, 1984), it appears that more serious offenders were in fact transferred to criminal court. However, the main limitation of this study was that violent offenders may simply have been the main ones who were sent to prison. In other words, this study does not address all juveniles who were initially transferred to criminal court, just those who were later sent to prison, which possibly could mislead one into believing that violent offenders constitute a majority of those transferred.

Another fairly recent study, though, examined all juveniles who were subject to being transferred to criminal court in Illinois from November 1992 to March 1994 (Clarke, 1996). In this study, researchers surveyed youth who passed through the Cook County Juvenile Temporary Detention Center and also used data from the handwritten entry logs maintained by the center. Results indicated that a large percentage of the transferred offenders were nonwhite (about 95%). In addition, over 60% of the waived youth were charged with either aggravated criminal sexual assault, armed robbery with a firearm, or murder. The remaining offenders (almost 40%) were charged with either a drug or weapon offense. Although this is only a descriptive study, the results suggest that violent offenders were more likely to be transferred than other types of offenders.

It should be noted that data for this research corresponded with the increase in violent juvenile crime that peaked in the mid-1990s. As previously mentioned, prior to the youth violence surge, property offenders were transferred at a higher rate than any other group of offenders (Bishop, 2000). However, subsequent to the increase in juvenile violence, many transfer laws were expanded to target violent offenders, making them the largest group of those transferred. Therefore, findings from more recent studies reflect the national trend of transferring greater numbers of violent youthful offenders to criminal court.

A final recent descriptive study examined juvenile transfer in Virginia (Clement, 1997). Data were collected from November 1986 to December 1991 on juveniles who were judicially waived from the Richmond Juvenile and Domestic Relations District Court to adult criminal court (n = 250). Of those who were transferred, 81% were 17 years old, 18% were 16, and 1% were 15. In addition to age, prior record also appeared to affect the transfer decision, whereas all of those waived had at least one prior appearance or petition before the court. In addition, race seemed to play some role. Almost all of the transferred offenders were African-American (97%), while other groups comprised only 3% of the offenders. This suggests that nonwhites are more likely to be transferred than white offenders, but rival explanations for this finding were not taken into account, due to the descriptive nature of the study.

Comparative Studies

Comparison studies improve upon some of the limitations inherent to descriptive studies. In the research discussed above, it was not possible to fully determine the variables that influenced the transfer decision, because only waived offenders were examined. In the following studies, a comparison group was employed, usually comprised of similar offenders who were retained by the juvenile court. Comparison studies allow researchers not only to describe the characteristics of transferred and retained offenders, but they also enable multivariate analysis, meaning more confidence can be placed in the results that indicate which factors impact on the transfer decision.

However, it also should be noted that comparison studies on juvenile waiver are not free from other limitations. Because many factors could influence the decision to transfer a case, unmeasured variables could account for some (or all) of the observed relationships found. Researchers often attempt to control for many factors in their statistical analyses, but it is virtually impossible to take all possible confounding variables into consideration (Shadish, Cook, & Campbell, 2002).

With this in mind, in an early study of juvenile offenders charged with homicide, Eigen (1981a, 1981b) attempted to examine the determinants of transfer. The sample consisted of all juveniles arrested for homicide in Philadelphia during 1970 (n = 154). Two groups emerged from this sample: those transferred to criminal court (n = 75) and those retained by the juvenile court (n = 79). A third comparison group was added of adults arrested for homicide (n = 139).

Offense seriousness was not found to impact on the transfer decision, as felony versus non-felony homicide charges did not distinguish transferred and non-transferred juvenile offenders. However, this may not be a good indication of the impact of offense seriousness on transfer, because of the limited variation in the homicide variable. Prior record also did not appear to strongly affect the likelihood of transfer, as 70% percent of the transferred offenders had a prior record, compared to 63% of the retained offenders. Again, a limitation of this finding is that the author only indicated whether offenders had a prior record, without noting how many prior contacts the offenders had. Therefore, the true effect of prior record on transfer was weakly assessed.

Finally, age did not appear to have a substantial impact on the transfer decision. Seventy percent of the 17-year old offenders were transferred to criminal court, but over one-half of the offenders 16 years old and under also were waived. This may suggest that age is not a significant determinant of the transfer decision, which is contrary to findings from most of the empirical research. However, because the sample was limited to offenders charged with homicide, this finding should be viewed with caution.

Regarding race, it was found that blacks not only were more likely than whites to be transferred, but the probability of waiver increased dramatically when blacks killed whites. This finding suggests that racial discrimination may be operating in the decision to transfer juveniles to criminal court, not only in terms of the race of the offender, but also with regard to race of the victim. However, although a comparison group was employed in this study, multivariate analysis was not conducted, limiting the strength of the conclusions.

In examining Minnesota's waiver statute, another study looked at demographic and case history data of offenders who fell into one of two categories: those who met presumptive criteria to be transferred to criminal court, and those who actually had waiver proceedings initiated against them (Osbun & Rode, 1984). In 1980, Minnesota established a classification scheme that defined an offender as being presumed to be unfit for juvenile court treatment. The criteria were based on age, alleged offense, and record of prior felony offenses. The researchers examined whether the new transfer law in Minneapolis "captured" the group of offenders for which it was intended. One hundred forty-five cases were examined in Hennepin County, Minnesota, during three six-month time periods, from 1978 to 1981. The first two six-month periods were prior to the new law, while the final six-month period was after implementation of the law.

The new law basically intended to transfer more serious offenders to criminal court. However, not only did most transferred offenders not come from the class of offenders the law was meant to target, but many juveniles that the law was supposed to target ended up not being transferred. Following the law's enactment, only 35% of those waived to criminal court met the presumptive transfer criteria set forth in the statute, which was an increase from the 22% transferred prior to the statute. On the other hand, approximately 65% of those transferred following the implementation of the statute did not meet the presumptive criteria, compared to 78% before the law. This suggests that although the law resulted in an increase in transfer for serious offenders, a substantial number of those transferred did not meet the criteria set forth in the statute.

A later study by Fagan and his colleagues (1987) compared violent youth who had transfer petitions filed against them by a prosecutor (n=201) with chronically violent delinquents for which no transfer petitions were filed (n=225), from 1981 to 1984 in four urban juvenile courts (Boston, Phoenix, Newark, and Detroit). The researchers attempted to match both groups on all characteristics except the petition for transfer. The results indicated that age and offense seriousness were significant predictors of having the transfer petition filed. The older the offenders were when the offense was committed, the more likely they were to be petitioned. Also, the more serious the offense committed, the more likely the offenders were to be petitioned. Specifically, it appeared as though murder was the offense targeted most often by prosecutors.

In this research, prior record was not significant in predicting petition for transfer. This finding was not as expected, based on previous research and because prior record is considered a legal variable that often is listed in the criteria for amenability to treatment. The main reason for the finding pertained to age at onset. In general, juveniles who start committing offenses at an early age will have a more extensive prior record than those who start offending at later ages. In this study, when age at onset was entered into the model, it diminished the relationship between prior record and transfer.

Race also was not significant when other variables were controlled (i.e., age of offender, age at onset, offense seriousness, and prior record). Minority youth, however, were more likely to have an extensive prior record, to be charged with a more serious current offense, and have an earlier age of onset, as compared to white offenders. Considering these other variables can directly impact on the transfer decision, one could infer from this study that race has an indirect effect. To the extent that police focus their attention on lower-class, high-crime neighborhoods, minorities may be more likely to be arrested, have a more extensive prior record, have an earlier age at onset, and be charged with a more serious offense, which then impacts directly on the transfer decision.

A follow-up study using the same data as Fagan et al. (1987) produced similar results in examining the same four urban courts from 1981-1984. Fagan and his colleagues originally examined offenders for which transfer petitions were filed by a prosecutor and compared them to other violent juvenile offenders. Fagan and Deschenes (1990) subsequently examined only the offenders who had the transfer petitions filed, and these offenders were separated into two groups: transferred and retained youth. In order to be included in the sample, the youth must have been charged with a violent offense (i.e., murder/attempted murder, rape/attempted rape, aggravated assault, armed robbery, arson of an occupied dwelling, or kidnapping). The offender also must have had a prior adjudication for a felonious person or property offense. This yielded a sample of 201 violent youth, of which 125 were retained by the juvenile court and 76 were transferred to criminal court.

The results showed that offense seriousness was an inconsistent predictor in the transfer decision across the four sites. For most of the violent offenses measured, offenders were transferred at different rates. For instance, none of the juveniles charged with murder were transferred in Boston. However, in Detroit, 40% of those charged with murder were transferred, compared to 67% in Newark and 80% in Phoenix. Similar results were found in transfer rates for armed robbery. None of those charged with armed robbery were transferred in Boston, while 29% were transferred in Detroit, 59% in Newark, and 86% in Phoenix. This suggests that although offense seriousness is a factor to consider in studying transfer to criminal court, its impact may vary across sites.

This study also examined the impact of prior record on the transfer decision. Those with a more extensive prior record initially were more likely to be transferred than those with a less extensive prior record. However, this effect was eliminated when age of onset (age when juveniles were arrested for delinquent behavior for the first time) was entered in the analysis, as those who had an earlier age of onset were more likely to have an extensive prior record than those who had a later age of onset. Juveniles who began committing delinquency at an earlier age were significantly more likely to be transferred than those who started at a later age. However, age at onset was coded as a binary variable in this study (13 and younger versus 14 and over), and this limited variation may have influenced the findings in some way.

In addition to age at onset having a significant effect, current age also was significant. Older offenders were more likely to be transferred than younger offenders. Finally, concerning race, the analysis revealed that although a greater percentage of nonwhites were transferred than whites, the difference was not statistically significant. Again, nonwhites generally were more likely to be charged with serious offenses and to have an earlier age of onset, which resulted in a greater likelihood of being transferred. Therefore, as previously mentioned, race could have an indirect effect on the transfer decision.

Other comparative research also attempted to gauge the impact of legal and extralegal variables on the decision to transfer. Barnes and Franz (1989) examined all juveniles who had waiver motions filed against them in a large metropolitan county in California between March 1978 and December 1983 (n = 206). Data were collected from juvenile court files, and the results showed that legal factors (i.e., previous commitment, offense seriousness, and prior record) were the most important factors in the transfer decision. Those who had more previous commitments and a more extensive prior record had a greater chance of being transferred, compared to those with few or no previous commitments and lesser prior records. In addition, the more serious the current offense, the greater was the likelihood of transfer. Current offenses were measured by placing them into one of three rank-ordered categories: 1) property offenses and victimless crimes, 2) personal offenses, and 3) aggravated personal offenses.

When race was examined, it was significant, but its impact was not as strong as the legal variables. Still, nonwhites were more likely to be transferred than whites. This finding is different from that of other comparative research (Fagan & Deschenes, 1990; Fagan et al., 1987), where it was found that when legal variables were controlled for in the analysis, the impact of race no longer was significant. The impact of race in this study did remain significant, even when controlling for legal variables.

Age also was examined in this study, and contrary to other research, it was not significant in predicting transfer. Although older juveniles were more likely to be transferred, the finding did not reach statistical significance. One reason may be the small sample size. Twenty independent variables were entered in the model, with 206 subjects. Having a vast number of independent variables with a fairly small sample size will influence the reliability of the coefficients, along with whether or not they reach statistical significance.

In a subsequent study, Lee (1994) used data from a cohort of all juveniles born in 1969 who later were referred to the Maricopa County Juvenile Court of Arizona. The sample size was 567, of which only 43 (roughly 7% of the sample) were transferred. Results showed that offense seriousness did not predict transfer to adult court, even for those with no prior record. Age also was examined, but the results showed that it was not significant. The author did mention that this finding might have been due to the lack of variability in age, as only one juvenile under age 16 was waived.

One salient finding of this study was that a prior record of waiver was significant in distinguishing the transferred and non-transferred cases, indicating that those who had a record of prior waiver were more likely to be waived again. Similarly, those with no record of prior waiver were more likely to be retained by the juvenile court. This finding may possibly be explained based on state law. Because Arizona is a state with a "once an adult, always an adult" provision (see Chapter 2), this might explain why the greatest predictor of transfer was prior waiver. Another limitation of this study was the small number of transfer cases compared to the large number of retained cases. It is difficult to draw adequate comparisons between groups with the size of one group being so small.

In one of the better comparative studies, Poulos and Orchowsky (1994) compared a random sample of transferred juveniles (n=364) with a random sample of juveniles who committed transferable offenses, but were retained by the juvenile court (n=363). All cases were processed in Virginia from 1988-1990. Also, all of the offenders in the sample were convicted, regardless of whether they were transferred or retained.

Multivariate analysis showed that the strongest predictor of transfer was number of prior felony property adjudications. The more prior felony property adjudications an offender had, the greater the likelihood of transfer. In addition, prior felony person offenses also had a significant positive effect. These two findings suggest that the more extensive the prior record of an offender, the greater the chance of being transferred. Furthermore, other variables also were significant in predicting transfer, including firearm use and age. Those who used a firearm were more likely to be transferred compared to when a firearm was not employed. It also appeared that older offenders were more likely to be transferred than younger offenders. The limitation with this finding, however, is that age was coded as a binary variable, measured simply as 17 years old or 16 and under.

Somewhat similar results were found by Kinder et al. (1995) in a comparison study of juveniles certified as adults (n=111) and a sample of juveniles adjudicated as delinquent for conduct that would constitute a felony if committed by an adult (n=111). The data were obtained from Family Court records in St. Louis, Missouri, from 1993. Two main findings emerged regarding predictors of transfer. First, transferred juveniles were more likely to have been arrested for a violent crime, while youth who were retained by the juvenile court were more likely to have been arrested for crimes involving drug possession or distribution. Second, older juveniles were more likely to be transferred than younger offenders. Approximately 74% of the transferred offenders were either 16 or 17 years old, while approximately 70% of the retained offenders were either 14 or 15 years old.

There are several limitations with this study that would lead one to question the findings. All of the transferred juveniles from 1993 were included in the study. However, the comparison group was a sample of offenders who were adjudicated for felonies in the age range of 14-16. No 17-year olds were included in the comparison group. Also, the study did not use control variables in the analysis, in an effort to account for differences between the groups. This leads to the possibility of other variables explaining away the presumed relationships that were revealed.

A more recent comparison study attempted to better examine the determinants of transfer (Podkopacz & Feld, 1996). In this research, data were gathered from juvenile court and probation files in Hennepin County, Minnesota, from 1986-1992, on juveniles who had reference (transfer) motions filed against them for the first time (n = 330). Of those who had referral motions filed, 115 were retained by the juvenile court, while 215 were transferred to criminal court.

Age again was a strong predictor, as older juveniles were more likely to be transferred than younger juveniles. Also, there were three categories of prior placement considered: no prior delinquency placements, one to three prior placements, and four or more prior placements. Offenders who had either no prior placements or one to three placements were significantly less likely to be transferred than were those with four or more placements. An interpretation of this finding is that juveniles may still be seen as amenable to treatment after few prior placements, meaning they are still likely to remain in the juvenile justice system. However, as prior placements then increase, offenders may no longer be thought of as being receptive to the treatment of the juvenile court, which likely will result in them being transferred.

In contrast to prior placements, offense seriousness was not found to be significant. There was no difference in the likelihood of the juvenile court judge transferring those charged with felony person offenses versus those charged with property offenses. However, if a weapon was used in the felony person offense, transfer was significantly more likely to occur. Also, although a disproportionate number of minorities were transferred to criminal court, the impact of race disappeared when legal variables (i.e., prior record and offense seriousness) were controlled for in the analyses.

Other research using 1994 data examined juvenile transfer in Pennsylvania (Myers, 2003b). In this study, 494 violent juvenile males were examined, all who would have been automatically transferred to criminal court had a subsequent 1996 legislative waiver law been in effect at that time. Seventy-nine offenders actually were judicially waived, while 415 were retained by the juvenile court. Prior record (a combination of prior referrals, prior adjudications, and prior placements) was a significant predictor of transfer. The more extensive the prior record, the more likely offenders were to be waived. Also, age was significant, as older offenders were more likely to be transferred than younger offenders.

It also was found that offenders who used a firearm were less likely to be transferred than those who did not use a firearm. However, a limitation of this finding is that victim injury was not taken into account, which could explain the negative relationship between firearm use and transfer. In other words, if offenders used a firearm, victims may not have been injured because they were more cooperative. If victims are not physically injured, it could be that offenders are less likely to be transferred to criminal court. Therefore, those who use a firearm, but without causing injury to the victim, may be less likely to be transferred than those who do not use a firearm, but do cause victim injury.

Finally, more recent research examined juvenile transfer in Virginia. In this study, Sridharan, Greenfield, and Blakley (2004) examined youth who met certain criteria to be transferred to adult court, via prosecutorial waiver. They focused on youth in 11 court service units (out of a total 35 court service units) in Virginia, who in 1997 and 1998, were eligible to be transferred to adult court (n = 1,148). The findings indicate that legal variables were significant in the prosecutor's decision to transfer a case to adult court. As offense seriousness increased and the more extensive the prior record, the greater the likelihood of transfer. In addition, those who used a firearm were more likely to be transferred, as compared to those who did not use a firearm. Also, those who used a knife during the offense had a greater likelihood of transfer. The results also indicated that those who dropped out of school had a significantly higher likelihood of transfer than youth who did not drop out of school. Finally, this research also added to the literature by examining the role of victim injury in the transfer decision. The more serious the victim injury during the offense, the greater the likelihood of youth being waived to adult court. It is likely that offenders who caused extensive injury to the victim may be viewed as a more serious offender and "deserving" of adult court sanctions. Although this research examined many independent variables during the analysis, the model explained 38% of the "variance" in transfer, suggesting that other unmeasured factors impact on prosecutors' decision to waive a case to adult court.

PREDICTORS OF DECERTIFICATION

As discussed in the last chapter, decertification (or reverse waiver) is the process of transferring originally waived offenders back to juvenile court (DeFrances & Strom, 1997; Griffin et al., 1998). In contrast to the transfer process, there has not been much research regarding the use of decertification, and little is known about the factors that predict which cases get decertified. To date, in fact, there has been only one known empirical study that focused on the determinants of reverse waiver.

In a comparison study, data were gathered on serious and violent juvenile offenders (n = 9,937) who were arrested in New York from

1978 to 1985 (Singer, 1996). In 1978, a new law statutorily excluded certain youth from juvenile court jurisdiction (based on the age and offense of the alleged offender) and automatically transferred them to the adult system. The offenses included were murder, kidnapping, rape, arson, robbery, assault, and burglary.

The multivariate results indicated that younger offenders were more likely to be decertified than older offenders. Also, females were more likely to be decertified than males. Regarding the legal variables, as offense seriousness increased, the likelihood of decertification decreased. Finally, similar results were reported concerning the effect of prior arrest. As the number of prior arrests increased, the likelihood of decertification decreased.

While this lone study focused on the determinants of decertification, other research only briefly examined this process. In Pennsylvania, data were examined on youth who fell under the state's new legislative waiver law (Act 33), which went into effect in March 1996 (Snyder et al., 2000). As discussed in Chapter 2, this new law excluded certain violent offenders from juvenile court and automatically transferred them to adult court jurisdiction. In order to be included in the study, the youth must have had a preliminary hearing between March 1996 and December 1996 (n = 473). Of these youth, 48% were charged with aggravated assault, 46% were charged with robbery, 1% was charged with a violent sex offense, and the remaining offenders were charged with various other offenses.

The results indicated that 149 youth (32%) were reversed waived (i.e., decertified) to juvenile court. Whites were more likely to be decertified, as compared to any other youth. Also, similar to research by Singer (1996), this study found decertified youth tended to be younger than those retained in the adult system. Using a firearm also seemed to increase the likelihood of a case remaining in criminal court. Concerning legal variables, prior record appeared to be associated with decertification, as those with no prior record seemed more likely to be decertified than those with a prior record. However, a major limitation of this study is that multivariate analysis was not employed, meaning the suggested relationships may be spurious.

Summary

Although earlier research revealed property offenders to make up the largest percentage of transferred youth (Bishop & Frazier, 1991; Bishop et al., 1989; Bortner, 1986; Champion, 1989; Gillespie & Norman, 1984), other more recent studies have found violent offenders now constitute the largest group (Clarke, 1996; Fritsch et al., 1996; Kinder et al., 1995). As discussed in this and the previous chapter, these findings are undoubtedly due to the sudden increase in youth violence that spanned a decade, beginning in the mid-1980s. During and following the increase, states made it easier to transfer juveniles to adult court (Zimring, 1998). Violent offenders were targeted with the new transfer laws, which explain the research findings regarding offense type.

With some exceptions, the findings generally are consistent regarding the predictors of transfer. Legal variables, such as prior record and offense seriousness, currently appear to be among the strongest determinants in the transfer decision. The more serious the offense and the more prior offenses juveniles exhibit, the less they may be viewed as amenable to juvenile court treatment. However, some research found that the impact of prior record was eliminated when age of onset was taken into consideration (Fagan & Deschenes, 1990; Fagan et al., 1987).

In general, juveniles who become involved in illegal acts at early ages are more likely to acquire an extensive offending record as they get older (Farrington, 1986; Farrington, 1998). Conversely, those who begin committing delinquent acts at later ages are less likely to produce an extensive record. As mentioned in Chapter 2, the peak in offending occurs during mid to late adolescence, after which offending declines (Blumstein, 1995). Overall, then, when juvenile offenders begin committing crime and being arrested at later ages, they generally will not have an extensive record of offending. Therefore, it may not be that prior record plays as strong a role in the transfer decision as believed; instead, age at onset could play a larger role.

When extra-legal variables are examined for their impact on transfer, they sometimes are shown to be statistically significant. Most of the research that considers age finds that older youth are more likely to be transferred than younger offenders (Eigen, 1981a; Fagan et al., 1987; Fagan & Deschenes, 1990; Kinder et al., 1995; Myers, 2003b;

Podkopacz & Feld, 1996; Poulos & Orchowsky, 1994). This most likely is due to older offenders approaching the age of majority (typically age 18), meaning they are viewed as "almost" an adult. In contrast, younger offenders may be perceived as still "salvageable."

The impact of race on transfer, when legal variables are controlled, typically is insignificant (Fagan & Deschenes, 1990; Fagan et al., 1987; Podkopacz & Feld, 1996). However, the conclusion cannot be reached that discrimination is not operating in the transfer process. According to Podkopacz and Feld (1996), a cumulative race effect may be operating throughout multiple decision points in the juvenile justice system. For example, African-Americans may be more likely than Caucasians to be held in pre-trial detention. Moreover, those who are held in pre-trial detention generally are more likely to receive severe sanctions than those who are released. Therefore, if a researcher is examining the impact of race on sentence severity, an original observed effect could be eliminated when pre-trial detention is considered. The same claim could be made for the impact of race on transfer. Although race does not appear to directly impact on transfer, it could be that the effect is indirect, through other decision making points in the transfer process.

Finally, not all cases initially placed in adult court remain in the criminal justice system. Some states allow for waived offenders to be decertified, resulting in a transfer back to juvenile court. Based on only two known studies (Singer, 1996; Snyder et al., 2000), the predictors of decertification seem similar to those of transfer. In these studies, younger offenders appeared more likely to be decertified than older offenders, possibly due to older offenders being closer to the age of majority. The criminal court judge, when deciding whether or not to decertify the case, may see little difference between older juvenile offenders and young adults. Also, younger offenders may be viewed as more amenable to treatment in the juvenile system.

The legal variables of offense seriousness and prior record also had the expected effect on the decertification decision. Much of the existing research suggests that as offense seriousness and prior record increase, the likelihood of transfer increases. Similarly, when criminal court judges are making the decision to decertify, the most serious offenders and those with extensive prior records appear more likely to remain in criminal court. Conversely, less serious offenders and those who do not have an extensive prior record may be viewed as still "salvageable," resulting in reverse waiver to juvenile court.

TRANSFER AND PRE-DISPOSITIONAL CUSTODY

A discussed in Chapter 2, the practice of transferring juveniles to adult court generally is expected to increase the accountability of the offender. In addition, harsher punishment and community protection also are goals of transferring youth. Following arrest, then, it would seem as though transferred offenders should be less likely to be released from pre-dispositional custody, because if granted liberty, accountability and punishment would be diminished and the community may be at risk for further illegal behavior by the offender.

There has been only one known empirical study that examined the pre-dispositional custody of transferred offenders. In a comparison study of 138 violent offenders transferred to criminal court and 419 violent offenders retained by Pennsylvania juvenile courts in 1994, it was found that transferred offenders were significantly more likely to be released from pre-dispositional custody than were non-transferred youth (Myers, 2001b; Myers & Kiehl, 2001). A possible explanation for this finding is that juveniles retained by the juvenile court are not entitled to bail, preventing their right to release from detention. However, once offenders are transferred to adult court, they are given the same constitutional rights as adults prosecuted in the criminal justice system, including greater bail rights and practices. In addition, they may generally be viewed as less serious offenders in the adult system, resulting in an increased likelihood of release.

The same study looked at county differences in pre-dispositional custody. The results showed that urban offenders were more likely to be released from pre-dispositional custody than were suburban and rural offenders. In general, holding facilities may be more likely to be overcrowded in urban areas as compared to suburban and rural areas. Therefore, urban judges could be more likely to release offenders from custody.

Finally, the study found that juveniles who used a firearm during their offense were less likely to be released, as compared to those who did not use a firearm. Juveniles who use a firearm may be viewed as more violent, resulting in them being denied release from pre-dispositional custody. Although firearm offenders were less likely to be released during the pre-dispositional time period, related research by Myers (2003b) also found that gun offenders were more likely to be retained by the juvenile court (rather than transferred).

Based on one study, it appears as though transferring violent offenders to adult court may not be effective in keeping these offenders detained until their case is disposed. Despite the goals of community protection and accountability, judges have to deal with limited jail space and a right to bail in the criminal justice system. In addition, because it appears to take transferred offenders longer to have their cases processed (as discussed later in this chapter), they may have more time to commit additional illegal acts when released from custody (Myers, 2001; Myers & Kiehl, 2001).

TRANSFER AND CONVICTION

When juveniles are transferred to criminal court, it commonly is thought that there will be a higher likelihood of conviction. The reason behind this is the belief that juveniles typically are transferred because they are serious or violent offenders who should be held accountable for their behavior and receive harsher punishments imposed in adult court. In order for transferred offenders to receive harsh sentences, they must first be convicted of an offense. Overall, there has been a great deal of research conducted that examined the extent to which transferred juveniles are convicted in adult court. However, these studies have been of varying levels of scientific rigor.

Descriptive Studies

As mentioned earlier, descriptive studies simply describe the characteristics of one group, in this case transferred offenders. Studies reviewed in this section only indicate the rate of conviction for juveniles in adult court. Because a comparison group of retained offenders was not used, it is not possible to conclude from these studies whether transfer actually increases the likelihood of conviction.

In examining transferred offenders from 1967 to 1980 in one district of Utah (n = 45), Gillespie and Norman (1984) found that 76% were convicted in adult court. Those not convicted (24%) were either found not guilty or had their cases dismissed. This finding generally suggests that transferred offenders have a high rate of conviction. Similar, but stronger, results were found by Thomas & Bilchik (1985). In studying transferred youth from 1981 in Dade County, Florida (n = 844), they found that approximately 90% of those transferred to criminal court were convicted. Other outcomes for the remainder of the cases were either dismissals or acquittals.

Other descriptive research has produced similar findings. Another Florida study examined all cases (n = 583) from two counties in which juveniles had charges filed against them in criminal court from January 1981 to December 1984 (Bishop & Frazier, 1991; Bishop et al., 1989). Results indicated that 96% of the transferred offenders were convicted in adult court. Slightly more moderate findings were produced by Champion (1989), who found that the conviction rate for transferred offenders steadily increased in four states (Tennessee, Virginia, Mississippi, and Georgia) from 1980 to 1988. In 1980, the conviction rate was approximately 62% for transferred offenders, but by 1988, the rate had increased to 78%.

Finally, in using available data on transferred offenders in New Mexico from 1981 to 1990 (n = 49), Houghtalin & Mays (1991) also found a high conviction rate for transferred youth. Convictions were obtained for 80% of the transferred offenders, of which most were charged with person offenses. The authors indicated, however, that most of those transferred not only had prior records, but also had prior records for serious offenses. Therefore, it may not be that transfer impacts on the likelihood of conviction; other factors such as prior record could explain the high likelihood of conviction.

Comparative Studies

In comparative studies, a second group is examined, in this case consisting of retained offenders. While descriptive studies suffer from the drawback of not being able to fully determine the impact of waiver on conviction, comparison studies allow for stronger conclusions to be made. In other words, by adding a second group of retained youth, researchers can better assess whether transfer actually increases the likelihood of conviction.

As discussed previously, although comparative studies use a second group, it does not follow that these studies are flawless. Because a true experiment cannot be readily used in this research (i.e., randomly assigning youth to either a transfer group or non-transfer group), there is no way of knowing with certainty that the possible observed differences between the conviction rate of the two groups is due to transfer. The best researchers can do is to control for other factors that can impact on conviction, thereby allowing for stronger conclusions.

In an early comparison study of transferred (n=75) and retained (n=79) homicide offenders in Philadelphia during 1970, Eigen (1981a, 1981b) found that 89% of the transferred juveniles were convicted, compared to 77% of the retained offenders. In addition to these two groups, a third group of adult homicide offenders was examined (n=200), which had an approximate 70% conviction rate. This suggests that transferred offenders had a higher likelihood of conviction than retained offenders. It also hints at transferred youth having a higher degree of punishment certainty than similar adult offenders in the criminal justice system. However, although this study was comparative, it did not control for other explanatory factors that could impact on the likelihood of conviction (e.g., prior record).

Other research by Rudman and his colleagues (1986) produced contrary findings. In this study, the sample consisted of 138 youths charged with violent offenses, who were considered for transfer in Boston, Newark, and Phoenix from 1981 to 1984 (n = 138). Of that group, 67 were transferred to criminal court, while 71 were retained by the juvenile court. It was found that 92.2% of the transferred offenders were convicted, as compared to 95.5% of the retained offenders. From this finding, it appears that regardless of whether violent youths are transferred or retained by the juvenile court, the probability of conviction is high. However, because multivariate analysis was not used, it was not possible to consider any other factors that could impact on the likelihood of conviction.

Subsequent research by Fagan (1995) found somewhat different results than those of Rudman et al. (1986). In this study, Fagan examined youth charged with robbery and burglary in four matched counties (2 counties in northern New Jersey and 2 counties in southeastern New York) from 1981-1982 (N = 800). Approximately half of the offenders were transferred (those from New York), while the other half was retained by the juvenile court (those from New Jersey). When examining conviction rates, those charged with robbery were significantly more likely to be convicted in adult court. However, regarding burglary, there was no statistically significant difference in conviction rates between the two groups. This finding suggests that those who commit violent offenses (e.g., robbery) may be more likely to be convicted in adult court, while those who commit non-violent offenses (e.g., burglary) may experience similar conviction rates in juvenile and adult court.

Similar results regarding violent offenders and the likelihood of conviction were found in the study by Myers (2001, 2003a) that utilized 1994 juvenile transfer data in Pennsylvania. Of the 557 violent offenders in this study, 138 were judicially waived to criminal court, while 419 were retained by the juvenile court. Multivariate analysis indicated that transferred offenders were significantly more likely to be convicted than were retained offenders, suggesting that transferring violent juveniles to adult court increases the certainty of conviction. In fact, the estimated probability of conviction for a waived offender was .89, while the estimated probability for a retained offender was .64, a difference of 25 percentage points. The impact of age on conviction also was significant, but negative, as older offenders were less likely to be convicted than younger offenders. Finally, race also was significant, as non-whites were less likely to be convicted than whites.

In this study, the impact of transfer also was significant on conviction of a target offense. Target offenses were defined as the alleged offense that actually triggered the waiver to adult court (i.e., robbery or aggravated assault). Transferred youth were significantly more likely to be convicted on target offenses than youth retained in juvenile court. For otherwise "average" offenders, the estimated probability of conviction on a target offense for a transferred youth was .90, while the estimated probability for a retained youth was .75, a difference of 15 percentage points.

Summary

When looking at the descriptive studies in this section, the results provide an incomplete picture, because they only suggest that transferred offenders have a high rate of conviction. Although this is true, it must be remembered that it does not necessarily follow that transfer increases the likelihood of conviction. When researchers use comparative studies to examine this issue, they can better determine whether transfer itself has an effect on conviction. Moreover, when multivariate analysis is employed, other factors that might impact on the likelihood of conviction can be examined as well.

The results of the comparison studies generally do indicate that violent transferred offenders experience a higher conviction rate than similar youth retained by the juvenile court (Eigen, 1981b; Fagan, 1995; Myers, 2001b; Myers, 2003a). Less difference may exist between the courts for nonviolent offenders. Considering that many contemporary transfer laws target violent youth, when these offenders are waived to adult court, prosecutors, judges, and juries may be less likely to dismiss or acquit them, because of their violent charge. Conversely, when juvenile offenders are charged with violent crimes, but retained in the juvenile court, prosecutors and judges may be more likely to approach the situation from a rehabilitation or treatment standpoint, as compared to one of deterrence or retribution.

In addition to violent transferred youth experiencing higher punishment certainty (i.e., conviction) than similar retained youth, transferred offenders also seem to receive a higher likelihood of conviction on target offenses. This is an indication of charges being less likely to be reduced in adult criminal court. In other words, transferred youth appear less likely to benefit from plea bargaining and more likely to be convicted of the crime that initiated waiver to adult court.

Although violent youth currently are the main target of transfer, less serious offenders also get waived to adult court. However, research does not support higher conviction rates for non-violent offenders who are transferred, as compared to similar retained youth (Fagan, 1995). This may be due to non-violent youth being viewed as "less-serious" by those in the criminal justice system. Although their crime was serious enough to result in transfer, prosecutors, judges, and juries in criminal court may not want to expose them to the harsh world of the adult system, resulting in a lower rate of conviction.

TRANSFER AND INCARCERATION

Because juvenile transfer is expected to provide harsher sanctions for youthful offenders, the rate of incarceration for waived youth should be somewhat high, since incarceration generally is viewed as a punitive sanction in our society. It then follows that if juvenile transfer is going to be viewed as effective, waived offenders should be incarcerated at a higher rate than retained offenders. Again, there has been a substantial amount of research that has examined this topic, including both descriptive and comparative studies.

Descriptive Studies

Regarding rates of incarceration, descriptive studies typically report the percentage of transferred (and sometimes transferred and convicted) offenders who received incarceration as their sentence. There is no comparison group, meaning there is no way of concluding from these studies whether transferred offenders are incarcerated at a higher rate than similar retained youth. Overall, though, this research does suggest fairly high rates of incarceration in adult court, with some exceptions.

In a study of Florida youthful offenders from 1981 (n = 844), Thomas and Bilchik (1985) found that 67% of the transferred offenders examined, all of which were charged with a felony (e.g., burglary and robbery), received incarceration as their sentence. Most of the other offenders were sentenced to probation. On the other hand, Bortner's (1986) study of 214 waived offenders in a western metropolitan state during 1980 and 1981 reported contrary results. In this study, the findings indicated that only 33% of the transferred and convicted offenders were incarcerated, while 67% received probation. These mixed findings likely are due to the fact that during this time period, many nonviolent offenders were being transferred to adult court.

Houghtalin & Mays' (1991) findings were more similar to those of Thomas and Bilchilk (1985). They found that most transferred and convicted offenders (64%) were incarcerated for their offenses, while only 28% received probation. Recall, however, that most of the New Mexico offenders in this study (approximately 77%) had prior records for serious offenses (measured as UCR Part I Index Crimes and Part II person offenses), which might explain why a majority of these youth were incarcerated.

Other descriptive research using Florida data from the 1980s also found that approximately 64% (n = 287) of the transferred and convicted offenders were incarcerated (Bishop & Frazier, 1991; Bishop et al., 1989). Of the remaining cases, 34% (n=150) were placed on probation, and 2% (n = 9) received juvenile sanctions, again suggesting that transferred offenders have a fairly high rate of incarceration. However, it is not clear from any of these studies if these incarceration rates are greater than those of similar offenders in juvenile court.

Comparative Studies

The following studies typically used a comparison group of retained offenders, meaning stronger conclusions can be made regarding whether transferred offenders have a higher rate of incarceration than retained youth. When using comparison groups, multivariate analysis also can be employed, to consider rival factors when attempting to determine the relationship between transfer and the likelihood of incarceration. However, because these studies do not use a true randomized experimental design, there is still the possibility that unmeasured factors could explain all, or part, of any presumed relationships.

In examining offenders charged with felony homicide, Eigen (1981a, 1981b) examined two groups: adult and transferred offenders. Of those charged with felony homicide, he found that 94% of the convicted adults (n = 31) were incarcerated, while all of the transferred and convicted youth (n = 22) were sentenced to some form of incarceration. With regard to youth who were transferred and convicted for non-felony homicide, it was found that 84% (n = 36) were incarcerated, while only 73% of the adults (n = 76) were incarcerated. However, when examining those offenders charged with robbery, Eigen studied transferred youth and similar defendants retained by the juvenile court. He found that 91% of the transferred and convicted youth (n = 29) were incarcerated, while only 28% (n = 14) of similarly convicted retained youth were incarcerated.

Rudman and his colleagues (1986) also found that violent transferred offenders were more likely to be sentenced to incarceration than violent retained youth. When examining those convicted in adult criminal court in four cities (Boston, Memphis, Newark, and Phoenix) from 1981 to 1984 (n = 62), 90% were incarcerated. Conversely, of the 68 retained youth who were convicted in juvenile court, 77% (n = 52) were sentenced to incarceration. This finding again suggests that there is a greater likelihood of incarceration for transferred violent offenders, as compared to violent retained youth.

Similar differences were revealed in other comparative research. In examining approximately 800 youth charged with robbery and burglary in four matched counties (2 in northern New Jersey and 2 in southeastern New York) in 1981 and 1982, Fagan (1995) found that of those youth convicted of robbery in juvenile court (n = 176), only 18% were incarcerated. However, of those convicted in adult court (n = 192), 46% were incarcerated. Similarly, regarding youth convicted for burglary in juvenile court (n = 21), 24% were incarcerated, while convictions for burglary in adult court (n = 43) resulted in 47% being incarcerated.

Podkopacz and Feld (1996) also found that transferred offenders were incarcerated at a higher rate than retained youth. In their study of 330 youth who had transfer motions filed against them for the first time in Hennepin County, Minnesota from 1986-1992, 85% of the transferred youth (n = 209) were sentenced to incarceration, while only 63% (n = 99) of the retained offenders were incarcerated.

Finally, in the study examining violent youth in Pennsylvania, where 138 were waived and 419 were retained by the juvenile court, Myers (2001, 2003a) found that transferred youth were significantly more likely to be incarcerated than retained offenders. After controlling for a variety of other possible explanatory factors, the estimated probability of incarceration for transferred and convicted offenders was .97, while the estimated probability of incarceration for retained and convicted youth was .66, a difference of 31 percentage points.

Summary

The general findings from the research discussed above suggest that transferred offenders are incarcerated at higher rates than are similar retained offenders, particularly in terms of those who commit violent offenses. This is consistent with one goal of contemporary transfer laws, which generally seek more punitive sanctions than typically are imposed in juvenile court. However, although there is a difference in incarceration rates between the two groups of offenders, the research is mixed regarding the percentage of transferred offenders incarcerated. Some studies indicate less than 50% of transferred and convicted offenders are incarcerated (Bortner, 1986; Fagan, 1995), while other research reports well over half (Bishop & Frazier, 1991; Bishop et al.,

1989; Houghtalin & Mays, 1991; Myers, 2003a; Podkopacz & Feld, 1996; Rudman et al., 1986; Thomas & Bilchik, 1985). Again, offense type and the time at which data were collected appear to play a role, as more recent studies that focus on violent offenders tend to find the greatest likelihood of incarceration in adult court.

TRANSFER AND INCARCERATION LENGTH

In addition to whether transferred offenders are more likely to be incarcerated than similar retained offenders, a related issue is whether waived youth are provided with longer sentences of incarceration than retained youth. One reason given for juveniles being transferred to adult court is that the juvenile court generally has a lesser ability to impose lengthy punishments. Therefore, in evaluating the effectiveness of transfer, waived offenders should be sentenced to longer incarceration time than those who remain in juvenile court.

Descriptive Studies

The studies in this section generally indicate the sentence length that transferred offenders receive, if they received incarceration as a sentence. Since comparison groups were not used in the following studies, the conclusions that can be reached are limited, as a determination cannot be made as to whether incarcerated offenders in adult court are sentenced to longer periods of confinement than are similar retained offenders in juvenile court.

When examining just transferred offenders in Dade County, Florida in 1981 (n = 844), Thomas & Bilchik (1985) found that the median incarceration length received for those who were convicted was approximately four years. Most of the convicted offenders who were sentenced to some period of incarceration had been charged with felonious crimes (e.g., robbery and burglary).

Other descriptive research found that in Florida, of those incarcerated (n = 287), a majority (54%) of the transferred offenders received between one and three years in prison (Bishop & Frazier, 1991; Bishop et al., 1989). Thirty-one percent of the offenders were sentenced to 4-6 years, while 15% received 7 or more years. Furthermore, most of these offenders (55%) were charged with felony property crimes. Twenty-nine percent of the offenders were charged with felony person crimes, while the remaining offenders (16%) were charged with either drug crimes or misdemeanors. It was pointed out, however, that although transferred youth were sentenced to fairly long periods of incarceration, because Florida has "generous gain time provisions," incarcerated offenders may serve much less time than ordered by the court.

Another more recent descriptive study by Clement (1997) found that of the transferred offenders sentenced to incarceration in Richmond, Virginia, from 1987-1991 (n = 250), 36% received a sentence of 1-4 years in prison. Only 4% received sentences of less than 6 months. The remaining breakdown was 5-6 years, 21%; 7-16 years, 30%; 20-62 years, 10%; and life sentences, less than 1%. Because of the generally long periods of incarceration imposed, one might conclude from this research that transferred offenders often are sentenced to long periods of confinement in adult court. However, comparisons with similar offenders retained in juvenile court provide a more complete picture of this situation.

Comparative Studies

Comparative studies in this section generally allow researchers to better determine whether waived youth are sentenced to longer periods of incarceration than similar retained youth. To begin, in comparing transferred youth (n = 22) and adult offenders (n = 33) charged with felony homicide, Eigen (1981a, 1981b) found that the two groups were given similar sentences. Twenty-three percent of the waived youth were sentenced to 1-2 years, while 27% of the adults were given that sentence. Twenty-two percent of the waived youth were sentenced to 3-5 years, while 16% of the adults were given the similar sentence. Both groups had 9% sentenced to 6-8 years. None of the waived youth were sentenced to 9-12 years, while 3% of the adults were given that sentence. Most of the offenders for both the transferred (36%) and adult (40%) groups were sentenced to life imprisonment. It also should be noted that 6% of the adults were sentenced to probation, and another 6% of this group were sentenced to death.

When comparing transferred and retained youth, larger differences were observed. Eigen found that of the retained youth charged with felony homicide (n = 20), approximately 25% were sentenced to probation, compared to none of the waived offenders. In addition, about 37% of the retained youth were sentenced to at least 1 year of confinement, compared to approximately 12% of those waived to adult court. Approximately 38% of the retained youth were sentenced to a minimum of 2 years of incarceration, compared to slightly less than 10% of the transferred offenders. The remaining transferred youth (well over half) were sentenced to periods of incarceration of at least 3 years. It also should be mentioned that because only group percentages were reported in this research, it cannot be strongly concluded that there were statistically significant differences in sentence length between the groups of offenders, as rival explanations for sentence lengths were not considered.

The study by Rudman et al. (1986) also found that the sanctions offenders received in adult court were more severe than those received in juvenile court. Among the violent youth examined, transferred offenders (n = 62) were sentenced to an average incarceration length of approximately 150 months, while retained offenders (n = 52) were sentenced to an average of approximately 30 months. This finding suggests that waived offenders receive substantially harsher sentences than those who remain in juvenile court.

However, Fagan's (1995) results did not support this finding. In his study, for those youth charged with robbery, the average sentence length in months was 22.9 for those in juvenile court, while for transferred offenders it was 21.4 months. Although retained offenders were sentenced to a slightly longer incarceration period, the difference was not statistically significant. Similar findings were revealed for those charged with burglary. The average sentence length for retained offenders was 22.4 months, while transferred offenders were sentenced to an average 20.7 months. Again, this difference was not statistically significant.

While most research in this section examined the length of incarceration imposed by either a juvenile or criminal court judge, very little attention has been given to actual time served. Fritsch et al. (1996) found that in general, transferred youth in Texas receive longer sentences in criminal court, as compared to similar offenders in juvenile court. However, when actual time served was taken in to consideration, the transferred youth only served approximately 27% of their sentence. The only transferred offenders who served at least one-half of their sentences on average were those convicted of aggravated assault.

More recently, though, Myers (2001, 2003a) found that transferred offenders were significantly more likely to serve longer sentences than similar retained youth. In his study of violent Pennsylvania youth, of those convicted and incarcerated, transferred offenders on average served a sentence of 32 months, while retained offenders served a sentence of about 11 months. This finding again suggests that transferred violent offenders generally are exposed to more punitive sanctions than are similar violent youth retained in juvenile court.

Finally, one other study examined transferred youth in Pennsylvania. In this research, Kurlychek and Johnson (2004) examined youth waived to adult court in Pennsylvania from 1997 through 1999 (n = 1,042) and compared them to young adult offenders during the same time frame, who were age 18 to 24 at the time of their offenses (n = 33,962). Data were gathered from Pennsylvania's Sentencing Commission. Sentence severity was measured by the length of confinement ordered by the court. The findings indicated that while controlling for both legal (e.g., offense severity and prior record) and extralegal (e.g., race and gender) factors, youth in adult court were sentenced to significantly longer confinement time than young adult offenders. Put differently, the results suggest that juveniles in adult court are given more punitive sanctions than young adult offenders, but conclusions cannot be drawn about the "harsh" effect of transfer, due to comparable youth in juvenile court being excluded from the analyses.

Summary

The results regarding transfer and incarceration length are somewhat mixed, but the general conclusion can be drawn that transferred offenders are sentenced to longer periods of incarceration than are similar retained juveniles. This suggests that transfer is effective in generating longer sentences for these offenders, as compared to those in juvenile court. However, most research has not taken actual time served into consideration.

Because the criminal justice system is overcrowded, many offenders are released early from confinement, after serving only a portion of their sentence. When transferred offenders become a part of the adult system, they are susceptible to the effect of jail and prison overcrowding, resulting in the potential for early release. Therefore, even though transferred offenders may be sentenced to longer periods of incarceration than retained youth, there is the possibility that the difference may be reduced or eliminated when actual time served is taken into account.

TRANSFER AND CASE PROCESSING TIME

It was mentioned earlier in this chapter that transferred cases generally take longer to process than those retained by the juvenile court. This basically is due to the slow nature of the adult criminal justice system. Because of court docket backlogs, along with the exercise of due process rights (e.g., bail and right to a jury trial), many cases take lengthy times to process in the adult system. However, only a small number of studies have examined the impact of being transferred on case processing time.

In Rudman et al.'s (1986) comparative study of 71 retained offenders and 67 transferred offenders from Boston, Newark, and Phoenix, it was found that it took transferred cases approximately 246 days to be processed from arrest to final disposition, while it only took retained cases approximately 98 days. Fagan (1995) found somewhat similar results in his study of youth charged with robbery and burglary. It took transferred cases approximately 145 days to be processed; however, retained cases took only 100 days. These findings also are consistent with the more recent study of violent offenders by Myers (2001, 2003a). In this research, the estimated time it took for transferred offenders to have their cases processed was 222 days, while retained offenders' cases took an estimated 45 days.

These studies generally show that transferred offenders experience longer case processing time than those who are retained in juvenile court. Unfortunately, longer case processing time can have an unintended negative effect. To begin, transferring juveniles to adult court is done partly for "community protection." However, as mentioned in Chapter 2, youth who remain in juvenile court are not entitled to bail. Conversely, once transferred to the adult system, juveniles are given all the procedural and due process rights that are granted to adults, including greater bail rights and practices. With this in mind, limited research has found that transferred offenders are more likely to be released from pre-dispositional custody, as compared to retained offenders (Myers, 2001b; Myers & Kiehl, 2001). Because transferred cases take a lengthy amount of time to process, when these offenders are released on bail, they have more time and opportunity to commit additional delinquent acts, which is the next topic of discussion.

TRANSFER AND RECIDIVISM

When examining the impact of transfer on recidivism, because juveniles are expected to be treated more harshly in adult court as compared to juvenile court, it generally is thought that transferred juveniles should recidivate less than retained juveniles. This is loosely based on the concepts and propositions of deterrence theory. From this perspective, if legal punishments are swift, certain, and severe, individuals should be deterred from committing criminal and deviant behaviors (Akers, 2000). As discussed above, it has been established fairly well that those who are transferred to criminal court experience longer case processing time than those who are retained by the juvenile court (Fagan, 1995; Myers, 2003a; Rudman et al., 1986), meaning punishment is not as swift. However, research also has shown that offenders who are transferred generally do have a high probability of conviction, which is an indicator of sanction certainty (Bishop & Frazier, 1991; Bishop et al., 1989; Myers, 2003a; Rudman et al., 1986; Thomas & Bilchik, 1985). Furthermore, as previously discussed, the general findings suggest that most transferred and convicted offenders are incarcerated (Bishop & Frazier, 1991; Bishop et al., 1989; Houghtalin & Mays, 1991; Podkopacz & Feld, 1996; Rudman et al., 1986; Thomas & Bilchik, 1985), and they tend to be sentenced to fairly long periods of confinement, which represents strong punishment severity.

With this in mind, the study by Fagan (1995) examined recidivism rates among the juvenile offenders from four matched counties (2 in New Jersey and 2 in New York). The transferred offenders not only recidivated more frequently, but did so more quickly, than did youth retained by the juvenile court. However, this only held true for those charged with robbery. When burglary offenders were examined, there was no significant difference in recidivism between the two groups. Recall that of the two types of offenders, those charged with robbery tended to experience greater punishment in adult court than in juvenile court, which was less true of those charged with burglary.

The study by Podkopacz & Feld (1996) also found evidence that transferred offenders' recidivated more than retained juveniles. In their comparative research, it was determined that 58% of the transferred youth committed additional offenses, while only 42% of retained youth committed new offenses. In this study, a conservative operationalization of recidivism was used. While many studies use rearrests as a measure of recidivism, actual adjudications or convictions were used in this research. This may have influenced the findings, because offenders may have been committing new crimes, resulting in an arrest. However, unless they were either adjudicated delinquent or convicted in criminal court, they would not have been considered as recidivists in the analysis.

Another study examined all juveniles (n = 3,151) who were transferred to criminal court in 1987 in Florida (Bishop et al., 1996). A matching procedure was used to generate a comparable group of retained offenders (n= 2,887). Matching criteria were based on such variables as offense seriousness, prior record, age, gender, and race. In examining recidivism, measured as rearrest over an approximate 1 year follow-up period, it was found that 30% of the transferred offenders were re-arrested, while 19% of the retained offenders were rearrested. Transferred offenders were significantly more likely to be re-arrested than retained offenders. Further analysis showed that transferred offenders also recidivated more quickly than retained offenders. The average number of days to rearrest for transferred offenders was 135 days, while the average number of days to rearrest for retained youth was 227 days.

Finally, Myers (2001, 2003b) found similar results in Pennsylvania. Using 18 months as a follow-up period, it was determined that transferred offenders were more likely to be rearrested, and were rearrested more quickly, as compared to similar retained offenders. This study also examined the impact of other variables on recidivism. Age at referral had a significant negative effect, as older offenders were less likely to get rearrested, as compared to younger offenders. The age at which offenders were initially referred to the juvenile court also had a significant negative effect, as the older a youth was when initially referred, the less risk of future rearrest.

Furthermore, offenders who were convicted experienced a greater likelihood of recidivism during the follow-up period, but incarceration length had a significant negative effect. The longer offenders were incarcerated, the less likely they were to recidivate, suggesting that the severity of sentencing plays a salient role in deterring future delinquent and/or criminal behavior among violent youthful offenders.

The main limitation with most of these studies was the short follow-up period, meaning recidivism over the long run was not examined. In a follow-up study of research previously conducted by Bishop et al. (1996), it was determined that when an extended time period was used, the probability of rearrest for retained juveniles caught up to that of transferred youth (Winner et al., 1997). However, a closer examination of the findings revealed that the similarity in probability of arrest between transferred and non-transferred offenders was offense specific. When looking exclusively at felony property crime, retained juveniles' recidivated more often than transferred offenders. However, when all other offenses were examined, the results were similar to that of past research. Transferred offenders recidivated more often and more quickly than offenders who remained in juvenile court.

Overall, it appears as though transferring juveniles to adult court is not effective in reducing recidivism. One reason may be that the criminal justice system is not as focused on rehabilitating offenders as the juvenile justice system. It also was found that older offenders and those with a later age of onset were less likely to recidivate than younger offenders and those with early onset. This is consistent with previous findings that people "age out" of committing illegal behavior during late adolescence (Blumstein, 1995), and that those who begin committing crime at older ages are less likely to commit future delinquent acts (Farrington, 1986; Farrington, 1998).

Finally, there was some support for specific deterrence in this section. In one study, as incarceration length increased, recidivism decreased (Myers, 2003b), indicating that sentence severity may have some effect on future illegal behavior. However, as noted earlier, most research regarding incarceration length examines the official sentence received. One study has found that juveniles in adult court may only serve approximately one-quarter of their original sentence (Fritsch et al., 1996). Therefore, there is a need for further research in this area.

TRANSFER AND GENERAL DETERRENCE

In addition to specific deterrence, it often is expected that because transferring juveniles to criminal court is supposed to result in harsh punishment, overall juvenile crime should decrease as a result of expanded transfer laws being implemented. In other words, if juvenile offenders know that committing crime can result in being transferred to adult court, it should deter them from being involved in illegal offenses. This again is loosely based upon deterrence theory. While specific deterrence focuses on punished offenders refraining from committing crime in the future, general deterrence is directed at preventing others in the population from committing crime, due to the punishment imposed on those who are caught (Akers, 2000).

To test this notion, one study evaluated the New York Juvenile Offender Law that was enacted in 1978 (Singer & McDowall, 1988). The law statutorily excluded violent juveniles, over age 13, from juvenile court jurisdiction, and automatically transferred them to criminal court (i.e., legislative waiver). The excluded offenses were murder, attempted murder, kidnapping, attempted kidnapping, arson, manslaughter, rape, sodomy, burglary, and assault. The researchers used monthly arrest totals that were reported to the FBI's Uniform Crime Reporting Division from 1974 to 1984. As a comparison city, the crime rates in Philadelphia also were examined during the same time. The general finding was that the law had no effect on the juvenile crime rate. Arrest rates for both homicides and assaults did not change as a result of the new law being implemented. The arrest rates for rape and arson did decrease in New York, but there also was a similar decline in the comparison city of Philadelphia, suggesting that there was a general decline in those juvenile crimes across other areas. In other words, the decrease in arrest rates for rape and arson did not appear to be due to the new transfer law.

Similar results were found in research by Jensen & Metsger (1994). A time-series design was used to determine the impact of an Idaho legislative waiver statute on violent juvenile crime (i.e., murder, forcible rape, robbery, and aggravated assault). Data were obtained from unpublished FBI sources. The new law went into effect in 1981; the years used for the analysis were 1976-1980 and 1982-1986. Montana and Wyoming also were used as comparison states. The results indicated that while violent juvenile crime decreased in the comparison states, it actually increased by 18% in Idaho. Stated differently, the transfer law did not produce a general deterrent effect on violent juvenile crime.

Finally, Risler, Sweatman, & Nakerud (1998) used a quasi-experimental cohort design to examine the impact of a new transfer law on serious juvenile crime. Georgia's Juvenile Justice Reform Act was passed in 1994; the years used for the analysis were 1992-1993 and 1994-1995. Results indicated that there was no significant difference in the mean arrest rates for serious juvenile crime (i.e., murder, rape, robbery, aggravated assault, and sex offenses) between the two time periods (prior to and after the law). This finding also suggests that transferring juveniles to adult court does not provide a general deterrent to youthful offending.

Similar to findings that transferring offenders to adult court does not appear to reduce recidivism among individual offenders (i.e., no specific deterrence), it also seems as though expanded transfer laws do not reduce overall juvenile crime (i.e., no general deterrence). In sum, based on a relatively small amount of research, the findings suggest that transferring offenders does not effectively prevent future delinquent and criminal activity, which is contrary to one of the main goals of transfer laws.

CONCLUSION

There has been a plethora of studies examining juvenile transfer to adult court. Overall, the research has found that the transfer decision often is made on the basis of legal variables, such as offense seriousness and prior record. However, other research suggests that extra-legal variables (e.g., race and age) may also be operating in the decision making process, which is cause for concern and further study.

Regarding the effectiveness of juvenile transfer, this process generally does not appear to be highly successful. Although many of those waived to adult court experience high conviction and incarceration rates, they may actually be serving only a portion of their sentence, which could be due to jail and prison overcrowding. Another problem with juvenile transfer is that waived offenders seem to have a higher recidivism rate than similar youth retained by the juvenile court. Because transferred offenders may be more likely to be released on bail, and due to the long amount of time until their cases are disposed, they also have greater opportunity to become involved in additional delinquent behavior. In addition, the adult system may not be focused on rehabilitating waived offenders. Therefore, when released back into the community, this may explain why transferred offenders are more likely to commit additional illegal offenses.

Finally, of the studies that examined whether juvenile crime decreased as a result of transfer laws being implemented, the findings were consistent. There was no reduction in juvenile crime following the introduction of new transfer laws. Considering the results of this empirical research, to date it seems as though transferring juveniles to adult court generally has been ineffective in reaching many of its intended goals.

THE CURRENT RESEARCH

As mentioned in this chapter, there has been only one known empirical study that focused on identifying the determinants of decertification (Singer, 1996). However, there were a number of limitations with this research. First, the data employed were based on offenders who were arrested prior to the increase in youth violence that began in the mid-1980s. Because of the current focus on violent juveniles, further research needs to be conducted that examines these types of offenders. Second, there were a small number of variables used in the analysis to predict decertification. Third, there was little comparison of court outcomes between the decertified and retained offenders. In order to better determine if transferred offenders are treated differently in adult court (in terms of certainty, severity, and swiftness of punishment), more comparative research must be done that examines similar offenders in both systems. Finally, there was no comparison between the decertified and retained youth regarding their recidivism. Considering that transfer laws generally are based on the expectation of deterrence, more research needs to be done in this area.

As a result of the legislative waiver law (Act 33) implemented in Pennsylvania in March 1996 (as discussed in Chapter 2), many violent youth have been automatically waived to adult court in this state (Snyder et al., 2000). However, there also is a provision in the statute that allows transferred youth to be sent back to juvenile court (i.e., decertification). With this in mind, the current study examined three critical areas. First, the predictors of the decertification decision were investigated. This part of the research is similar to that of Singer (1996), except the data used for the current study were subsequent to the youth violence surge that began in the mid-1980s, and both quantitative and qualitative research was conducted. Second, this study compared the court outcomes between decertified and retained youth regarding the certainty, severity, and swiftness of punishment. Finally, the current research compared the two groups of offenders in terms of recidivism. In addition to quantitative analyses, findings are reported from interviews with key players involved in the decertification process (i.e., prosecutors, public defenders, and judges), and courtroom observations were conducted. It is believed that the findings from the interviews and observations shed further light on the highly under-researched area of decertification, and that this study fills a gap in the large body of transfer literature.

CHAPTER 4

Labeling or Deterrence

In the previous chapter, the empirical research regarding juvenile transfer was examined. Among the many salient issues discussed regarding transfer, two emerged that are most relevant to the current research. First, there is a possibility that extra-legal factors, as well as legal factors, impact on the waiver decision and on subsequent case outcomes. For instance, older offenders appear more likely to be transferred than those who are younger, and nonwhites may be more likely to be transferred than whites. Second, despite generally harsh sanctioning, research to date has indicated that transferred offenders exhibit greater recidivism than youth retained in juvenile court.

The purpose of this chapter is to examine these issues within a theoretical framework. The two theoretical perspectives that are most applicable are labeling and deterrence. Although the present study does not directly test these theories, it is important to provide a theoretical background for conducting this research. Labeling theory's status characteristics hypothesis provides the framework regarding certain characteristics being associated with more formal or harsher justice system processing. Labeling theory also provides a deviance amplification hypothesis, which will be one framework for studying the recidivism of transferred and retained offenders. In addition, this chapter discusses the theoretical opposite of labeling's deviance amplification hypothesis, as provided by deterrence theory.

Because labeling theory's deviance amplification hypothesis and the propositions relevant to specific deterrence predict opposite outcomes, support for one theory, in essence, results in non-support for the other. This being the case, when discussing research relevant to the deviance amplification hypothesis, the studies that provide empirical support are discussed. Conversely, when discussing specific deterrence, studies providing supportive evidence are examined.

EVOLUTION OF LABELING THEORY

Like virtually all theories, labeling theory has undergone various changes since originally being developed. Tannenbaum (1938) initially claimed that children often engage in deviant behavior for fun or play, usually in the form of minor mischief (e.g., breaking windows, skipping school, and annoying others). Although most children are involved in these behaviors, the community generally views these activities as delinquent or even evil. Therefore, attention is given, often by the police and the juvenile justice system. As the behavior continues, the community demands for the act(s) to be suppressed. A shift soon occurs from the behavior being viewed as evil and delinquent, to the juvenile being viewed as evil and delinquent. This results in all behavior by the youth being looked upon suspiciously.

It is at this point that Tannenbaum (1938) stated that the "dramatization of evil" could take place, and "the first dramatization of the 'evil' which separates the child out of his group for specialized treatment plays a greater role in making the criminal than perhaps any other experience" (p. 19). From this perspective, after children have been labeled "delinquent," their entire world is different. They no longer see themselves as they did previously, and others also may begin to look at them negatively. Once they realize they are "different," they begin to self-identify with the new label. Eventually, they develop attachments to others similarly labeled, and become further involved in delinquent or criminal activities. The youth then become the very people they were described as being.

Tannenbaum also mentioned that it does not matter whether the label is applied as the result of punishment or reform. If the emphasis is on the behavior, a similar end could result, regardless of the purpose of sanctioning. The more society seeks to reform the "evil," the greater the evil will become. Therefore, in order to diffuse the evil, less has to be said about the behavior.

Lemert (1951) subsequently built upon Tannenbaum's theory in two main ways. First, he expanded upon the reasons why youth commit initial deviance, prior to being labeled. Second, he clarified the process by which someone becomes more deviant, after being labeled by society. In Tannenbaum's version of labeling theory, he referred to the early deviance of youth as play or mischief. Lemert claimed that there are different reasons, identified in a variety of theories, as to why youth initially commit deviant acts (e.g., because of various biological, psychological, and sociological factors). These beginning acts are "primary deviance." According to Lemert, primary deviance is sporadic and unorganized; those who commit this deviance rationalize their behavior, because they still think of themselves within the "normal" and socially accepted role.

Lemert also stated that it could not be known how long primary deviance will continue. Tannenbaum had claimed that after being labeled, a youth might begin to self-identify with that label, resulting in more deviant acts. Lemert stated that it likely would take more than one negative societal reaction for this to occur, as it generally is a process of action and reaction. If primary deviance continues, and there is an increase in social reactions and penalties when the deviance occurs, the juvenile may begin to self-identify with a deviant label. At this point, labeled youth no longer will view themselves within the same role, and then may adopt another role, based on the deviant label. The deviance that occurs as a result of the new role is "secondary deviance." According to Lemert, "when a person begins to employ his deviant behavior or a role based upon it as a means of defense, attack, or adjustment to the overt and covert problems created by the consequent societal reaction to him, his deviation is secondary" (p. 76).

Following up on Lemert's work, Becker (1963) further specified that deviance is created by society. He then clarified this statement by saying he did not mean the etiology of delinquent behavior is located in the social situation, or that social factors cause the behavior. Instead, he proposed that "social groups create deviance by making the rules whose infraction constitutes deviance, and by applying those rules to particular people and labeling them as outsiders" (p. 9).

There are two central ideas within this statement. First, deviance does not refer to the act of the person, but rather it is the result of the application of others. Deviance is simply the behavior that social groups label as such. The second idea is that the rules are applied unequally to certain people, subsequently resulting in them being more likely to be labeled. Although Becker did not go into great detail about which groups or individuals are more likely to get labeled compared to others, he did allude to socio-economic factors and race playing a role in determining who would be labeled:

Rules tend to be applied more to some persons than to others....Boys from middle-class areas do not get as far in the legal process when they are apprehended as do boys from slum areas....This variation occurs even though the original infraction of the rule is the same in the two cases....Similarly, the law is differentially applied to [blacks] and whites. It is well known that a [black person] believed to have attacked a white woman is much more likely to be labeled than a white man who commits the same offense. (Becker, 1963, pp. 12-13)

With this theoretical perspective in mind, the next section will examine the empirical evidence regarding one of the central tenets of labeling theory: the status characteristics hypothesis. In other words, are certain characteristics associated with a greater likelihood of labeling?

THE STATUS CHARACTERISTICS HYPOTHESIS

Overall, the status characteristics hypothesis posits that certain groups or individuals are more likely to be labeled than others (Paternoster & Iovanni, 1989). This suggests discrimination, because people who possess certain characteristics have an increased risk of becoming labeled. However, in assessing the state of labeling theory in the 1970s, mainly with regard to juveniles, Wellford (1975) argued that there was "overwhelming evidence" that extralegal variables (e.g., race, class, and demeanor) had little or no impact on the decision to arrest, determination of guilt, or sentencing. He further contended that offense related variables were the most important in determining case outcomes. Furthermore, concerning research that had found extralegal effects on police and court outcomes, he claimed that the analyses were flawed, due to a failure to properly control for the impact of legal variables (e.g., offense seriousness and prior record).

Paternoster and Iovanni (1989) later reached different conclusions than those of Wellford. In their review of studies that tested the status characteristics hypothesis, they found mixed support. However, unlike Wellford, who dismissed the research that supported extralegal factors as having an effect on court outcomes, they asserted that, "the only reasonable inference that can be drawn from this literature is that there are data of uneven quality and rigor which both support and refute the hypothesis" (p. 372).

In addition, Paternoster and Iovanni (1989) provided two suggestions that would allow better empirical testing of the status characteristics hypothesis. First, researchers should consider the relevant conditions under which status characteristics would have the most impact. For example, as suggested earlier by Becker (1963), there likely may be a difference in court outcomes depending upon the characteristics of both the offender and victim (e.g., black offender/black victim versus black offender/white victim). Second, instead of examining the effect of status characteristics at single decision points (e.g., arrest, detention, and conviction), researchers should investigate the cumulative effects over the entire process. In other words, there may be a series of small discriminatory effects operating in the justice system, which accumulate as cases get processed further. Therefore, only by examining the whole process will researchers be able to fully understand the effect of status characteristics on justice system processing.

Modern Status Characteristics Research

In this section, modern empirical research regarding labeling theory's status characteristics hypothesis will be examined. Most of the following studies attempted to determine whether extra-legal variables (e.g., race, gender, and age) had an effect on case outcomes for juvenile offenders in the juvenile justice system. Consistent with the arguments of Paternoster and Iovanni (1989), contemporary studies have uncovered evidence in support of the hypothesis.

In a comparative study of juvenile offenders, data were collected from a subset of cases referred to the juvenile justice intake division of the Florida Department of Health and Rehabilitative Services (HRS) in 1979 (Smith & Paternoster, 1990). The data were obtained from the central planning and research division of HRS for 31 counties in the state. The researchers only examined white and black juvenile offenders who were referred to HRS for felonies or misdemeanors (n = 3180). Two groups were compared: those subsequently referred to juvenile court and those not referred to juvenile court.

The results indicated that after controlling for legal variables (prior record and offense seriousness), age and race were significant predictors of the juvenile intake officer's decision to refer a case to juvenile court. Older youth were more likely to have their cases referred than younger juveniles. In addition, black youth were more likely to be referred than whites. One weakness of this study, however, is that there was a lack of variation within the offense seriousness variable; it was measured simply as a felony or misdemeanor.

A subsequent study by Triplett (1993) found similar, but not identical, results. The data for this research came from the National Youth Survey, based on a national probability sample of households from 1976 to 1980. All households with children aged 11 to 17 were eligible; the total number of youth included was 1,324. This study was different than previous research in one distinctive way: it examined parental labeling. In other words, factors were considered that determined whether parents labeled their children delinquent. The results indicated that race and age were significant predictors. Contrary to Smith and Paternoster (1990), however, older children were less likely to be labeled than younger children. On the other hand, blacks again were more likely to be labeled than whites. Gender was not significant, meaning there was no difference between males and females in the likelihood of parental labeling. Finally, socioeconomic status also was not a significant predictor in the labeling decision.

Another study sought to examine the impact of race on detention decisions (Wordes, Bynum, & Corley, 1994). The researchers used a combination of juvenile court and police records from five counties in an unknown state. A stratified random sample was drawn (based on race, gender, offense category, and disposition), resulting in a final sample size of 2,225 (728 felony cases from police records and 1,497 felony cases from juvenile court records). The results indicated that after controlling for legal variables (i.e., offense seriousness and prior record), race, gender, and age had significant effects on detention at the intake stage and the preliminary hearing stage. Black and Latino youth were more likely to be detained than were whites; males were more likely to be detained as compared to females; and older youth were more likely to be detained than were younger offenders.

Frazier & Bishop (1995) also found substantial extralegal effects at key stages in juvenile court processing. They examined case files of youth referred to juvenile justice intake units in Florida from 1985 to 1987 (n = 137,028). Their results indicated that while controlling for legal variables (i.e., prior record and offense seriousness), youth who were detained prior to disposition were significantly more likely to get referred to juvenile court, as compared to those who were released. Although race had little direct impact on referral to juvenile court, nonwhites were significantly more likely to get detained than were whites. Therefore, there appeared to be an indirect race effect on court referral, operating through pre-dispositional custody. In addition, older offenders and males were more likely to be detained prior to disposition. Finally, regarding court referral, males were more likely to be referred as compared to females.

The same study also found significant effects of the extralegal variables on subsequent case dispositions, including transfer to adult court. Again, controlling for legal variables, nonwhites were more likely to get either committed to a residential facility or waived to adult court, as compared to white offenders. Also, males were more likely to get committed or transferred, as compared to females. Finally, the older the offender, the greater the likelihood was of being committed or transferred.

Another study from the mid-1990s sought to examine possible racial disparities in an urban juvenile court. Feld (1995) used data from the Minnesota Supreme Court's Judicial Information System to investigate decision making in Hennepin County during 1986 (n = 3,385). The results indicated that blacks were more likely to be detained prior to disposition than non-blacks. Although offense seriousness and prior record also were significant determinants of the detention decision, race had a greater impact than prior record, but less impact than offense seriousness.

In addition to assessing the effect of race on the detention decision, Feld (1995) also examined the impact of extralegal variables on disposition. After controlling for legal factors, detention, and presence of an attorney, both blacks and Native Americans were significantly more likely to receive out-of-home placements, as compared to whites. When examining secure confinement, males were significantly more likely to receive this type of sentence than were females. Finally, older offenders were more likely to be sentenced to secure confinement than were younger youth.

Similar results regarding the detention decision were found by Leonard & Sontheimer (1995). In their research, they examined the 14 counties in Pennsylvania with the highest proportions of black and Latino youth residents. These counties reported 20,325 delinquency cases during 1989, which comprised 70% of all delinquency cases involving black, Latino, and white youth in Pennsylvania for that year. After controlling for legal variables, race and age had significant effects on the detention decision. Latino youth were significantly more likely to be detained than any other race, followed by blacks. In addition, older offenders were more likely to be detained than younger offenders. Gender had no effect, as there was no difference in the likelihood of detention between males and females.

Later research examined a random sample of juvenile cases in Pennsylvania (but not including Philadelphia) during 1990 (n = 4,683) (DeJong & Jackson, 1998). The results indicated that after controlling for offense seriousness, type of charge (i.e., property, violent, drug, or other), prior record (since 1985), and population density, there was no significant difference in the referral rate between whites and blacks. However, Hispanics were significantly more likely to be referred to juvenile court than whites. Also, older offenders were significantly more likely to be referred, as compared to younger youth.

The same study examined factors that potentially could affect secure placement. There was no significant difference between blacks and whites on the likelihood of being placed. Contrary to the findings regarding referral, there also was no difference between placement rates for Hispanics and whites. Finally, age had no significant effect in the placement model.

Finally, in a recent study, McGuire (2002) sought to investigate the potential cumulative effects of race on court outcomes. He examined the records of all cases that were referred to the juvenile courts of Missouri during 1997, but only used cases of children who were either black or white. Also, in order to be in the analysis, cases had to represent either status or delinquent offenses, resulting in a total sample 64,466. The findings indicated that after controlling for many variables (i.e., offense seriousness, having multiple charges, prior record, age, and the presence of a detention facility in the processing jurisdiction), race was a significant predictor of detention. Blacks were more likely to be detained prior to disposition than whites. However, whites were significantly more likely to be adjudicated than blacks, after controlling for the other factors (including pre-dispositional detention). It also should be pointed out that those who were detained were more likely to be adjudicated and committed, compared to those who were released. As with the detention stage, blacks were more likely to be committed as compared to whites. Regarding the effect of age, older offenders were significantly more likely to be detained, adjudicated, and committed, as compared to younger youth.

Summary

There does appear to be substantial contemporary research on juvenile offenders that supports labeling theory's status characteristics hypothesis. However, the general findings regarding the effect of extralegal variables on case outcomes is somewhat mixed, depending upon the explanatory factors and case outcomes examined. Most of the research does suggest that older offenders are more likely to get sanctioned than younger offenders (DeJong & Jackson, 1998; Frazier & Bishop, 1995; Leonard & Sontheimer, 1995; McGuire, 2002; Wordes et al., 1994), and that males are more likely to get sanctioned than females (Frazier & Bishop, 1995; Minor, Hartmann, & Terry, 1997; Wordes et al., 1994).

The effect of race on formal sanctions is not quite as clear. While various studies suggest that race has a significant effect, (Feld, 1995; Leonard & Sontheimer, 1995; Minor et al., 1997; Smith & Paternoster, 1990; Triplett, 1993; Wordes et al., 1994), other research indicates that the relationship is indirect (Frazier & Bishop, 1995), or that it depends on the particular decision making stage (McGuire, 2002). Minorities could be more likely to receive formal sanctions than whites, and there also may be an indirect effect through earlier decision-making stages (e.g., pre-dispositional detention). However, in order to effectively gauge the true effect of race on court outcomes, more research should be conducted according to the suggestions of Paternoster & Iovanni (1989), which include examining status characteristics in the context under which the potential effects could be maximized and looking at the entire justice process, instead of single decision points.

DEVIANCE AMPLIFICATION VERSUS SPECIFIC DETERRENCE

This section will examine both labeling theory's deviance amplification hypothesis and propositions derived from deterrence theory. After discussing each, their empirical support also will be examined. This congruent discussion is based on contrary theoretical predictions. In general, the deviance amplification hypothesis states that sanctions and punishments will increase the likelihood of deviance, while deterrence theory holds that sanctions and punishments will decrease deviance.

Deviance Amplification and Empirical Support

As mentioned above, the deviance amplification hypothesis states that as a result of being labeled, people commit more deviance than they otherwise would have, had they not been labeled. According to Paternoster and Iovanni (1989), the process from labeling to secondary deviance occurs as follows: after getting publicly labeled, people may begin to self-identify with the label; they also may be excluded from conventional opportunities and may be more likely to develop deviant associates; finally, they then may commit further deviance as a consequence of the labeling process. In other words, while situational or personal factors can cause primary deviance, from this perspective societal reactions increase the likelihood of secondary deviance occurring. Arriving at secondary deviance is therefore a complex process, which is one reason why this theory is difficult to test empirically. Not surprisingly, then, most of the existing research simply focuses on whether those who are labeled commit more deviant acts than those who are not labeled.

Research on the deviance amplification hypothesis generally has sought to determine the possible effect of formal sanctions on recidivism. Most of the relevant studies with juvenile offenders did not use random assignment to treatment and control groups, meaning definitive conclusions cannot be made regarding the effect of formal sanctions on subsequent offending. However, in order to allow for greater confidence in the findings, many researchers did attempt to control for various other explanatory factors.

One early study attempted to determine the impact of labeling on future shoplifting (Klemke, 1978). Questionnaires were given to students in four high schools in small communities in the Pacific Northwest (n = 1189; no timeframe was given regarding year of data collection). Descriptive results indicated that approximately 40% of those apprehended by store personnel continued shoplifting. The deviance amplification hypothesis states that people will commit more crime after being labeled, compared to if the labeling had not taken place. Therefore, the study also compared shoplifting rates of those "labeled" with those who were not "labeled." While controlling for gender, the findings were not statistically significant regarding the impact of labeling on subsequent shoplifting. However, although the effect was not significant, labeled youth did have a higher reported rate of future shoplifting than did non-labeled youth.

The same study also examined the impact of police intervention on shoplifting. Those who had experienced police intervention shoplifted more times in the future than did those who had no police intervention. These findings also did not reach statistical significance, but the relationship was in the expected direction. A major limitation of this study is that the researcher did not control for other explanatory factors that could impact future shoplifting (e.g., prior offending).

A subsequent longitudinal study from the same time period examined 215 youth in London who were given self-reported questionnaires at ages 14, 18, and 21 (Farrington, Osborn, & West, 1978). By age 21, 109 of the subjects had been convicted of a crime, while the remaining youth (106) were not convicted. The results generally indicated that those convicted experienced an increase in criminal behavior following the conviction, while those who were not convicted displayed no increase. However, as with the prior study (Klemke, 1978), because this research did not account for factors that could have influenced re-arrest (e.g., prior offending), the results are questionable.

Another study used cluster sampling to collect data from high school students (2,147 juniors and seniors; no specific year given) at 13 schools in Virginia Beach and at nine schools in Portsmouth, Virginia (Thomas & Bishop, 1984). A questionnaire was administered both at the beginning of the school year and at the end. Examples of delinquent acts measured were truancy, theft, simple assault, vandalism, breaking and entering, vehicular theft, and assault with a weapon. When examining the impact of both formal and informal sanctions on delinquency, the results indicated that as sanctions increased, delinquent acts significantly increased. In addition, consistent with the deviance amplification hypothesis, this research found that increased sanctions were moderately associated with a delinquent self-identification. However, because the researchers did not consider the effect of confounding variables (e.g., age and gender) the results must be interpreted with caution.

Klein (1986) subsequently assessed the effect of labeling on a cohort of juvenile offenders who were randomly assigned by police (an anonymous department) to one of four groups: released, referred to a community agency, released to a community agency with purchase of service, or petitioned to juvenile court (n = 306). Using 6 months as an initial follow-up period, the findings indicated that the more stigmatizing the label, the greater the recidivism. Moreover, using 27 months as a follow-up period, the petitioned youth recidivated more often than the released offenders. Overall, the strength of this randomized study provides solid evidence of a deviance amplification effect.

Schneider and Ervin (1990) also found support for labeling's deviance amplification hypothesis, in a study 876 adjudicated delinquents from six juvenile courts (Washington, DC; Ventura, CA; Madison, WI; Oklahoma City, OK; Jonesboro, GA; and Boise, ID). The researchers interviewed the subjects, along with examining their official records. After controlling for confounding variables (e.g., prior record, age, and gender), they found that the severity of punishment (i.e., number of days incarcerated) had a significant effect on recidivism, as measured in a 2 to 3 year follow-up period. In general, the more severe the punishment received, the greater the recidivism.

In examining informal parental labeling, Matsueda (1992) found similar results using data from the National Youth Survey (NYS) of 1976. Of the households included in the survey, 73% of the eligible youths participated in the study (n = 1,725). The findings were that parental appraisal (i.e., whether parents believed their child was sociable, likely to succeed, distressed, or a rule violator) had a strong effect on delinquency. As parental appraisal became more positive, delinquency decreased. Furthermore, part of the effect was mediated by youth-reflected appraisals. In other words, parental appraisals also influenced youth-reflected appraisals, which subsequently affected the child's delinquency.

Similar findings were revealed in research attempting to determine the effect of other informal sanctions on delinquency (Ward & Tittle, 1993). In this study, data were collected, via survey, from juniors and seniors in a southeastern state university (n = 270). In order to establish causal ordering, the questionnaires were given at three separate points over the course of a year (from spring of 1987 to spring of 1988). The variables measured were primary deviance (prior cheating), informal sanctions (severity of reaction by school peers), labeling (social reactions from informal audience or peers), deviant identity (whether the students conceived of themselves as academic cheaters), risk perception (perceived chances of other students learning about it if the student was to cheat), and subsequent deviance (number of times they cheated during the subsequent semester).

The findings were consistent with labeling theory. Primary deviance had a significant positive effect on sanctions by peers. Sanctions had a significant positive effect on labeling. Labeling had a significant positive effect on deviant identity. Finally, deviant identity had a significant positive effect on subsequent deviance. While most previous studies focused simply on secondary deviance, this research examined the entire labeling process and indicated that when informal sanctions are considered, labeling theory is supported.

Finally, Paternoster & Piquero (1995) also found support for labeling theory. In this study, questionnaires were administered to all 10th-grade students in nine high schools in a southeastern city. The questionnaires were first distributed in the students' English class during the fall of 1981 (n = 2,700). One year follow-up questionnaires were given during the fall of 1982 in the junior-year English class, of which 1,600 of the original 2,700 were enrolled. Sample attrition was due to absenteeism on the day the questionnaire was distributed, students taking a non-traditional English class their junior year, or students moving out of the school district.

The results indicated that punishment (i.e., being apprehended by the police, taken to the police station, arrested, or taken to juvenile court) had a significant positive effect on substance use (i.e., number of times students had drank liquor and used marijuana during the subsequent 12 months). Students who were punished reported more future substance use as compared to those who were not punished.

Summary

A significant amount of research on young people tends to support the deviance amplification hypothesis. In general, these studies suggest that as the severity of sanctions increase, the likelihood of recidivism also increases. A number of reasons can be put forth to explain these findings. First, the deviance amplification process could, in fact, be taking place. However, until further research examines the entire labeling process (i.e., primary deviance, reaction of society, self-identity, and secondary deviance), the existing findings should be viewed with caution. Second, most of the existing studies did not randomly assign offenders to groups. Therefore, other unmeasured and unconsidered factors may be affecting recidivism, other than being "labeled." Third, when offenders are formally sanctioned, they may become more visible to the police because of being apprehended in the past. Meanwhile, non-sanctioned offenders are not a focus of law enforcement, meaning they may be committing illegal acts, but they are undetected by formal agencies and therefore not identified in official records. Regardless of whether the findings are due to one or more of these reasons, stronger research designs are needed to better test the deviance amplification hypothesis.

Origins of Deterrence Theory

As mentioned previously, specific deterrence is the theoretical opposition of labeling theory's deviance amplification hypothesis. In this section, the origins of deterrence theory initially will be discussed. Following this historical discussion, the empirical support for specific deterrence will be examined.

Deterrence theory is rooted in the classical school of criminology, which can be traced to the mid 1700s (Empey et al., 1999). According to pure classical school theorists, there is no need to examine extraneous causes of criminal behavior; the assumption from this perspective regarding human behavior is that people are rationale beings who try to maximize their pleasure, while minimizing their pain. The person given the most credit for leading the classical school of thought was Cesare Beccaria (1963), who proposed that punishment should be fair and equal for everyone.

According to Beccaria, people can be deterred from committing crime if punishments are swift, certain, and proportionate to the crime committed. Punishment should be swift for two reasons. First, if the punishment is given soon after the commission of the crime, criminals are spared from uncertainty, which can contribute to them feeling tormented and weak. Second, if the punishment closely follows the criminal act, there will be a strong association between the two, in the mind of the criminal. Beccaria (1963) summed up his belief on the swiftness of punishment as follows:

Of utmost importance is it, therefore, that the crime and the punishment be intimately linked together, if it be desirable that, in crude, vulgar minds, the seductive picture of a particularly advantageous crime should immediately call up the associated idea of punishment. Long delay always produces the effect of further separating these two ideas: thus, though punishment of a crime may make an impression, it will be less as a punishment than as a spectacle, and will be felt only after the horror of the particular crime, which should serve to reinforce the feeling of punishment, has been much weakened in the hearts of the spectators. (p. 57)

Beccaria also stated that punishment should be certain. He claimed that, "the certainty of a punishment, even if it be moderate, will always make a stronger impression than the fear of another which is more terrible but combined with the hope of impunity" (p. 58). In other words, crime does not have to be overly severe in order for potential offenders to be deterred. If they strongly believe that they will be punished for their actions (i.e., high certainty), they are likely to refrain from committing crime.

Finally, punishment should be proportionate to the crime. Beccaria stated, "For a punishment to attain its end, the evil which it inflicts has only to exceed the advantage derivable from the crime" (p. 43). Therefore, in order for deterrence to be effective, there should not be a barrage of severe sanctions for acts that do not equally injure society. Each sanction should fit a specific crime.

As discussed in Chapter 2, the modern approach generally used to address juvenile crime has been to "crack-down" and "get tough." As a result of the youth violence surge that began in the mid-1980s, many states passed laws that resulted in increased penalties for juvenile offenders, including making it easier to transfer many to adult court (Taylor et al., 2002). In other words, states sought to increase the severity, and, to a lesser extent, certainty of punishments. This method of addressing crime appears contrary to the views set forth by Beccaria. While current policies mainly attempt to increase the severity of punishment, Beccaria placed much greater emphasis on the swiftness and certainty of punishment.

Specific Deterrence Research

Although Beccaria (1963) originally distinguished between general and specific deterrence in the mid 1700s, neither type of deterrence was tested empirically until approximately 40 years ago. As mentioned in Chapter 3, specific deterrence occurs when an individual offender is punished and is deterred from committing future illegal acts, while general deterrence occurs when people in the general population are deterred from committing crime, due to the knowledge of laws and punishments of those who are caught (Akers, 2000). The current study will be focused more on specific deterrence, with regard to the recidivism of violent youthful offenders in juvenile and adult court.

It first should be pointed out that the empirical research on specific deterrence is somewhat limited, particularly when examining juvenile offenders. Although there are three main propositions to deterrence theory, based on punishment certainty, severity, and swiftness, the existing literature typically examines offenders who were formally sanctioned, as compared to those who were not, in an attempt to determine whether the sanctioned group had a lower recidivism rate than the non-sanctioned group. Put differently, studies tend to focus most on the severity element of deterrence theory. In addition, the results from these studies differ from those in the last section regarding deviance amplification, as the following research shows some evidence of a specific deterrence effect.

In an early study, Murray and Cox (1979) examined arrest data for a cohort of boys born in Chicago in 1960. They used a random sample of those who were arrested at least once by the Chicago police (n = 484). Only arrests prior to the offenders' 17th birthday were considered. These youth either were sentenced to informal supervision (n = 155), probation (n = 52), put in a community program (n = 131), or institutionalized (n = 146). The general findings were that the institutionalized group experienced lower re-offending rates than did the other groups. In other words, harsher sanctions were associated with a lower rate of recidivism. The main limitation with this study is that rival causal factors were not controlled for in the analysis, meaning the suggested relationship may have been spurious.

Brown and his colleagues later examined 500 delinquent youth who were randomly selected from the files of the juvenile probation office in Dauphin County, Pennsylvania, from the years 1960 to 1975 (Brown, Miller, & Jenkins, 1987; Brown, Miller, Jenkins, & Rhodes, 1989; Brown, Miller, Jenkins, & Rhodes, 1991). Follow-up information could be obtained only for 476 juveniles in the sample. The findings indicated that those who were adjudicated at first referral (n = 243) were significantly less likely to be imprisoned later as an adult, in compared to those who did not go to juvenile court until a subsequent referral (n = 233). Put differently, those who were formally sanctioned at their first referral were less likely to be incarcerated as an adult, as compared to those who were not sanctioned until subsequent referrals.

In a more elaborate study, Wooldredge (1988) examined the effect of 12 dispositions on the recidivism of juvenile offenders. The data were obtained from four counties in Illinois (McLean, Sangamon, Champaign, and Vermillion) from 1978 to 1982. The sample consisted of all delinquents who committed misdemeanor and felony offenses, and who subsequently were processed by the juvenile court (n = 2,038). There was a 3 to 7 year follow-up for recidivism (1985 was the cut-off year employed). The findings generally indicated that some sort of intervention (e.g., short term incarceration and short term court supervision) was more effective in reducing recidivism, compared to the cases that were dismissed. The research found that a combination of court supervision and community treatment was better at reducing recidivism than any other disposition examined, including dismissing the case.

Another longitudinal study also found some support for specific deterrence (Smith & Gartin, 1989). This research used police contact histories of all males who were born in Racine, Wisconsin, during 1949, who also maintained continuous residence in that area until age 25 (n = 325). To be included in the sample, the males must have had at least one police contact for a misdemeanor (not including status offenses, traffic violations, or suspicion) or felony. In examining the effect of arrest on future police contact rate, as the number of arrests increased, there was a consistent decrease in the rate of police contacts. This relationship, however, was less pronounced among repeat offenders, as compared to non-chronic offenders.

In a subsequent study of the effects of three different types of sanctions, Gottfredson & Barton (1993) looked at the impact of the closing of a juvenile correctional institution on recidivism. They examined data for three groups: a group committed to the Montrose Training School during the time it was being closed (the transition group; n = 355); a group who was both committed to and completed their time at Montrose prior to the closing (the pre-closing group; n = 318); and a group referred to Department of Juvenile Services after the last admission to Montrose, who also likely would have been committed to Montrose (the post-closing group; n = 254).

Recidivism was examined using official records for a 2.5-year follow-up period. The findings indicated that after controlling for other variables (i.e., age at first referral, age at release from Montrose, prior record, and a seriousness ranking for the most serious alleged crime), those in the pre-closing group had significantly fewer re-arrests for both property and person crimes, as compared to those in the post-closing group. Also, the transition group had significantly fewer re-arrests for property offenses, compared to the post-closing group. When examining recidivism for serious offenses (e.g., auto theft, breaking and entering, assault and battery, murder, rape, and distribution of narcotics), the general findings were the same: the pre-closing and transition groups had significantly fewer re-arrests than the post-closing group.

The same study also examined group differences in recidivism using self-report data. Though the relationships generally remained significant, the coefficients were not as large, as compared to when official reports were used. Gottfredson and Barton (1993, pp. 603-604) gave three reasons for the discrepancy. First, there was a longer follow-up period for the self-reports than for official records. Second, the youth interviewed may have been more delinquent than those who were not interviewed. The number of offenders in the sample using official records was 927, while the self-report sample only consisted of 458 of those original offenders. Third, the self-report questionnaire included minor crimes, which would not have been captured fully by official records. Although factors seemed to lessen the differences between the groups, in general, the pre-closing and transition groups recidivated less than the post-closing group.

In addition to studies focusing on juvenile offenders, there also has been some empirical support for specific deterrence with adult offenders. Sherman & Berk (1984) originally conducted an experiment in Minnesota where suspects for simple domestic assault were randomly assigned to one of three outcomes: arrest, separation, or some form of advice. The experiment ran from March 1981 to August 1982, and ended with a total usable sample of 314 cases. When examining both official records and victim self report data, the results indicated that arrested offenders committed significantly fewer repeat assaults than those who were separated from their victims or given advice.

However, in similar subsequent domestic violence studies, the results were mixed (Berk, Campbell, Klap, & Western, 1992; Dunford, Huizinga, & Elliot, 1990; Pate & Hamilton, 1992); see also Sherman & Eck, 2002). Some research found evidence of a deterrent effect, while other studies found a deviance amplification effect from arrest or no effect. This body of research further suggested an interaction between arrest and employment. In general, it was found that those who were employed and were arrested exhibited less recidivism, while those who were unemployed and were arrested displayed greater recidivism.

A different type of study with adult offenders study examined all men (n = 14,358) born in Copenhagen, Denmark, between 1944 and 1947, who were arrested by 1973 (Brennan & Mednick, 1994). Recidivism was measured by examining official records. While controlling for age, time in prison, recidivism risk, and type of offense, offenders who were sanctioned committed significantly fewer future offenses than those who were not sanctioned. However, the severity of initial sanctions had no significant effect on recidivism.

Finally Deng (1997) studied all offenders referred by the court to a Stop Shoplifting School in a northeastern metropolitan area from 1987 to 1990 (n = 3,974): The school was designed for first time shoplifters. After controlling for gender, the 3,494 offenders who attended the program had significantly fewer rearrests for shoplifting, compared to the 480 who did not attend the program. However, the main weakness of this study was that explanatory factors other than gender, which may have impacted on recidivism (e.g., prior record and age), were not controlled for in the analysis, meaning the presumed relationship between the sanction and recidivism may have been spurious.

Summary

It appears as though a significant amount of research provides support for a specific deterrent effect from formal sanctions. In the studies reviewed above, sanctioned offenders tended to recidivate less than those receiving lesser or no sanctions. One explanation for this finding is that as a result of being punished, sanctioned offenders actually are deterred from committing future crime. However, it must also be noted that much of the research on specific deterrence is not a true test of the theory.

Beccaria (1963) stated that in order for people to be deterred from committing crime, three criteria must be met: swiftness, certainty, and proportionality of punishment. Much of the existing research simply compares sanctioned and non-sanctioned offenders, meaning certainty and swiftness are not examined. In addition, Beccaria stated that the punishment should be proportionate to the crime. The current specific deterrence literature generally does not acknowledge this component. Therefore, although specific deterrence appears to be supported in the literature reviewed in this section, the above studies do not provide a full test of the theory.

CHAPTER SUMMARY

Overall, there is empirical support for both labeling theory and deterrence theory, particularly when examining youthful offenders. Regarding the status characteristics hypothesis, early research tended to be either flawed or suggested that there were little or no extralegal effects on court outcomes (Wellford, 1975). However, contemporary studies have indicated that extralegal factors can have both a direct and indirect effect on key decision-making stages in the juvenile justice system. Minorities tend to be more negatively impacted than whites, and older juveniles are more likely to be adversely effected than those who are younger. With some exceptions, these effects usually remain after legal variables are considered, suggesting the existence of bias in the juvenile system. In other words, there is empirical support for labeling theory's status characteristics hypothesis, meaning some groups and individuals are more likely to get labeled as compared to other groups and individuals.

There also is conflicting empirical support for labeling theory's deviance amplification hypothesis and for specific deterrence. However, as can be seen from the research discussed in this chapter, at least slightly more of the empirical findings seem to be toward labeling theory. This literature suggests that formal sanctions tend to increase, rather than decrease, future delinquency. Although there is substantial empirical evidence for deviance amplification, much of this research must be viewed with caution. In interpreting the findings, as discussed by Smith & Paternoster (1990), "a statistically significant positive coefficient could emerge [between formal sanctions and recidivism] because of a positive correlation between the variable indicating whether one is referred to court and the disturbance term in the recidivism equation—a selection artifact" (p. 1111). In other words, there may be unmeasured factors that affect the formal sanction decision and also result in the labeled group being more likely to recidivate than the non-labeled group. It may not be the labeling, then, that causes deviance amplification, but other unmeasured factors. This possibility points out the need to develop well-specified models that account for factors that can influence both the decision to sanction and subsequent offending behavior.

The general belief in specific deterrence also is supported in the literature. Many people may question, then, as to why there is empirical evidence for both deviance amplification and specific deterrence, considering each theory predicts opposite outcomes. Sherman (1993) has attempted to address this dilemma. In doing so, he claimed that both labeling and deterrence theories have their limitations, as deterrence theory fails to account for why sanctions sometimes increase criminal behavior, and labeling theory fails to explain why sanctions sometimes decrease illegal behavior.

Two of the factors Sherman set forth to explain the conflicting findings are perceptions of unfair treatment and having a stake in conformity. First, if an offender views a sanction as unfair, any possible deterrent effect may be weakened or eliminated. Therefore, future conduct may be unaffected, or even adversely affected, by the sanctioning event. For a sanction to be perceived as unfair, it can be viewed as arbitrary, discriminatory, undeserved, or excessive. In addition, perceived unfairness can be the result of the sanctioning agent disrespecting offenders, or a group to which they belong.

Second, concerning a stake in conformity, if offenders are poorly bonded to society (i.e., weak attachments to significant others and weak commitments to conventional activities), they may have no reason to remain law-abiding citizens. It then becomes a matter of having nothing to lose by violating the law. Overall, from this perspective, offenders who perceive unfair treatment and have a weak stake in conformity would be at a higher risk for recidivism, while perceptions of fair treatment and stronger social bonds would be associated with lesser recidivism. This might not only explain the conflicting findings from labeling and deterrence research, but also the results from juvenile transfer research that suggest greater recidivism on the part of waived youth (i.e., these offenders may perceive unfair treatment, have a weaker or broken stake in conformity, or both).

In sum, it appears as though labeling theory and deterrence theory are incomplete as separate theoretical perspectives. While each focuses on the effect of sanctions imposed on offenders, it seems that much more has to be considered in the prevention of future criminal behavior. With this in mind, researchers should be careful to incorporate measures of control variables and intervening variables into their studies (such as stakes in conformity and perceptions of fairness), so that clearer findings regarding deviance amplification and deterrence can be revealed.

This chapter focused on both labeling and deterrence theories, both of which can be applied to the topic of juvenile transfer. Labeling's status characteristics hypothesis would hold that youth with certain characteristics may be more likely to be waived to adult court (or decertified to juvenile court) and may be more likely to receive harsher case outcomes. Furthermore, labeling theory's deviance amplification hypothesis would predict that transfer to adult court and subsequent harsher sanctions will eventually lead to increased illegal behavior. On the other hand, deterrence theory can be applied in examining the certainty, severity, and swiftness of sanctions in juvenile and adult court, as well as the specific deterrent effect produced by waiver to the adult criminal system.

CHAPTER 5

Research Agenda

The current study, which employed a combined quantitative and qualitative design, examined three main areas: the process and determinants of decertification (i.e., reverse waiver), case processing outcomes for decertified youth and similar offenders retained in adult court, and the recidivism of decertified and adult court youthful offenders. Past empirical research, labeling theory, and deterrence theory were the foundations for the proposed hypotheses discussed in this chapter.

In general, this research first examined whether violent young offenders with certain characteristics are more or less likely to get decertified than other offenders, as suggested by the status characteristics hypothesis of labeling theory. This part of the theory posits that certain people are more likely to be labeled than others. Regarding the current research, the "label" will involve adult "criminal" court processing versus juvenile court processing as a result of decertification.

In addition, the present study examined whether young violent offenders are treated more harshly in the adult system (i.e., in terms of their case processing outcomes), as compared to similar youth who are decertified. It generally is believed that the juvenile court is unable to impose severe sentences that are "appropriate" for serious and violent offenders. The current research attempted to further determine whether this belief is empirically supported. In addition, other offender characteristics that impact on case outcomes also will be considered.

Finally, the study looked at whether offenders in the adult system exhibited greater recidivism than decertified youth (i.e., deviance amplification from transfer to adult court) or whether the findings are reversed (i.e., specific deterrence from transfer to adult court). Most research on the recidivism of serious and violent youthful offenders indicates a deviance amplification effect from transfer to adult court. However, relatively few studies have examined this issue, and none have compared the recidivism of decertified offenders with similar youth retained in adult court.

QUANTITATIVE HYPOTHESES

When considering the predictors of juvenile transfer, legal variables generally are believed to be the most important. As discussed in Chapter 2, when the juvenile court first began, it mainly exercised jurisdiction in cases in which youth committed less serious offenses. Those who committed serious and violent crimes usually were tried in adult criminal court (Tanenhaus, 2000). A great deal of modern research also has found legal variables (e.g., offense seriousness, prior record, or both) to be significant factors in the transfer decision (Barnes & Franz, 1989; Fagan et al., 1987; Fagan & Deschenes, 1990; Kinder et al., 1995; Lee, 1994; Myers, 2003b). It seems likely that these same factors would be important at the decertification stage. Therefore, the first two research hypotheses were as follows:

H_a (1): As offense seriousness increases, the likelihood of decertification decreases.

H_a (2): As prior record increases, the likelihood of decertification decreases.

Although there is empirical support for legal variables significantly affecting the transfer decision, there also is research suggesting that extra-legal variables can have an effect. For example, age has been shown to have a fairly consistent and significant positive impact on wavier to adult court (Eigen, 1981a; Fagan & Deschenes, 1990; Fagan et al., 1987; Kinder et al., 1995; Myers, 2003b; Podkopacz & Feld, 1996; Poulos & Orchowsky, 1994). In general, as offenders get older, the likelihood of transfer increases.

Concerning race, many descriptive studies have found that non-whites comprise a large majority of those transferred to adult court (see, e.g., Clement, 1997; Keiter, 1973; Thomas & Bilchik, 1985). When examining comparison studies, at the bivariate level, non-whites appear more likely to be transferred than whites. However, once legal variables are controlled for in multivariate analyses, this relationship often disappears (see, e.g., Fagan & Deschenes, 1990; Fagan et al.,

1987; Poulos & Orchowsky, 1994). Although the statistical relationship may become insignificant, it cannot be concluded then that race has no effect on transfer. As mentioned in Chapter 3, race also may have an indirect effect through other variables (Podkopacz & Feld, 1996). Along these lines, when examining the effect of race in other stages of juvenile justice processing, this variable has been shown to significantly impact on such case outcomes as court referral, detention, and disposition (Feld, 1995; Leonard et al., 1995; Minor et al., 1997; Smith and Paternoster, 1990), all of which may have a subsequent effect future waiver decisions.

Based on the above discussion regarding the effects of age and race on transfer, along with the status characteristics hypothesis of labeling theory and corresponding research, the next pair of research hypotheses included:

H_a (3): As age increases, the likelihood of decertification decreases.

H_a (4): Race will have either a direct or indirect effect on the decertification decision.

The next group of hypotheses deals with the possible effect of transfer on case outcomes (i.e., conviction, incarceration, incarceration length, and case processing time). First, in examining the likelihood of conviction, research generally has found that transferred offenders are more likely to be convicted as compared to those in the juvenile system (see e.g., Eigen, 1981a, 1981b; Fagan, 1995; Myers, 2003a). This seems particularly true for violent offenders. Fagan (1995), for example, also found that there was no difference in conviction rates in adult and juvenile court for non-violent offenders. Since this study will examine violent offenders, the research hypothesis was as follows:

H_a (5): Decertified violent youth will have a lower likelihood of conviction than similar youth in adult court.

Although overall conviction rates may appear higher in adult court than in juvenile court, it may be that offenders are convicted on lesser offenses, not the charge that triggered the waiver. When examining violent juvenile offenders, Rudman et al. (1986) found that conviction rates on target offenses (i.e., the offense specified for transfer to occur) were similar in both juvenile and adult court, but were slightly greater in juvenile court. Myers (2001), however, found contrary results. In his research on violent juvenile offenders in Pennsylvania, it was found that transferred offenders were significantly more likely to be convicted on target offenses as compared to youth retained in juvenile court.

Because of this limited and contradictory research, the next research hypothesis stated:

H_a (6): There is a significant difference in the likelihood of conviction on a target offense for decertified youth and those retained in adult court.

One reason given for juveniles being transferred to adult court is that transfer is expected to result in harsher punishment than typically is provided by the juvenile court. Most of the existing literature suggests that convicted, transferred youth are more likely to be sentenced to incarceration, as compared to those who are convicted in juvenile court (Fagan, 1995; Myers, 2003a; Podkopacz & Feld, 1996; Rudman et al., 1986). A related issue is the length of incarceration. If juvenile transfer is effective in providing harsh punishment, it then should follow that waived youth should be sentenced to and serve longer periods of incarceration than those imposed in the juvenile system. The research generally shows that violent transferred offenders are in fact sentenced to longer periods of incarceration than are similar offenders in juvenile court, although differences in actual time served are somewhat debatable (Fritsch et al., 1996; Myers, 2001; Myers, 2003a; Rudman et al., 1986). Therefore, based on the previous literature, the next two research hypotheses included:

H_a (7): Decertified violent youth who are adjudicated delinquent have a lower likelihood of incarceration than similar youth who are convicted in adult court.

H_a (8): Decertified violent youth who are adjudicated delinquent are sentenced to and serve shorter periods of incarceration than similar youth convicted in adult court.

Another reason commonly given for juvenile transfer is to deter future illegal acts by offenders. If deterrence is a goal, according to Beccaria (1986) punishment should be swift. However, past research is not supportive of punishment being faster in adult court. A few comparative studies have shown that transferred youth experience longer periods of case processing time than do retained youth (Fagan, 1995; Myers, 2001; Rudman et al., 1986). It then follows that the next research hypothesis stated:

H_a (9): Decertified violent youth will experience shorter case processing time than similar youth in adult court.

The final set of hypotheses deals with the possible effect of transfer on recidivism. As mentioned above, juvenile waiver is meant to provide a specific deterrent for those who are transferred. Therefore, waived offenders should recidivate less than those who are retained by the juvenile court. However, the research in this area seems quite clear and in the opposite direction. Transferred offenders appear to recidivate not only at a higher rate, but do so more quickly than similar youth retained in juvenile court (Bishop et al., 1996; Fagan, 1995; Myers, 2001; Myers, 2003b; Podkopacz & Feld, 1996; Winner et al., 1997).

Although this research strongly suggests that juvenile transfer is associated with greater recidivism, it does not necessarily provide conclusive evidence that transfer causes recidivism. As discussed in Chapter 4, a selection artifact may be operating, whereby unmeasured explanatory factors (e.g., parental criminality) may have impacted on the transfer decision, resulting in the transfer group being more likely to recidivate (due to the unmeasured variables, rather than transfer itself). In other words, the act of being transferred does not necessarily cause recidivism; an unmeasured variable could be the true cause.

Furthermore, there also is support in the literature for specific deterrence from harsher sanctions (Brown et al., 1987; Brown et al., 1989; Brown et al., 1991; Gottfredson & Barton, 1993; Smith & Gartin, 1989). In these studies, youth who received more formal or greater sanctions recidivated less than those who received lesser or no sanctioning. Because of this mixed research and the possibility of selection bias, directional alternative hypotheses would not seem appropriate. Therefore, the research hypotheses were as follows:

H_a (10): For violent youth released from confinement following final disposition, there is a significant difference in the likelihood of post-dispositional recidivism between decertified and adult court offenders.

H_a (11): For violent youth released from confinement following final disposition, there is a significant difference in the seriousness of post-dispositional recidivism between decertified and adult court offenders.

H_a (12): For violent youth released from confinement following final disposition, there is a significant difference in the time to post-dispositional recidivism between decertified and adult court offenders.

QUALITATIVE RESEARCH QUESTIONS

Prior to quantitatively testing the above hypotheses, qualitative methods initially were used to gain an understanding of the decertification process and to collect rich descriptive information that will supplement the quantitative findings. The model used was that which Creswell (1994) refers to as the "dominant-less dominant design." In this model,

> The researcher presents the study within a single, dominant paradigm with one small component of the overall study drawn from the alternative paradigm....The advantage of this approach is that it presents a consistent paradigm picture in the study and still gathers limited information to probe in detail one aspect of the study. (p. 177)

As mentioned in Chapter 2, 23 states currently have a mechanism in place that allows initially transferred cases to be decertified or reverse waived back to juvenile court (DeFrances & Strom, 1997; Griffin et al., 1998). There only have been two known studies that briefly examined decertification. One study (Singer, 1996) relied upon quantitative data that preceded the youth violence surge of the latter 1980s and early 1990s. The other (Snyder et al., 2000) was rather brief and descriptive, and did not utilize multivariate statistical techniques or qualitative methods in considering various determinants of decertification. Considering the modern crackdown on youth violence and the expanded use of juvenile transfer laws that often automatically place certain youth in adult court, research on the decertification process is long overdue. Therefore, while the quantitative portion of this research examined the statistical predictors of decertification, the initial qualitative portion of the study was devoted to gaining a better understanding of this process. This research not only provided contextual information about decertification, but it also assisted with interpreting the results produced by subsequent quantitative analyses.

The qualitative methods included both observations and interviews. The observations were of decertification hearings, where a criminal court judge determined whether waived youth should be transferred back to the juvenile court. Because these hearings are held in the criminal court system (i.e., the youth are considered "adults" at that point), members of the general public are allowed to observe the proceedings. The interviews were with key players in the decertification process (i.e., prosecutors, defense attorneys, and judges). The interviews were directed at, but also went beyond, the decertification issue. Questions also were asked that tie into the other areas of the current research.

As mentioned above, the qualitative results helped with the interpretation of the quantitative findings. The quantitative portion of this research was based on the 12 hypotheses discussed earlier, with the initial dependent variable being decertification to juvenile court. Decertification then was used as the central independent variable, allowing comparisons to be made between decertified and retained youth. It is believed that through this combined (qualitative and quantitative) research design, a known gap in the empirical transfer literature was filled.

The general questions (which pertain to the three main areas of research discussed previously and an additional area) answered through the qualitative approach were as follows:

First area of research: Decertification.

1. What types of cases generally are successful in getting decertified?

2. What factors seem to impact most on judges in deciding whether to decertify a case?

3. What are the conditions under which some youth may not request a decertification hearing?

4. Do you see any inherent problems in the decertification process?

Second area of research: Case outcomes.

1. Do transferred youth in adult court have a higher likelihood of conviction than decertified youth in juvenile court?

2. Do transferred youth generally have a higher conviction rate on target offenses as compared to decertified offenders (i.e., does plea bargaining or charge reduction more often take place in one system over the other)?

3. Do transferred offenders typically receive harsher sentencing outcomes in criminal court (i.e., a greater chance of incarceration and longer periods of incarceration) as compared to offenders decertified to juvenile court?

4. Do transferred cases typically take longer to process in adult court than those decertified to juvenile court?

Third area of research: Recidivism.

1. Is Act 33 generally effective in reducing recidivism among transferred offenders?

2. Are transferred youth generally re-arrested for more serious offenses than decertified youth, both prior to and following disposition?

Additional category of overall effectiveness.

1. Overall, how effective is Act 33 in achieving the goals of increased offender accountability and greater public safety?

2. If many offenders are decertified, is there a reason to keep Act 33 in place?

3. What are the strengths and weaknesses of Act 33 as compared to discretionary judicial waiver?

RESEARCH SITES

There were three sites used in Pennsylvania for the proposed qualitative and quantitative research: Allegheny County (Pittsburgh), Dauphin County (Harrisburg), and Philadelphia County. As discussed in Chapter 2, in 1995 the Pennsylvania legislature enacted legislation (Act 33) that statutorily excludes certain violent youthful offenders from the jurisdiction of the juvenile court. In order for juveniles to be legislatively waived to criminal court, three conditions must be met. First, the juvenile must be at least age 15 at the time of the offense. Second, the offender must be charged with a violent crime (i.e., rape, involuntary deviant sexual intercourse, aggravated assault, aggravated indecent assault, robbery, robbery of a motor vehicle, voluntary manslaughter, kidnapping; or an attempt, conspiracy, or solicitation to commit any of these crimes). Last, the youth must have either used a deadly weapon in the offense, or have been previously adjudicated for an excluded offense other than aggravated assault.

In order to quantitatively consider the factors that best predict decertification, data were employed from the previously mentioned research conducted by Snyder et al. (2000), which utilized the same three research sites as in the current study. This data was housed by the National Center for Juvenile Justice (NCJJ), and permission was granted for its use. The data set originally was built by NCJJ researchers gathering the names of all youth who had preliminary hearings between March 1996 (the date of Act 33's implementation) and December 1996, and who were determined to meet Act 33's criteria for juvenile court exclusion (n = 447).[1] These names were identified on-site through the assistance of local court and probation personnel in the respective counties.

After eligible offenders were distinguished, data were gathered on each youth with the assistance of local magistrates, juvenile courts, clerk of courts, and probation offices. Examples of such data include variables measuring offense and offender characteristics, prior offending, and whether the youth was decertified. When this data was used in the original study (Snyder et al., 2000), it was indicated that 18% of the cases (n = 80) were dismissed at the preliminary hearing stage. Of the cases remaining (n = 367), 153 were decertified to juvenile court, while 209 were retained in the adult system (4 cases were unidentifiable and 1 case was refiled in juvenile court). Although the study indicated the number of youth who were decertified and discussed some of their characteristics, multivariate analysis was not utilized to determine significant predictors of decertification, which was a central goal of the current research.

In order to compare case outcomes between decertified youth and those retained in adult court, the same dataset was employed (Snyder et al., 2000). Case outcome information (e.g., conviction and incarceration) originally was collected with the assistance of both juvenile and adult court personnel. However, follow-up data last were obtained in January of 1998, at which time a number of cases remained open. When the study originally was reported, 12 (8%) of the decertified cases and 46 (19%) of the cases retained in adult court remained unresolved.

---

[1] After numerous visits were made to each research site to complete the data set, and following the "cleaning" of the data, the total sample size decreased by 24. The sample was reduced for several reasons. First, some offenders were not at the age required to be eligible for transfer under Act 33 (i.e., some youth were either under age 15 or at least age 18). Second, some offenders in the initial dataset were arrested for offenses that were not targeted by Act 33 (e.g., murder). Finally, several youth were included in the dataset more than once, due to being arrested more than once in 1996 for an Act 33 offense in Pennsylvania. After inappropriate cases were removed from the dataset, the final sample size was 423, of which 34% (n = 145) were decertified to juvenile court.

With regard to the current research, key contacts were made in Allegheny County (via the juvenile probation office), Dauphin County (via the juvenile probation office, the District Attorney's Office, and the Public Defender's Office), and in Philadelphia (via the Public Defender's Office and juvenile probation). Officials from these offices agreed to provide and facilitate access within their own offices and with other county agencies in an effort to collect and update data that were missing from the original study. Being able to obtain data on cases that were open provided a more complete picture of the case outcomes of those falling under Act 33 during the time period of the study. Also, additional explanatory variables (e.g., attorney type) were added to the existing dataset that would improve subsequent multivariate analyses.

Finally, the current study examined the recidivism of those offenders included in the study. The original research (Snyder et al., 2000) did not measure recidivism, which likely was due to the short follow-up period that ended in January 1998. The current study used an 8-year follow-up period. To measure recidivism, in addition to official county records, the Pennsylvania Commission on Crime and Delinquency (PCCD) provided a statewide criminal record background check on the offenders, given that all of them currently would be over the age of 18. To obtain these records, the names and other identifying information of the offenders were given to PCCD, allowing them to produce records on all the youth.

Even though state criminal records were obtained for all of the offenders in the dataset, youth who were decertified may have had a subsequent juvenile record of offending, because they would have been considered minors until age 18. With this in mind, the data on juvenile recidivism were provided by the Center for Juvenile Justice Training and Research (CJJT&R), which is located at Shippensburg University in Pennsylvania. The CJJT&R runs a Statistical Analysis Center, which collects offender data from county juvenile courts in Pennsylvania and publishes an annual report on juvenile court operations across the state. Because CJJT&R maintains statewide, offender-based juvenile records, official juvenile recidivism can be measured and analyzed.

HUMAN SUBJECT PROTECTIONS

There were a number of human subject protections associated with both the qualitative and quantitative parts of the current research. The qualitative portion of the study was conducted by observing decertification hearings and interviewing the key players involved in the decertification process (i.e., public defenders, prosecutors, and judges). Because decertification hearings are open to the public, there were not any serious human subject risks associated with this observation. The purpose of the observation simply was to develop an understanding of how decertification hearings operate, and to identify themes and characteristics of these hearings that could be further discussed during the interviews. No individual or offender names, or any other identifiers, were recorded or reported as a result of courtroom observations.

However, a central human subject issue is voluntary participation in the interviews. The subjects were given an informed consent form, which detailed the purpose of the study. In addition, the form indicated that participation was completely voluntary, and participants could withdraw from the study at any given point in time, with no penalty. There were two consent forms. Each participant was required to sign one prior to the beginning of the interview, and the other was for their personal records. For two participants, the signed consent forms were faxed to the researcher, due to telephone interviews being employed (discussed shortly).

A second concern with the qualitative interviews was confidentiality, because the researcher knew the identity of those interviewed. In order to maintain confidentiality of participants during data collection, the researcher did not use any names or identifying characteristics when tape recording the interview. The participants were encouraged strongly to do the same. The only identifiers mentioned were their profession (i.e., public defender, prosecutor, or judge) and the county in which they were employed. After each interview, the audio tapes were transcribed, with the only identifiers being the profession and county. Audio tapes were maintained in a locked filing cabinet, in a locked and secure office at Indiana University of Pennsylvania. Following transcription and coding of the data, each tape was destroyed.

Also, due to the schedules of several criminal justice professionals, face-to-face interviews were not always possible. However, telephone interviews were employed, allowing detailed notes to be taken, instead of audio taping. Following each telephone interview, the notes were transcribed, with the only identifiers being profession and county. When reporting the results at the conclusion of the study, only the participants' responses were revealed. There were no mention of names (or any other identifiers), assuring the participants' confidentiality.

The quantitative portion of the research also has a human subject issue: confidentiality of juvenile records and adult criminal histories. In order to update the variables in the existing dataset and to obtain measures of offender recidivism, the identities of the offenders were known to the researcher. With regard to updating the data and adding possible variables, names only were used at the time of collecting that particular information. As mentioned earlier, the original dataset (Snyder et al., 2000) reported results with a number of cases still open, and various explanatory variables were not fully measured and contained missing data in the previous research. In order to complete the dataset and maintain the confidentiality of the youth, the new data collected were coded and directly entered onsite (i.e., in Allegheny, Dauphin, and Philadelphia counties). The dataset is stored on the researcher's personal laptop, and all names and other personal identifiers were stripped and destroyed upon completion of data collection. In addition, the data subsequently was analyzed in aggregate form, meaning no individual cases were examined or reported on specifically.

Regarding rearrest information, data were provided by the Pennsylvania Commission on Crime and Delinquency (PCCD) and the Center for Juvenile Justice Training and Research (CJJT&R). While data collection was taking place, all paper records were kept in a locked filing cabinet, in a locked and secure office at Indiana University of Pennsylvania. Criminal history data was quantified and entered into a statistical program without any identifying information included, and later it was analyzed in aggregate form for the purposes of the current research. Following the data collection process, all paper records identifying particular individuals were destroyed, preventing the researcher from having further knowledge of offender identities.

VARIABLES

Table 1 presents statistical descriptions (i.e., means, standard deviations, and ranges) of all the variables used in the current study, based on all youth in the final data set (n = 423). Table 2 provides a comparison of descriptive statistics for the offenders, based on decertification status (i.e., decertified and retained offenders).

Decertification

The first key variable examined in the current study was decertification (DECERT). This variable does not represent a true "treatment," for it was not possible to randomly assign subjects to a treatment and control group for this research. If an offender was decertified, the variable was coded as a 1. Cases that were not decertified were coded as a 0. For the current study, 34% of the total 423 youth were decertified to juvenile court.

Case Outcomes

There were five dependent variables measuring case outcomes in the analyses: 1) conviction, 2) conviction on a target offense, 3) incarceration, 4) incarceration length, and 5) case processing time.

Conviction and conviction on an excluded offense both pertain to punishment certainty. In general, if youth are convicted at a high rate, this suggests a stronger likelihood of punishment. With regard to the current research, conviction (CONVICT) refers to whether any charges were substantiated in either juvenile or adult court.[2] This variable was coded as 0 for dismissals and acquittals, and 1 if any charges were substantiated in either juvenile or adult court. Of all of the offenders in the dataset, 56% were convicted on any offense. However, when examining youth by decertification status, a significantly higher

---

[2] For the current study, there were 5 cases in which data on this variable were missing. Due to there being no information available at the research sites supporting that the youth were convicted, these 5 cases were coded as 0 (i.e., not convicted).

Table 1: Descriptive Statistics for all Variables

Variable	Mean	SD	Min.	Max.	N
DECERT	0.34	0.48	0.00	1.00	423
AGE	16.73	0.81	15.01	18.00	423
GENDER	0.87	0.34	0.00	1.00	423
RACE	0.88	0.33	0.00	1.00	420
PRIORREF	1.78	2.27	0.00	13.00	423
PRIORVIO	0.60	0.98	0.00	5.00	423
AGGRAV	0.43	0.50	0.00	1.00	423
ROBBERY	0.51	0.50	0.00	1.00	423
OTHEROFF	0.06	0.24	0.00	1.00	423
ROLEPRIM	0.68	0.49	0.00	1.00	423
ROLENON	0.03	0.19	0.00	1.00	423
ROLEUNK	0.29	0.45	0.00	1.00	423
FIREARM	0.54	0.50	0.00	1.00	423
NONFIRE	0.27	0.45	0.00	1.00	423
FIREUNK	0.19	0.39	0.00	1.00	423
PUBDEF	0.49	0.50	0.00	1.00	423
ALLEGH	0.21	0.41	0.00	1.00	423
DAUPHIN	0.05	0.23	0.00	1.00	423
PHILLY	0.74	0.44	0.00	1.00	423
CONVICT	0.56	0.50	0.00	1.00	423
EXCONV	0.83	0.38	0.00	1.00	235
INCARCER	0.77	0.42	0.00	1.00	235
INLENGTH	36.29	33.65	2.00	216.00	181
LNINLENG	3.15	0.99	0.41	5.38	181
PROCESS	243.38	232.85	1.00	1440.00	423
LNPROCES	4.86	1.33	0.00	7.27	423
POSTARR	0.60	0.49	0.00	1.00	404
POSTVIO	0.33	0.47	0.00	1.00	404
RISKTIME	80.47	24.48	3.07	104.10	404
TIMEARRD	602.94	602.37	0.00	2860.00	242

Table 2: Descriptive Statistics by Decertification Status

Variable	Mean	SD	Min.	Max.	N
		Decertified Offenders			
AGE	16.58	0.81	15.01	17.99	145
GENDER	0.87	0.34	0.00	1.00	145
RACE	0.81	0.39	0.00	1.00	144
PRIORREF	1.19	1.60	0.00	9.00	145
PRIORVIO	0.47	0.89	0.00	5.00	145
AGGRAV	0.40	0.49	0.00	1.00	145
ROBBERY	0.54	0.50	0.00	1.00	145
OTHEROFF	0.06	0.24	0.00	1.00	145
ROLEPRIM	0.65	0.48	0.00	1.00	145
ROLENON	0.09	0.29	0.00	1.00	145
ROLEUNK	0.26	0.44	0.00	1.00	145
FIREARM	0.43	0.50	0.00	1.00	145
NONFIRE	0.41	0.49	0.00	1.00	145
FIREUNK	0.16	0.37	0.00	1.00	145
PUBDEF	0.54	0.50	0.00	1.00	145
ALLEGH	0.22	0.42	0.00	1.00	145
DAUPHIN	0.06	0.24	0.00	1.00	145
PHILLY	0.72	0.45	0.00	1.00	145
CONVICT	0.68	0.47	0.00	1.00	145
EXCONV	0.78	0.42	0.00	1.00	98
INCARCER	0.64	0.48	0.00	1.00	98
INLENGTH	12.12	6.91	2.00	39.00	63
LNINLENG	2.34	0.58	0.74	3.67	63
PROCESS	200.75	160.15	7.00	697.00	145
LNPROCES	4.94	0.92	1.95	6.55	145
POSTARR	0.68	0.47	0.00	1.00	144
POSTVIO	0.34	0.48	0.00	1.00	144
RISKTIME	87.68	9.45	55.13	103.60	144
TIMEARRD	694.65	612.23	0.00	2505.00	98

Table 2 (continued)

Variable	Mean	SD	Min.	Max.	N
	Non-Decertified Offenders				
AGE	16.80**	0.80	15.00	18.00	278
GENDER	0.87	0.34	0.00	1.00	278
RACE	0.91**	0.29	0.00	1.00	276
PRIORREF	2.09***	2.50	0.00	13.00	278
PRIORVIO	0.67*	1.02	0.00	4.00	278
AGGRAV	0.44	0.50	0.00	1.00	278
ROBBERY	0.50	0.50	0.00	1.00	278
OTHEROFF	0.06	0.23	0.00	1.00	278
ROLEPRIM	0.69	0.46	0.00	1.00	278
ROLENON	0.01**	0.09	0.00	1.00	278
ROLEUNK	0.30	0.46	0.00	1.00	278
FIREARM	0.60**	0.49	0.00	1.00	278
NONFIRE	0.20***	0.40	0.00	1.00	278
FIREUNK	0.20	0.40	0.00	1.00	278
PUBDEF	0.46	0.50	0.00	1.00	278
ALLEGH	0.20	0.40	0.00	1.00	278
DAUPHIN	0.05	0.22	0.00	1.00	278
PHILLY	0.75	0.43	0.00	1.00	278
CONVICT	0.49***	0.50	0.00	1.00	278
EXCONV	0.86	0.35	0.00	1.00	137
INCARCER	0.86***	0.35	0.00	1.00	137
INLENGTH	49.19***	35.14	2.00	216.00	118
LNINLENG	3.58***	0.89	0.41	5.38	118
PROCESS	265.62**	260.42	1.00	1440	278
LNPROCES	4.82	1.50	0.00	7.27	278
POSTARR	0.55*	0.50	0.00	1.00	260
POSTVIO	0.32	0.47	0.00	1.00	260
RISKTIME	76.48***	28.95	3.07	104.10	260
TIMEARRD	540.52*	589.55	4.00	2860.00	144

* p < .05
** p < .01
*** p < .001

percentage of decertified offenders were convicted (68%), as compared to the non-decertified offenders (49%; $p < .001$).

Conviction on an excluded offense (EXCONV) involves whether a youth was convicted on the statutorily excluded offense that triggered the initial waiver to criminal court. According to Pennsylvania's legislative waiver law (Act 33), a youth automatically can be transferred for a number of violent offenses: rape, involuntary deviant sexual intercourse, aggravated assault, aggravated indecent assault, robbery, robbery of a motor vehicle, voluntary manslaughter, kidnapping; or an attempt, conspiracy, or solicitation to commit any of these crimes (Pennsylvania Juvenile Court Judges' Commission, 1996; Snyder et al., 2000). If the youth was not convicted on a target offense, the variable was coded as 0. If the youth was convicted on a target offense, it was coded as 1. Of the entire group of offenders who were convicted in either juvenile or adult court ($n = 235$), 83% were convicted on an excluded offense. When comparing based on decertification status, decertified youth experienced a lower conviction rate on excluded offenses (78%) than non-decertified youth (86%), but the difference was statistically insignificant.

The next two dependent variables are incarceration and incarceration length. These variables pertain to sentence severity, and they mainly apply to youth who had charges substantiated against them in either juvenile or adult court. Incarceration (INCARCER) refers to whether convicted offenders ($n = 235$) were sentenced to secure confinement. Those who were not incarcerated were coded as 0, and those who were sentenced to some period of incarceration were coded as 1. Of the convicted offenders, 77% were incarcerated. In addition, when examining the two groups of offenders, there was a statistically significant difference between the incarceration percentages, with 64% of the decertified youth being incarcerated and 86% of the non-decertified youth being incarcerated ($p < .001$).

Incarceration length (INLENGTH) mainly applies to youth who were incarcerated. It is the length of time for which incarcerated offenders experienced secure confinement. The measure of this variable depended upon whether the offender was decertified or remained in adult court. Juvenile courts in Pennsylvania use indeterminate sentencing (Myers, 2001), whereby offenders are placed (and remain) in secure facilities until they are considered suitable for release by a juvenile court judge. In other words, there is no minimum term of incarceration initially imposed by juvenile court judges. The juvenile court also can maintain jurisdiction over an adjudicated delinquent until the youth is 21 years old. Because sentences are indeterminate in juvenile court, the actual time served (in months) in a correctional facility functioned as the measure of incarceration length for decertified youth. For youth in adult court, the minimum sentence (in months) imposed by the criminal court sentencing judge served as the conservative estimate of incarceration length.[3] The mean incarceration length for the entire group of incarcerated offenders (n = 181) was 36.29 months. However, when examining each group based on decertification status, the decertified group served significantly less time in secure confinement (12.12 months)[4] than the non-decertified group (49.19 months; $p < .001$).

Due to this variable being positively skewed, the natural log of incarceration length (LNINLENG) was used as the dependent variable in the multivariate analysis. The mean natural log of incarceration

---

[3] In Pennsylvania's criminal courts, judges use indeterminate sentencing, where a minimum and maximum period of incarceration is imposed on the offender. County-level sentences are those in which a defendent is sentenced to 2 years or less, to be served in a county jail. However, a maximum period of incarceration of 2 or more years is considered a state-level sentence, typically served in a state prison. For those serving a county-level sentence, county judges possibly can order parole prior to the minimum sentenced being served (e.g., if "good time" system is in place). However, for offenders with a state-level sentence, at least the minimum term of incarceration imposed by the judge must be served prior to consideration of parole. Therefore, when examining incarceration length for non-decertified offenders, most of the offenders would have served at least their minimum sentence and often more, making it a conservative estimate of incarceration length.

[4] For 11 decertified youth, there was no indication of their release date from secure confinement, based on site visits and state juvenile data, though they were incarcerated. For the purpose of providing values for the 11 missing cases, the mean incarceration length for decertified youth (12 months) was used.

length for the entire group of offenders was 3.15 (or 23.33 months). When examining each group based on decertification status, the decertified youth still experienced significantly less incarceration time (natural log of 2.34, or 10.38 months), as compared to the non-decertified youth (natural log of 3.58, or 35.87 months; $p < .001$).

Case processing time (PROCESS) pertains to the swiftness of punishment for the offenders. For all offenders, this variable represents the length of time from arrest to final disposition. Similar to incarceration length, this variable was measured continuously, but in days. The mean case processing time for all offenders was 243.38 days. When examining each group, decertified youth experienced significantly shorter case processing time (200.75 days) than non-decertified youth (265.62 days; $p < .01$).

This variable also was positively skewed, resulting in the current study using the natural log of case processing time for multivariate analysis. The mean natural log of case processing time for the entire group of offenders was 4.86 (or 129.02 days). When looking at each group of offenders, decertified youth now experienced very similar case processing time (natural log of 4.94, or 139.77 days) as non-decertified youth (natural log of 4.82, or 123.97 days), but the difference was insignificant.[5]

Recidivism

The current research also measured offender recidivism following final disposition, along with the seriousness and timing of recidivism. In addition to county records, there were two main sources used to obtain recidivism indicators. First, the Center for Juvenile Justice Training and Research (CJJT&R) provided data on recidivism for youth in the juvenile justice system (i.e., those who were decertified and were

---

[5] It should be noted that based on the original case processing time variable, decertified youth experienced significantly shorter processing time than non-decertified youth ($p < .01$). However, when the variable was transformed to its natural log, the significant difference disappeared. This is due to the original variable having extreme outliers (i.e., it is positively skewed), which increased the mean, especially for those in adult court (i.e., non-decertified offenders).

rearrested prior to their 18th birthday). As previously mentioned, the CJJT&R collects offender data from all county juvenile courts in Pennsylvania. Also, the Pennsylvania Commission on Crime and Delinquency (PCCD) provided state criminal records for all offenders in the dataset, as they all would have exceeded their 18th birthday at the time of the criminal record check, conducted on October 21, 2004.

In examining recidivism, not all offenders would have had the same amount of time to be rearrested during the follow-up period. In other words, each of them would have had their case disposed and been released from secure custody at different times, resulting varying exposure times for potentially getting rearrested. To control for these differences, time at risk (RISKTIME) was considered in the analyses. This variable indicated the time (in months) between the date of release from secure custody and the end of the follow-up period (10/21/2004). Over 95% of the offenders were released during the follow-up period (n = 404), but a small number continued to be incarcerated in adult prison on the original Act 33 conviction (n = 19). The entire group of released offenders experienced a mean risk time of 80.47 months. When comparing across groups, decertified youth experienced a significantly longer time at risk (87.68 months), as compared to non-decertified youth (76.48 months; $p < .001$).

Measures of post-dispositional recidivism were examined for those offenders who either were not incarcerated or were released on parole prior to when the state criminal records were obtained. The first variable of this type measured whether youth were rearrested on any charge following final disposition. In measuring post-dispositional arrest (POSTARR), offenders who were not rearrested were coded as 0, while those rearrested were coded as 1. For the current sample, this variable only included those youth who were able to be captured in the 8-year follow-up period (n = 404). In examining all offenders who were "on the street," 60% were rearrested following final disposition. Somewhat surprisingly, when looking at each group based on decertification status, a significantly higher percentage of decertified youth were rearrested following final disposition (68%), as compared to the non-decertified youth (55%; $p < .05$).

Violent recidivism (POSTVIO) also was measured during the post-dispositional period. This variable was defined as a rearrest for murder or any violent offense targeted by the Act 33 statute (i.e., rape, involuntary deviant sexual intercourse, aggravated assault, aggravated indecent assault, robbery, robbery of a motor vehicle, voluntary manslaughter, kidnapping; or an attempt, conspiracy, or solicitation to commit any of these crimes). If offenders were not rearrested for a targeted offense following final disposition, post-dispositional violent arrest was coded as 0, while those rearrested for any of these offenses were coded as 1. This variable, again, only included youth who were "on the street." For the entire group of offenders (n = 404), 33% were rearrested for a violent offense. Similarities emerged between the two groups, whereas 34% of the decertified youth and 32% of the non-decertified group were rearrested for a violent offense (p = .667).

Finally, time to failure or time to rearrest (TIMEARRD) was measured as the length of time (in days) that it took for offenders to be rearrested following their post-dispositional release (i.e., this variable is based on the 242 offenders who were rearrested during the follow-up period). This continuous measure was used to asses how quickly decertified and adult court youth recidivated following their final court processing. Of the youth who were rearrested, the mean time to rearrest was 602.94 days, or slightly more than one-and-a-half years. However, a significant difference arose when examining each group. Decertified youth, on average, experienced a longer time to rearrest (694.65 days, or almost 2 years), as compared to non-decertified youth (540.55 days, or about one-and-a-half years; $p < .05$).

INDEPENDENT/CONTROL VARIABLES

As mentioned earlier, the current study is a quasi-experimental or non-equivalent group design, meaning there is no random assignment to treatment and control groups. Due to this type of design, selection bias is a plausible threat to the results of the study (Shadish et al., 2002). However, every attempt was made to control for factors that have been empirically shown to impact on the dependent variables used in the study. Nevertheless, the findings should be interpreted with caution.

In previous research, a number of factors have been found to impact on each of the case outcome and recidivism variables. Examples include age at referral, gender, race, firearm use, offense seriousness, prior record, and county location (see e.g., Fagan, 1995; Fritsch et al., 1996; Myers, 2001; Myers and Kiehl, 2001; Podkopacz &

Feld, 1996). Similar to the model that was used to predict decertification, a variety of additional variables also were employed in the case outcome and recidivism models to determine their impact on the dependent variables.

The first control variable was age at referral (AGE). Previous literature has found that older offenders are more likely to be given harsher sentences, as compared to younger offenders (see e.g., Wolfgang, Figlio, and Sellin, 1972). In addition, research has found that older youth tend to have a greater likelihood of being transferred to adult court, in comparison to similar youth in juvenile court (Eigen, 1981a; Fagan & Deschenes, 1990; Fagan et al., 1987; Kinder et al., 1995; Myers, 2003b; Podkopacz & Feld, 1996; Poulos & Orchowsky, 1994). For the current study, age at referral was measured as a continuous variable, and the average age of the entire group of offenders was 16.73 years. When making comparisons across groups, the average age for decertified youth (16.58) was less than that of the non-decertified group (16.80), with the difference between means being statistically significant ($p < .01$).

Gender (GENDER) also was used as a control variable. Although only a few juvenile transfer studies have examined the effect of gender on transfer (e.g., see Keiter, 1973), general research has produced mixed results regarding its impact on court outcomes (Leonard & Sontheimer, 1995; Wordes et al., 1994). In regard to the current research, males were coded as 1, and females were coded as 0. Of the entire group of youth, 87% were male (13% were female). The breakdown was equal across the two groups of offenders, with 87% of both the decertified and non-decertified youth being male.

Race (RACE) also was used as a variable in the statistical models. Prior research findings have been mixed when examining the possible effect of race on court outcomes. Some research has found the minorities are more likely to experience harsher court outcomes, as compared to whites (see, e.g., Feld, 1995; Leonard et al., 1995; Minor et al., 1997; Smith and Paternoster, 1990), while other research has found that once legal variables are controlled for in the analyses, the direct race effect disappears (see, e.g., Fagan & Deschenes, 1990; Fagan et al., 1987; Poulos & Orchowsky, 1994). For the current study, whites were coded as 0, while non-whites were coded as 1. Of the entire cohort of youth, 88% were non-white.[6] When looking at each group separately, a significantly larger group of non-whites were in the non-decertified group (91%) as opposed to the decertified group (81%; $p<.01$).

The number of prior referrals to juvenile court (PRIORREF) was used as an indicator of general prior offending. The research has been clear and consistent in that the more extensive a youth's prior record, the greater the likelihood of both transfer and harsher court outcomes (Barnes & Franz, 1989; Fagan et al., 1987; Fagan & Deschenes, 1990; Kinder et al., 1995; Lee, 1994; Myers, 2003b). For the present study, the number of prior referrals to juvenile court was measured continuously, with the entire cohort of youth previously being referred an average of 1.78 times. When examining each group separately, the non-decertified youth had a significantly higher average number of prior referrals (2.09) than the decertified youth (1.19; $p < .001$).

It was also expected that the number of times youth previously were referred to the juvenile court for a violent offense (PRIORVIO) could impact on case outcomes. Prior research indicates that a record of prior violent offending has a significant effect on court outcomes (Myers, 2001). For the present study, a prior violent offense included murder, non-negligent manslaughter, negligent homicide, manslaughter, criminal homicide, forcible rape other violent sex offenses, sodomy, robbery, aggravated assault, and kidnapping. Of the entire group of offenders, the mean number of prior referrals for a violent offense was 0.60. However, a difference-between-means test revealed that that the average number of prior referrals for serious person offenses for the non-decertified youth (0.67) was significantly higher than the average for the decertified youth (0.47; $p<.05$).

The type of weapon (WEAPON) used during the commission of the crime also has been shown to impact on the decision to transfer a youth to adult court and on other court outcomes and recidivism (Myers, 2001, 2003b). The use of a firearm also can be used as an indicator of offense severity, as compared to other weapons used in a crime. Unfortunately, due to limitations in the data, it was not possible

[6] While 88% of the offenders in the dataset were nonwhite, they also were predominantly African-American (over 90% of the nonwhites).

to determine the type of weapon used for 19% of the offenders. When deciding whether to combine those missing cases with either the "firearm" or "non-firearm" group, numerous statistical analyses were performed to determine whether there was a difference between the "unknown" group and the other two groups. The results indicated that there were statistically significant differences between all three groups on numerous dependent variables. Stated differently, combining cases into two weapons groups would not have been appropriate. Therefore, the "unknown" category was used as its own separate group, resulting in three dichotomous weapons variables being developed (i.e., firearm, non-firearm, and unknown).

Of the entire sample, 54% used a firearm, 27% used other deadly weapons (e.g., bats, knives, etc.), and 19% were unknown. It was further found that a significantly lower percentage of youth using a firearm existed in the decertified group (43%), as compared to the percentage of youth who were in the non-decertified group (60%; $p < .01$). In regard to those using other deadly weapons (i.e., non-firearm), a significantly higher percentage of decertified youth used other deadly weapons (41%), as compared to the non-decertified group (20%; $p < .001$). Finally, there was no significant difference between decertified and non-decertified offenders with regard to the "unknown" weapon variable ($p = .419$).

With regard to the present study, it was not possible to examine a direct measure of offense severity using only the offense the youth was charged with, due to Act 33 targeting violent felony offenses. In general, it is difficult to claim that one violent felony offense is more (or less) serious than another violent felony offense. Furthermore, in Pennsylvania in 1996, most Act 33 youth (approximately 95%) were charged with either aggravated assault or robbery. Therefore, offense was measured as three dichotomous variables: aggravated assault, robbery, and other offenses. For the entire sample, 43% were charged with aggravated assault, 51% were charged with robbery, and 6% were charged with other violent offenses. When examining offenders based on decertification status, there were no significant differences in offenses across the two groups, as 40% of the decertified youth were charged with aggravated assault (44% of the non-decertified youth; $p = .44$), 54% of the decertified youth were charged with robbery (50% of the non-decertified youth; $p = .50$), and 6% of both the decertified and non-decertified youth were charged with other violent offenses ($p = .85$).

The county of the offender also was used as a control variable in the analyses. Prior research has found that the type of county (i.e., rural, suburban, or urban) has an impact on court outcomes and recidivism (Myers, 2001). The current study, therefore, dichotomized each county into its own separate variable. Of the entire cohort of youthful offenders, 21% were from Allegheny County, 5% were from Dauphin County, and 74% were from Philadelphia. There was no statistically significant difference between the non-decertified and decertified groups, in terms of county location, as 22% of the decertified group came from Allegheny County (20% of the non-decertified group; $p = .58$), 6% of the decertified group came from Dauphin County (5% of the non-decertified group; $p = .62$), and 72% of the decertified group came from Philadelphia (75% of the non-decertified group; $p = .44$).

A neglected area of research when examining court outcome data has been the potential effect of the role a youth played in the offense. It is possible that judges in both juvenile and adult court may hold offenders more accountable if they played a central role in the offense, as compared to those offenders who did not play as big a part. In the current research, this potential relationship was explored. Similar to the "weapon" variable, limitations in the data resulted in 29% of the values for this variable to be missing. Statistical examinations also revealed that the "unknown" (i.e., missing) group was significantly different from both those who played a primary role and those who played a non-primary role in terms of several dependent variables. Therefore, this variable was treated similarly to the "firearm" variable, resulting in 3 dichotomous "role" variables: primary role, non-primary role, and "unknown."

Of the entire group of offenders, 68% played a primary role in the offense, 3% played a non-primary role, and 29% were unknown. A significant difference emerged when examining the non-primary group, based on decertification status. Nine percent of the decertified group played a non-primary role in the offense, while only 1% of the non-decertified youth played a non-primary role in the offense ($p < .01$), suggesting that those who do not play a primary role in offenses are more likely to get decertified to juvenile court. There were no significant differences across the means for the other two variables, with 65% of the decertified youth playing a primary role (69% of the non-decertified youth; p = .46) and 26% of the decertified youth being unknown (30% of the non-decertified youth; p = .30).

A final variable that tends to be neglected in research is the potential effect of attorney type on court decisions. Some defense attorneys may be more experienced in certain types of cases, which undoubtedly influences the effectiveness of their representation for their clients. For instance, conversations with the Public Defender's Office in Philadelphia revealed a belief that the public defenders in this county are better able to handle Act 33 cases than most private attorneys, due to their juvenile division that specializes in juvenile cases (i.e., private attorneys, in comparison, take cases that cover a wide variety of areas). For the current study, attorney type was measured as whether or not the offender's attorney was a public defender (PUBDEF).[7] In examining all the youth, 49% used a public defender (51% used a non-public defender). There was no statistically significant difference between the two groups in attorney-type, with 54% of the decertified youth and 46% of the non-decertified youth having used a public defender (p = .131).

---

[7] Two separate issues were considered at this stage. First, the original coding of the variable included public defenders, private attorneys, and court-appointed attorneys. However, statistical tests revealed no statistical differences between private and court appointed attorneys in cases outcomes. In addition, court appointed attorneys are private attorneys who are hired by the court to take cases. Therefore, private and court appointed attorneys were combined into a non-public defender group. Second, 14% of the cases had missing values for attorney. Further statistical analyses showed no significant differences in case outcomes for the "unknowns" and both court appointed and private attorneys. It also was revealed that the public defender group had the same differences (at the bivariate level) with the private attorneys, court appointed attorneys, and "unknowns" on the dependent variables. Therefore, the "unknowns" were combined with the non-public defender group.

STATISTICAL ANALYSIS PLAN

Multivariate analyses were used to test all 12 hypotheses in the quantitative component of the study. These analyses allowed for the statistical examination and control of various explanatory factors that could influence each of the dependent variables. The specific statistical technique used depended upon the nature of the dependent variable (i.e., whether it was continuous or dichotomous). The following discussion of the analysis plan is broken down by research area: decertification, case outcomes, and recidivism.

Decertification

Decertification was coded as a dichotomous variable, and Hypotheses 1-4 utilized it as the dependent variable. In order to determine the simultaneous effect of numerous independent variables or predictors (e.g., age, race, offense seriousness, and prior record) on a dichotomous dependent variable, multivariate logistic regression is appropriate (Menard, 2002). The resulting coefficients from the logit analysis indicate the change in the log odds of an event (e.g., decertification) occurring due to a one-unit increase in each independent variable, while controlling for the other explanatory factors.

Because it is somewhat difficult to interpret log odds, logistic regression coefficients can be transformed into odds ratios (or exponentiated coefficients), which show the change in the simple odds of an event occurring, in response to a one-unit increase in each independent variable. At its basic level, an odds ratio is "the probability [that an event] will occur to the probability that it will not...[For instance] the odds of getting a diamond on a single draw from a card deck are 0.25/0.75 = 1/3" (Norusis, 1997, p. 42). In the decertification model, the odds ratios will show the change in the simple odds of decertification occurring as a result of a one-unit increase in each independent variable in the model, while controlling for the others. In general, positive coefficients and odds ratios greater than 1.0 indicate that an increase in an independent variable is associated with a greater likelihood of an event occurring, while negative coefficients and odds ratios less than 1.0 show than an increase in an independent variable is associated with a lower likelihood of an event occurring. A major goal of this research was to develop a logistic regression model that did a solid job of explaining or predicting decertification to juvenile court.

Another way logistic regression models can be employed is to use them to calculate estimated probabilities of an event occurring, based on different values of a variable of interest (Menard, 2002). For example, Hypothesis 2 stated that as prior record increases, the likelihood of decertification decreases. With this in mind, the coefficients produced from the logistic regression analysis can be used to compare probabilities of decertification, based upon different values of an explanatory variable. To illustrate, the probability of decertification for an offender with 5 prior court referrals could be compared with the probability of decertification for an offender with 2 prior court referrals, while controlling for the other explanatory factors (which typically are held constant at their means).

The same type of procedure can be used for a dichotomous independent variable. For instance, Hypothesis 3 examines the potential impact of race on the decertification decision. If white youth are coded as 0 and non-whites are coded as 1, comparisons could be made regarding the estimated probability of decertification for whites versus non-whites, again while controlling for the other explanatory factors. The equation used to calculate these probabilities is as follows:

$$P(Y=1) = \frac{e^{(a_0 + b_1x_1 + b_2x_2 + b_3x_3 + \ldots b_kx_k)}}{1 + e^{(a_0 + b_1x_1 + b_2x_2 + b_3x_3 + \ldots b_kx_k)}} \quad (1)$$

where a_0 is the constant, b represents each slope estimate, and x is the value of each independent variable (Menard, 2002). Overall, while the basic results of the multivariate logistic regression model will for a determination of which explanatory factors are significant in predicting decertification, using the above formula allows for comparisons to be made regarding the specific probabilities of decertification to juvenile court, based on specific values of independent variables of interest (e.g., those that turn out to be statistically significant predictors of decertification).

Case Outcomes

Hypotheses 5-7 consider the effect of decertification on various case outcomes. The measurement of the case outcome determined the appropriate statistical analysis to employ. Hypothesis 5 (conviction), Hypothesis 6 (conviction on target offense), and Hypothesis 7 (incarceration) involved dichotomous dependent variables, making multivariate logistic regression the appropriate technique to determine the impact of decertification on these outcomes, while controlling for other possible explanatory factors. As discussed above, the coefficients obtained from the analyses indicate the change in the log odds of an event (i.e., the outcome) occurring, as a result of a one-unit increase in each independent variable.

Numerous independent variables were included in each model to determine their effect on the dependent variable, while controlling for the others. However, the main goal was to asses the impact of decertification on each dependent variable. In order to further accomplish this goal, the logit coefficients were used to make separate estimates of the probability of each outcome occurring when decertification equals 0, and also when decertification equals 1, while setting all other explanatory variables in the model at their mean. Put differently, when decertification is set to 0 (i.e., to represent youth remaining in the adult system), the probability of the case outcome occurring was estimated. Similarly, when decertification is set to 1 (i.e., to represent youth decertified to juvenile court), the probability of the case outcome occurring also was estimated. The difference in these probabilities further demonstrate the impact of decertification on each case outcome.

Hypothesis 8 (incarceration length) and Hypothesis 9 (case processing time) both involved continuous dependent variables. Therefore, ordinary least squares (OLS) multiple regression was the most appropriate multivariate statistical technique (Lewis-Beck, 1980). OLS regression was used to determine the impact of decertification on these two case outcomes, while controlling for the other explanatory factors. In these models, unstandardized slopes indicate the change in the dependent variable that occurs in response to a one-unit increase in each independent variable.

As mentioned above, even though the effect of all independent variables on the dependent variables was assessed, the central variable of interest was decertification. Similar to techniques employed with logistic regression results, OLS regression results can be used to estimate separate predictions of each dependent variable based on different values of an independent variable of interest. For example, separate predictions can be made with decertification set at 0 and at 1, with all other explanatory variables set at their mean. The possible difference in the predicted values of the dependent variables can provide further clarification of the effect of decertification on the particular case outcomes examined. The OLS formula used to make these predictions is:

$$\hat{y} = a_0 + b_1x_1 + b_2x_2 + b_3x_3 + \ldots b_kx_k + e \quad (2)$$

where a_0 is the constant, b is the unstandardized slope estimate, and x is the value of each independent variable (Lewis-Beck, 1980).

Recidivism

The final research area will considered recidivism. Hypothesis 10 (post-dispositional rearrest) and Hypothesis 11 (violent post-dispositional rearrest) both contained dependent variables measured as dichotomies. As discussed earlier, when a dependent variable is dichotomous, multivariate logistic regression is appropriate. This will allow for a determination of the impact of decertification and the other explanatory variables on the likelihood of recidivism. The resulting coefficients from the analyses reveal the change in the log odds of an event (e.g., rearrest) occurring, based on a one-unit increase in each independent variable.

Again, the central independent variable to be examined is decertification, as the main goal here is to assess the effect of decertification on recidivism. Using Equation 1 presented above and the results of the logistic regression analyses, the probability of each type of rearrest can be calculated when decertification is set at 0, and then when it is set at 1, while holding all other explanatory variables constant at their means. The potential difference in probabilities can assist in determining the effect of decertification on each type of rearrest.

Finally, Hypothesis 12 examined time to rearrest. In order to test this hypothesis, survival analysis is the most appropriate statistical technique. If OLS regression was used to examine time to re-arrest, many cases would be "censored" (excluded), due to those offenders not experiencing the event (i.e., rearrest); this would produce biased coefficient estimates (Allison, 1984; SPSS Advanced Statistics 7.5, 1997). Using Cox's proportional hazards model, censored cases can be handled and included while considering the impact of various explanatory variables on time to rearrest.

When using Cox regression, a minimum of three variables must be employed. The dependent variable actually is based on two separate variables: a survival time indicator, such as time to rearrest; and a status indicator, which specifies whether or not an event, such as rearrest, occurred (Allison, 1984; SPSS Advanced Statistics 7.5, 1997). In general, the dependent variable in Cox regression represents the risk of failure at any given point in time in the follow-up period; more specifically, it is the natural log of the hazard function (Allison, 1984). There also must be at least one independent variable utilized. Again, although other explanatory factors were entered into the model and assessed for their impact, the key independent variable of interest was decertification.

If a coefficient produced for an explanatory variable in the model is positive, this indicates that an increase in that variable is associated with an increased risk of failure at any point in time during the follow-up period. In other words, positive coefficients are associated with decreased survival time, or quicker failure (e.g., faster time to rearrest). On the other hand, a negative coefficient indicates that an increase in the explanatory variable is associated with a decreased risk of failure at any point in time during the follow-up period, or increased survival time or time to failure. With this in mind, the coefficient for decertification in the Cox regression model will indicate whether this variable impacts on the risk of rearrest at any particular point in time during the follow-up period, while controlling for the other factors.

To further interpret Cox regression results, model coefficients also can be exponentiated (which produces their antilogs), and they then can be interpreted as the relative risk of failure associated with a one-unit increase in the independent variable of interest (Allison, 1984). Any exponentiated coefficient greater than 1.0 shows that an increase in the independent variable is associated with an increased risk of failure, while coefficients less than 1.0 indicate that an increase in the independent variable is associated with a decreased risk of failure. Moreover, the exponentiated coefficient indicates the percentage change in relative risk that results from a one-unit increase in the explanatory factor. For instance, if the exponentiated coefficient for an independent variable is 1.25, it can be interpreted that for every one-unit unit increase in that variable, the relative risk of failure increases by 25%. Similarly, if the exponentiated coefficient for the independent variable was 0.75, it would indicate that for every one-unit increase in that variable, the relative risk of failure decreases by 25%.

The above interpretations assume that the independent variable is continuous, or that it is able to experience multiple one-unit increases. Exponentiated coefficients for dichotomous explanatory variables are interpreted in a slightly different manner. For a dichotomous independent variable, the exponentiated coefficient indicates the relative risk of failure for the two groups represented by the values of the variable, while controlling for the other explanatory factors (Allison, 1984). For instance, if the exponentiated coefficient for decertification is 1.50, it could be interpreted that decertified youth had a 50% greater risk of rearrest at any point in time during the follow-up period, as compared to youth who remained in adult court. This would indicate that decertified youth experienced shorter survival times (to rearrest) than did youth in adult court. Conversely, if the exponentiated coefficient for decertification was .50, it could be interpreted that decertified offenders had a 50% lower risk of rearrest as any point in time during the follow-up period, as compared to youth in adult court. In this case, decertified youth would experience greater survival times (to rearrest) than would adult court offenders. In the current research, the potential effect of decertification on time to rearrest was assessed in this manner, based on the size of the relative risk associated with the variable.

Split Models

Finally, "decertification specific" models also were estimated, using the full models for both decertified and non-decertified youth. In other words, two statistical models were produced for each of the case outcome and recidivism measures: one model for decertified offenders (i.e., youth in juvenile court) and one model for non-decertified offenders (i.e., youth in adult court). Using the coefficients from each of these models allowed for the testing of statistical differences between the coefficients, based on the following formula:

$$z = \frac{b_1 - b_2}{\sqrt{(se_1)^2 - (se_2)^2}} \qquad (3)$$

where b_1 is the unstandardized slope for group 1, b_2 is the unstandardized slope for group 2, se_1 is the standard error for b_1, and se_2 is the standard error for of b_2 (Brame, Paternoster, Mazerolle, & Piquero, 1998; Paternoster, Brame, Mazerolle, & Piquero, 1998).

Each group, essentially, will have variable effects on case outcomes and recidivism that are specific to its group (i.e., either decertified or non-decertified). The above formula allowed for the testing of interaction effects, meaning it could be determined whether certain factors had significantly more or less influence on particular court outcomes and recidivism in one court, as compared to the other court.

QUALITATIVE ANALYSIS PLAN

The qualitative component contained both observations and interviews. The observations were of two decertification hearings in Philadelphia. Due to limited knowledge and advanced notice of the time and place of relatively small numbers of decertification hearings in both Allegheny and Dauphin Counties, observations of decertification hearings were not possible at those two research sites. During the courtroom observations, field notes were taken. The model used was that described by Creswell (1994), whereby a dividing line was drawn down the middle of a single page. One side contained descriptive notes (e.g., concerning critical players in the decertification hearings, demographic characteristics of both the critical players and the defendants, and the content of court discussions), while the other side contained reflective notes, which were ideas and thoughts of the researcher. One advantage of conducting observations was that it allowed for the recording of information as it occurred (Creswell, 1994). All field notes then were transcribed immediately.

The interviews were with the critical players in the decertification process (i.e., prosecutors, defense attorneys, and judges) in each of the three research sites. However, not all of these individuals in each county were available to be interviewed. In Allegheny County, a criminal court judge and a group of four prosecutors were interviewed, but the public defender handling Act 33 cases declined the interview request. When interviewing the judge, a face-to-face interview was conducted, and the interview was audiotape-recorded. Due to the group of prosecutors being apprehensive about the interview, they strongly discouraged the use of their specific county name when reporting the results. In addition, they did not allow the interview to be audiotape-recorded, resulting in the researcher taking notes during the interview. The researcher also verbally paraphrased and confirmed the responses, in order to ensure the reliability and validity of the notes.

In Dauphin County, a criminal court judge, prosecutor, and defense attorney were interviewed. All interviews were face-to-face, and each interview was audiotape-recorded. Finally, in Philadelphia, a criminal court judge and defense attorney were interviewed, but the prosecutor handling Act 33 cases declined the interview request. The judge was interviewed via telephone, due to his limited availability for a face-to-face interview. Therefore, notes of his responses were taken during the interview. When interviewing the defense attorney, a face-to-face interview was conducted. Notes were also taken during this interview, due to the respondent not feeling comfortable being tape-recorded. Throughout both interviews with respondents in Philadelphia, the researcher verbally paraphrased and confirmed the responses, in order to ensure the reliability and validity of the resulting notes.

It was believed that these individuals would be able to provide valuable insight into the Act 33 statute and the decertification process, considering they regularly encounter juveniles waived under Act 33 as part of their professional duties. The interviews consisted of open-ended questions reflective of the quantitative hypotheses, as predictors of decertification were sought, along with comparisons of decertified and non-decertified youth in terms of court outcomes and recidivism. The open-ended questions further asked respondents their views on the overall effectiveness of Act 33, and their answers were probed as necessary to explore potential themes. While each interview was taking place, the researcher recorded the thoughts and ideas that developed.

Analysis of the qualitative data began immediately following the first interview and observation. In order to analyze these data, the first step was to read the interview transcripts and observational notes (Maxwell, 1996). This enabled the researcher to produce further notes and memos, allowing for the initial development of ideas and potential relationships. Following this process, the data were coded into themes that emerged as a result of examining the interview and observation transcripts. In analyzing the qualitative data, comparisons of the interview responses then were made, based mainly on the profession of the interviewees.

CHAPTER 6

Quantitative Findings

This chapter presents the quantitative findings for the tests of the 12 hypotheses contained in Chapter 5. First, the bivariate correlations for all of the variables are revealed and discussed. Second, the results from the multivariate analyses are shown and highlighted. Finally, the chapter concludes with a summary of the quantitative findings.

BIVARIATE RESULTS

Table 3 presents the estimated correlations between all the variables used in the current study. In examining these correlations, it must be remembered that the values in the table only indicate the statistical association between two factors (i.e., does the value of one variable increase or decrease as the value of the other variable changes), without controlling for the potential effect of other variables. Nevertheless, correlations can provide a picture of the general relationships between the variables.

In considering the bivariate correlations among the independent/control variables, two coefficients hint at multicollinearity being a salient concern.[8] Further statistical tests (i.e., tolerance statistics and variance inflation factors) were performed to determine whether there was serious collinearity among any of the independent variables. According to Mernard (2002), "A tolerance of less than .20 is cause for concern" (p. 76). Furthermore, Kutner, Nachtsheim, Neter, & Li (2005) state that, "A maximum VIF value in excess of 10 is

[8] The coefficient between the number of prior referrals and the number of prior referrals for violent offenses was .67. The coefficient between unknown firearm use and unknown role was .74.

Table 3: Estimated Correlations Between All the Variables

Variable	1	2	3	4	5
1 DECERT	1.00				
	(423)				
2 AGE	-.13**	1.00			
	(423)	(423)			
3 GENDER	.00	.05	1.00		
	(423)	(423)	(423)		
4 RACE	-.14**	.02	-.02	1.00	
	(423)	(423)	(423)	(423)	
5 PRIORREF	-.19**	.14**	.11*	.12*	1.00
	(423)	(423)	(423)	(423)	(423)
6 PRIORVIO	-.10*	.12*	.05	.12*	.67**
	(423)	(423)	(423)	(423)	(423)
7 AGGRAV	-.04	.03	-28**	-.12*	.00
	(423)	(423)	(423)	(423)	(423)
8 ROBBERY	.03	-.04	.24**	.14**	-.01
	(423)	(423)	(423)	(423)	(423)
9 OTHER	.01	.03	.07	-.06	.02
	(423)	(423)	(423)	(423)	(423)
10 ROLEPRIM	-.04	.03	-.12*	.05	.13**
	(423)	(423)	(423)	(423)	(423)
11ROLENON	.21**	-.06	.00	-.12*	-.05
	(423)	(423)	(423)	(423)	(423)
12 ROLEUNK	-.05	.00	.12*	.00	-.11*
	(423)	(423)	(423)	(423)	(423)
13 FIREARM	-.16**	.01	.21**	.26**	.14**
	(423)	(423)	(423)	(423)	(423)
14 NONFIRE	.22**	-.04	-.31**	-.30**	-.02
	(423)	(423)	(423)	(423)	(423)
15 FIREUNK	-.04	.03	.10*	.01	-.15**
	(423)	(423)	(423)	(423)	(423)

N's are in parentheses

* $p < .05$, ** $p < .01$

(Continued...)

Table 3 (continued)

Variable	1	2	3	4	5
16 PUBDEF	.07 (423)	-.01 (423)	-.07 (423)	.13** (423)	.09 (423)
17 ALLEGH	.03 (423)	.00 (423)	-.06 (423)	-.17** (423)	.16** (423)
18 DAUPHIN	.03 (423)	-.09 (424)	.03 (423)	-.07 (423)	.03 (423)
19 PHILLY	-.04 (423)	.04 (423)	.05 (423)	.19** (423)	-.16** (423)
20 CONVICT	.18** (423)	-.05 (423)	.16** (423)	-.13** (423)	.06 (423)
21 EXCONV	-.11 (235)	.00 (235)	.11 (235)	.19** (235)	-.02 (235)
22 INCARCER	-.26** (235)	.01 (235)	.14* (235)	.28** (235)	.23** (235)
23 LNINLENG	-.60** (181)	.02 (181)	.12 (181)	.28** (181)	.08 (181)
24 LNPROCES	.04 (423)	.02 (423)	.20*** (423)	-.02 (423)	-.02 (423)
25 POSTARR	.12* (404)	-.10* (404)	.13** (404)	-.01 (404)	.19** (404)
26 POSTVIO	.02 (404)	-.12* (404)	.14** (404)	.10 (404)	.14** (404)
27 RISKTIME	.22** (404)	-.04 (404)	-.18** (404)	-.08 (404)	-.08 (404)
28 TIMEARRD	.13* (242)	.04 (242)	-.19** (242)	.05 (242)	-.14 (242)

N's are in parentheses

* p < .05
** p < .01

(Continued…)

Table 3 (continued)

Variable	6	7	8	9	10
6 PRIORVIO	1.00 (423)				
7 AGGRAV	-.06 (423)	1.00 (423)			
8 ROBBERY	.08 (423)	-.89** (423)	1.00 (423)		
9 OTHER	-.03 (423)	-.22** (423)	-.26** (423)	1.00 (423)	
10 ROLEPRIM	.03 (423)	.10* (423)	-.07 (423)	-.06 (423)	1.00 (423)
11ROLENON	-.04 (423)	-.01 (423)	.03 (423)	-.05 (423)	-.28** (423)
12 ROLEUNK	-.01 (423)	-.10* (423)	.06 (423)	.09 (423)	-.92** (423)
13 FIREARM	.09 (423)	-.32** (423)	.35** (423)	-.07 (423)	.34** (423)
14 NONFIRE	-.02 (423)	.40** (423)	-.39** (423)	-.02 (423)	.22** (423)
15 FIREUNK	-.09 (423)	-.06 (423)	.00 (423)	.11* (423)	-.68** (423)
16 PUBDEF	.07 (423)	.08 (423)	-.01 (423)	-.14** (423)	.10* (423)
17 ALLEGH	-.04 (423)	.12* (423)	-.09 (423)	-.05 (423)	.18** (423)
18 DAUPHIN	.04 (423)	.05 (423)	-.02 (423)	-.06 (423)	.12* (423)

N's are in parentheses

"." Is printed is coefficient could not be computed.

* p < .05
** p < .01

(Continued...)

Table 3 (continued)

Variable	6	7	8	9	10
19 PHILLY	.02	-.13*	.09	.08	-.22**
	(423)	(423)	(423)	(423)	(423)
20 CONVICT	.04	-.10*	.11*	-.04	-.01
	(423)	(423)	(423)	(423)	(423)
21 EXCONV	.02	-.12	.16*	-.10	.02
	(235)	(235)	(235)	(235)	(235)
22 INCARCER	.17**	-.19**	.15*	.08	-.14*
	(235)	(235)	(235)	(235)	(235)
23 LNINLENG	.08	.07	-.10	.07	-.08
	(181)	(181)	(181)	(181)	(181)
24 LNPROCES	.08	-.10*	.05	.11*	-.11*
	(423)	(423)	(423)	(423)	(423)
25 POSTARR	.11*	.01	.04	-.05	.06
	(404)	(404)	(404)	(404)	(404)
26 POSTVIO	.09	.02	.04	-.11*	.06
	(404)	(404)	(404)	(404)	(404)
27 RISKTIME	-.08	.18**	-.14**	.08*	.07
	(404)	(404)	(404)	(404)	(404)
28 TIMEARRD	-.01	.13*	-.10	-.07	.07
	(242)	(242)	(242)	(242)	(242)

N's are in parentheses

"." Is printed is coefficient could not be computed.

* p < .05
** p < .01

(Continued...)

Table 3 (continued)

Variable	11	12	13	14	15
11ROLENON	1.00				
	(423)				
12 ROLEUNK	-.12*	1.00			
	(423)	(423)			
13 FIREARM	-.05	-.33**	1.00		
	(423)	(423)	(423)		
14 NONFIRE	.14**	-.28**	-.67**	1.00	
	(423)	(423)	(423)	(423)	
15 FIREUNK	-.09	.74***	-.52**	-.30**	1.00
	(423)	(423)	(423)	(423)	(423)
16 PUBDEF	.02	-.11*	.01	.07	-.09
	(423)	(423)	(423)	(423)	(423)
17 ALLEGH	.28**	.30**	-.13**	.35**	-.23**
	(423)	(423)	(423)	(423)	(423)
18 DAUPHIN	.07	-.15**	.05	.04	-.12*
	(423)	(423)	(423)	(423)	(423)
19 PHILLY	-.29**	.35**	.09	-.34**	.27**
	(423)	(423)	(423)	(423)	(423)
20 CONVICT	.09	-.03	.01	-.01	.01
	(423)	(423)	(423)	(423)	(423)
21 EXCONV	-.15*	.06	.17*	-.22**	.04
	(235)	(235)	(235)	(235)	(235)
22 INCARCER	.04	.13*	.19**	-.33	.13*
	(235)	(235)	(235)	(235)	(235)
23 LNINLENG	-.17*	.16*	.09	-.24**	.13
	(181)	(181)	(181)	(181)	(181)

N's are in parentheses

"." Is printed is coefficient could not be computed.

* p < .05
** p < .01

(Continued...)

Table 3 (continued)

Variable	11	12	13	14	15
24 LNPROCES	-.02 (423)	.12* (423)	.03 (423)	-.14** (423)	.13** (423)
25 POSTARR	-.04 (404)	-.04 (404)	.08 (404)	-.01 (404)	-.10 (404)
26 POSTVIO	-.10* (404)	-.02 (404)	.09 (404)	-.08 (404)	-.02 (404)
27 RISKTIME	.06 (404)	-.09 (404)	-.13** (404)	-.25** (404)	-.12* (404)
28 TIMEARRD	.01 (242)	-.08 (242)	-.21** (242)	.25** (242)	-.03 (242)

N's are in parentheses

"." Is printed is coefficient could not be computed.

* p < .05
** p < .01

(Continued...)

Table 3 (continued)

Variable	16	17	18	19	20
16 PUBDEF	1.00 (423)				
17 ALLEGH	.11* (423)	1.00 (423)			
18 DAUPHIN	.00 (423)	-.12* (423)	1.00 (423)		
19 PHILLY	-.10* (423)	-.86** (423)	-.40** (423)	1.00 (423)	
20 CONVICT	-.02 (423)	-.04 (423)	.17** (423)	-.05 (423)	1.00 (423)
21 EXCONV	-.03 (235)	-.26** (235)	.07 (235)	.19** (235)	.
22 INCARCER	-.03 (235)	-.09 (235)	-.08 (235)	.13* (235)	.
23 LNINLENG	-.25** (181)	-.34** (181)	.15* (181)	.20** (181)	.
24 LNPROCES	-.28** (423)	-.33** (423)	.10* (423)	.25** (423)	.49** (423)
25 POSTARR	.17** (404)	.15** (404)	-.03 (404)	-.13* (404)	-.07 (404)
26 POSTVIO	.16** (404)	.04 (404)	.00 (404)	-.04 (404)	-.06 (404)
27 RISKTIME	.17** (404)	.21** (404)	-.13* (404)	-.13 (404)	-.54** (404)
28 TIMEARRD	-.01 (242)	.01 (242)	-.02 (242)	.00 (242)	-.03 (242)

N's are in parentheses

"." Is printed is coefficient could not be computed.

* p < .05
** p < .01

(Continued...)

Table 3 (continued)

Variable	21	22	23	24	25
21 EXCONV	1.00				
22 INCARCER	.26**	1.00			
	(235)	(235)			
23 LNINLENG	.19	.	1.00		
	(181)		(181)		
24 LNPROCES	.22**	.16*	.41**	1.00	
	(235)	(235)	(181)	(423)	
25 POSTARR	-.06	-.05	-.42**	-.10*	1.00
	(216)	(216)	(162)	(404)	(404)
26 POSTVIO	-.12	-.04	-.32**	-.08	.57**
	(216)	(216)	(162)	(404)	(404)
27 RISKTIME	-.27**	-.49**	-.91**	-.57**	.25**
	(216)	(216)	(162)	(404)	(404)
28 TIMEARRD	.12	-.29**	-.19	.05	.
	(123)	(123)	(90)	(242)	

N's are in parentheses

"." Is printed is coefficient could not be computed.

* p < .05
** p < .01

(Continued...)

Table 3 (continued)

Variable	26	27	28
26 POSTVIO	1.00		
	(404)		
27 RISKTIME	.20**	1.00	
	(404)	(404)	
28 TIMEARRD	-.24**	.10	1.00
	(242)	(242)	(242)

N's are in parentheses

"." Is printed is coefficient could not be computed.

* $p < .05$
** $p < .01$

frequently taken as an indication that multicollinearity may be unduly influencing the least squares estimates" (p. 409). For the current study, all tolerances were greater than .4 and all variance inflation factors were less than 2.5.

In examining the bivariate relationships between decertification and the potential explanatory variables, many significant relationships emerge. The negative coefficient for age indicates that the older the offender, the lesser the likelihood of decertification. Non-whites, also, were less likely to be decertified than whites. Both prior record indicators were significant, indicating that as the number of prior referrals and the number of prior referrals for violent offenses increase, the lower the likelihood of decertification.

As mentioned in Chapter 5, the potential effect of "role" has been unexplored in research. For the current study, offenders who played a non-primary role in the offense were more likely to be decertified, as compared to those who played a primary role and those whose role was unknown. A proxy measure for offense seriousness, weapon, also was significant at the bivariate level. Youth who used a firearm were less likely to be decertified than youth who either used other deadly weapons or whose weapon type was unknown. If youth used other deadly weapons (i.e., no firearm), the likelihood of decertification increased, as compared to those who used a firearm and those whose weapon type was unknown.

Decertification now will be considered as the independent variable of interest, with regard to its potential effect on the other eight dependent variables. In examining the coefficients, decertification had a significant bivariate relationship with most of the dependent variables. Decertified youth were significantly more likely to be convicted, as compared to non-decertified youth. Of those who were convicted, decertified youth were less likely to be incarcerated, as compared to similar non-decertified youth. Of those youth who were incarcerated, decertified youth were incarcerated for significantly shorter periods of time.

In regard to the effect of decertification on recidivism, the positive and significant coefficient indicates that decertified youth were more likely to be rearrested during the post-dispositional follow-up period than non-decertified youth. It also is worth noting that the weak positive coefficient for decertification and rearrest for a violent offense suggests that decertified youth were more likely to be rearrested for a violent offense, but the relationship was far from being statistically significant ($p = .67$). Finally, in contrast to the other recidivism variables, for those youth who were rearrested following final disposition, decertified youth had a significantly longer time to rearrest than non-decertified youth.

In examining the bivariate correlations between the independent/control variables and the dependent variables, several significant relationships emerged. First, age only was significantly correlated with recidivism. The negative coefficients suggest that the older the youth, the lower the likelihood of rearrest, both on any offense and for a violent offense.

Concerning gender, males were significantly more likely to be convicted than females. Of those convicted, males were more likely to be incarcerated, as compared to females. It also took males longer to have their cases processed. Regarding the relationship between gender and recidivism, males were more likely to be rearrested following final disposition and also more likely to be rearrested for a violent offense. Finally, males experienced a shorter time to rearrest than females.

In examining the effect of race, non-whites were less likely to be convicted than whites, but among those who were convicted, non-whites were more likely to be convicted on a violent offense and more likely to be incarcerated. Among those who were incarcerated, non-whites were confined for a longer period of time than whites. There were no significant differences between whites and nonwhites on any of the recidivism variables.

The prior record indicators also exhibited several significant associations. The more times youth were referred to the juvenile court and the more times youth were referred for violent offenses, the greater the likelihood of incarceration (among those who were convicted). Both prior referral indicators also had a significant positive relationship with recidivism, as increases in both were associated with a greater likelihood of post-dispositional arrest. Finally, only the number of prior referrals had a significant relationship with post-dispositional violent recidivism, as increased prior referrals was associated with an increased likelihood of rearrest for a violent offense.

Type of offense also was significantly associated with numerous case outcomes. Youth charged with aggravated assault were significantly less likely to be convicted than youth charged with either robbery or other violent offenses. Those who were charged with aggravated assault and convicted had a lower likelihood of incarceration than those charged with robbery and other violent offenses. Finally, youth charged with aggravated assault experienced significantly lower case processing time.

If youth were charged with robbery, they were more likely to be convicted on any charge, convicted on a violent offense (among those who were convicted), and incarcerated (among those who were convicted), as compared to those charged with aggravated assault and other violent offenses. However, those charged with robbery and incarcerated were sentenced to shorter incarceration periods than those charged with aggravated assault and other violent offenses, but this relationship was not significant.

If youth were charged with "other" violent offenses, they experienced significantly longer case processing time, as compared to those who were charged with aggravated assault or robbery. In addition, those charged with "other" violent offenses were less likely to be rearrested for a violent offense, as compared to those charged with aggravated assault or robbery.

The role youth played in the offense also was significantly associated with numerous dependent variables. Convicted youth who played a primary role in the offense were less likely to be incarcerated than those played either a non-primary role or those whose role was unknown. Primary role offenders also experienced shorter case processing time than the other two groups of offenders. Also, those who played a non-primary role were less likely to be convicted on a target offense (among those who were convicted) than those who played either a primary or unknown role. In addition, those who played a non-primary role were less likely to be rearrested for a violent offense, as compared to those who played either a primary or unknown role. As for those whose role was unknown in the offense, they were more likely to be incarcerated (among those who were convicted) and incarcerated for a longer period of time (among those who were incarcerated), as compared to those who did not play either a primary or non-primary role. Finally, those whose role was unknown in the original offense experienced longer case processing time than those who played either a primary or non-primary role.

Weapon, an indicator of offense-seriousness, was significantly correlated with several dependent variables. Those who were convicted and used a firearm had a greater chance of being convicted on a target offense and incarcerated, as compared to those who did not use a firearm or whose weapon was unknown. Of those who were rearrested during the follow-up period, firearm users had a shorter time to rearrest than those who were in the other two groups.

Those who used other deadly weapons (i.e., non-firearm) were less likely to be both convicted on a target offense and incarcerated (among those who were convicted), as compared to those who used a firearm or whose weapon type was unknown. Also, those who used a non-firearm experienced shorter case processing time. As for those whose weapon type was unknown, they were more likely to be incarcerated (among those who were convicted), as compared to those who used either a firearm or non-firearm. Finally, those whose weapon type was unknown experienced longer case processing time.

The type of attorney also was significantly related to numerous dependent variables. Youth using public defenders were incarcerated for shorter periods of time (among those who were incarcerated) than youth who used another type of attorney. In addition, youth who used a public defender experienced shorter case processing time. Finally, if a public defender was used, youth not only were more likely to be rearrested, but also more likely to be rearrested for a violent offense, as compared to youth who used another type of attorney.

The specific county in which the youth initially were charged with an Act 33 also was significantly related to some of the outcomes. Among those convicted, Allegheny youth were less likely to be convicted on a target offense than Dauphin and Philadelphia youth. Among those incarcerated, Allegheny youth were confined for significantly shorter time than youth from Dauphin and Philadelphia.

The negative and significant coefficient also indicates that youth from Allegheny County had shorter case processing time the youth from the other two counties. Regarding the recidivism variables, Allegheny youth were more likely to be rearrested following disposition, as compared to youth from Dauphin and Philadelphia.

Youth in Dauphin County were more likely to be convicted than youth in Allegheny and Philadelphia Counties. Among those who were incarcerated, Dauphin County offenders were sentenced to longer periods of incarceration than those in Allegheny and Philadelphia Counties. The county of Philadelphia also was significantly related to numerous dependent variables. Among those who were convicted, Philadelphia youth were more likely to be both convicted on a target offense and incarcerated, as compared to Allegheny and Dauphin County youth. Offenders in Philadelphia also experienced longer case processing time than Allegheny County youth. Finally, youth in Philadelphia were less likely to be rearrested following final disposition.

The length of time a youth was "on the street" was associated with both dichotomous measures of post-dispositional recidivism. The longer youth were at risk following final disposition, the more likely they were to be rearrested on any offense and to be rearrested for an excluded offense.

In closely examining other bivariate relationships involving the recidivism measures (i.e., post-dispositional rearrest, post-dispositional rearrest for a violent offense, and time to recidivism), several case outcome variables also can be viewed as explanatory variables (e.g., conviction, incarceration length, and case processing time). Whether or not a youth either was convicted on any offense or convicted on a target offense had no significant bivariate relationship with any of the recidivism measures. Of the youth who were incarcerated, as confinement time increased, the likelihood of rearrest on both any offense and on an excluded offense decreased. Case processing time also was significantly related to recidivism, as an increase in case processing time was associated with a decreased likelihood of rearrest on any offense.

Finally, when examining incarceration length at the bivariate level, the coefficients in Table 3 were based only on those offenders who were incarcerated, excluding those who either were not convicted, or convicted but not incarcerated. In order to consider the impact of incarceration length on recidivism of all of the offenders who were "on the street" following final disposition, incarceration length was recoded for multivariate analyses. Offenders who were either not convicted or convicted but not incarcerated were coded as 0 (i.e., they served no incarceration time), while the length of incarceration for those imprisoned continued to be coded in months. In examining the bivariate relationship between this variable and recidivism, the associations were statistically significant. The lengthier the incarceration period, the lesser the likelihood of rearrest both on any offense ($r = -.27$; $p < .001$) and on a violent offense ($r = -.19$; $p < .001$).

MULTIVARIATE RESULTS

It must be remembered that the correlations discussed above only indicate the association between two variables. Stated differently, bivariate correlations do not control for the effects of other explanatory variables; therefore, they cannot be used to make causal inferences. However, to help account for some of the limitations of correlations, multivariate analyses were employed, which allows for the effects of specific independent variables to be examined while controlling for the effects of other independent variables. It is still stressed, however, that due to the current study not being a true experiment, cause-and-effect cannot be fully established, but stronger conclusions can be made than were possible at the bivariate level.

In order to appropriately test the 12 hypotheses discussed in Chapter 5, numerous statistical analyses were used: ordinary least squares regression, logistic regression, and survival analysis. Hypotheses 1-4 will be examined in two decertification models. Hypothesis 5-12 resulted in three models being developed to test each hypothesis: a full model and two decertification-specific models. The full models test the additive effects of the independent variables, and the decertification-specific models test for the potential interaction between decertification and the other explanatory variables.

Hypotheses 1-4: Determinants of Decertification

Due to the first four hypotheses all being focused on the potential effect of various factors on decertification, they all will be considered in the same models. The first hypothesis stated that as offense seriousness increases, the likelihood of decertification decreases. It must be remembered that Pennsylvania's Act 33 statute targets violent felony offenses, so it was difficult to rank-order the offenses by severity. Therefore, as mentioned earlier, the offenses were coded as three dichotomous variables: aggravated assault (the reference group), robbery, and other offenses. However, weapon type can be used as another indicator of offense seriousness, as a firearm being used during the commission of a crime may be viewed as a more serious offense than one in which another weapon was used. In addition, the role of the offender also may be seen as an indicator of offense seriousness, as youth who played a primary role in the offense may be viewed more seriously by the court than someone who did not play a primary role.

At the bivariate level, robbery was not significantly associated with a greater chance of decertification, as compared to being charged with either aggravated assault or other violent offenses. In addition, "other" violent offenses was not significantly associated with decertification, as compared to being charged with either robbery or aggravated assault. The coefficient for robbery, however, was significant in logistic regression model, as shown in Table 4.

Those charged with robbery were more likely to be decertified, as compared to those charged with aggravated assault ($b = .63$; $p < .05$), while controlling for other factors. However, the coefficient for

Table 4: Logistic Regression Estimates for the Determinants of Decertification (n = 423)

Variable	B (SE)	|Wald|	Exp(B)
AGE	-.247 (.140)	3.133	.781
GENDER	.530 (.367)	2.077	1.698
RACE	-.411 (.363)	1.285	.663
PRIORREF	-.266 (.093)	8.132**	.766
PRIORVIO	.172 (.182)	.897	1.118
ROBBERY	.632 (.279)	5.113*	1.881
OTHEROFF	.711 (.503)	1.996	2.036
ROLENON	2.477 (.817)	9.199**	11.904
ROLEUNK	-.174 (.383)	.206	.841
FIRENON	1.402 (.331)	17.957***	4.064
FIREUNK	.199 (.439)	.206	1.220
PUBDEF	.476 (.233)	4.178*	1.609
DAUPHIN	.417 (.549)	.577	1.517
PHILLY	.583 (.344)	2.867	1.791
Constant	2.137 (2.398)	.794	8.478
Log-likelihood	473.738		
Model X^2	70.129***		
Cox & Snell R^2	.153		
Nagelkerke R^2	.211		

* $p < .05$
** $p < .01$
*** $p < .001$

while controlling for other factors. However, the coefficient for "other" violent offenses ($b = .71$; $p = .16$) still did not reach the level of statistical significance, although it was in the same direction as the robbery coefficient. The logistic regression results indicate, then, that offenders charged with aggravated assault were the least likely to be decertified to juvenile court.

When examining the effect of weapon on decertification, another significant effect emerged. In the bivariate correlations, those who used a non-firearm (i.e., other deadly weapons) were significantly more likely to be decertified than those who either used a firearm or whose weapon type was unknown. In the full logistic model, the significant positive coefficient for FIRENON indicates that while controlling for other explanatory factors, those who used a non-firearm were more likely to be decertified than those who used a gun ($b = 1.40$; $p < .001$). Put differently, the adult court was more likely to retain those who used a firearm. The coefficient for "unknown weapon," however, was weak and insignificant in the full model, suggesting these offenders were viewed more like gun offenders than non-gun offenders.

Because of the high significance of the non-firearm coefficient, using Equation 1 from Chapter 5, the estimated probability of decertification was calculated with non-firearm equal to 0 (i.e., a firearm was used in the offense) and with non-firearm equal to 1 (i.e., a firearm was not used in the offense), with all other explanatory factors set at their mean. The estimated probability of decertification when offenders used a firearm was .24, while the estimated probability for those who did not use a firearm was .56, a large difference of 32 percentage points. In other words, those who used a firearm had a much lower chance of decertification.

Finally, the role of the offender also was significant in predicting decertification. At the bivariate level, those who played a non-primary role were significantly more likely to be decertified, as compared to those who either played a primary or unknown role. This factor remained significant in the full logistic model, as those who played a non-primary role were significantly more likely to be decertified, as compared to those who played a primary role ($b = 2.48$; $p < .01$). Again, stated differently, the adult court was more likely to retain those who played a primary role. In addition, the coefficient for "unknown role" was weak and insignificant in the full model, again suggesting those offenders were viewed more like primary offenders than non-primary offenders.

Hypothesis 2 stated that prior record would have a negative effect on decertification. The current research examined both prior referrals to juvenile court and the number of prior referrals for violent offenses. In the bivariate correlations, both prior record indicators had a significant and negative association with decertification. However, in the full model, only prior referrals remained significant when controlling for other factors (b = -.27; p < .01). As the number of prior referrals increased, the likelihood of decertification decreased. As just stated, the original significant bivariate relationship between prior referrals for violent offenses and decertification disappeared when other factors were taken into account (b = .18; p = .34), though it is interesting that the relationship is positive. In general, having a greater number of prior referrals significantly decreases the likelihood of decertification, regardless of whether these referrals were for violent offenses.

Hypothesis 3 sought to determine the effect of age at referral on decertification. Specifically, age was expected to have a significantly negative effect on decertification. At the bivariate level, this association was supported. As can be seen in Table 4, the unstandardized logistic regression coefficient for age is negative (-.25), which is in the expected direction. However, when controlling for other factors, the effect of age did not quite reach statistical significance (p = .08), though it is worth noting.

Hypothesis 4 examined the effect of race on decertification. At the bivariate level, race had a significant and negative relationship with decertification, whereby nonwhites were less likely to be decertified than whites. When looking at the full model, the negative coefficient suggests that non-whites were less likely to be decertified than whites, but while considering other factors, the effect of race did not reach statistical significance (b = -.41; p = .26). However, there may be an indirect race effect on decertification. When examining the bivariate correlations, nonwhites were significantly more likely to have a greater record of prior offending and to use a firearm, and less likely to play a non-primary role, as compared to whites. Furthermore, prior record, firearm, and non-primary role all had a significant effect on decertification. Therefore, the race effect appears indirect through these legal variables.

One other factor that was significant in the decertification model was public defender. In the bivariate correlations, having a public defender was not significantly associated with decertification.

However, in the full model, when accounting for other factors, the effect reached statistical significance. Those who used a public defender were more likely to be decertified than those who did not use a public defender ($b = .48$; $p < .05$).

Another possible effect worth considering is the impact of county of jurisdiction on decertification. At the bivariate level, the coefficient for Philadelphia youth was negative and insignificant. When examining the full model, as youth in Philadelphia were more likely to get decertified than youth in Allegheny County (the reference group), though the relationship did not quite reach the traditional level of significance. In addition, although the positive coefficient for Dauphin County suggests that those youth are more likely to get decertified than Allegheny County youth, the effect also was not statistically significant ($b = .42$; $p = .45$).

The pseudo r-squares in Table 4 indicate that the model explains between 15.3% and 21.1% of the "variance" in decertification, suggesting that there are other unmeasured factors that impact on this outcome. When examining the predictors of decertification, it should be noted that the statistical model presented in Table 4 included cases that proceeded to prosecution, as well as those cases that were dismissed at the initial preliminary hearing stage. In this model, the dismissed cases ($n = 78$) were treated as "not decertified." Therefore, an argument could be made that there may be a difference in the findings if the dismissed cases were excluded from the analysis, since they had no opportunity for decertification. To examine this potential difference in results, a separate decertification model was developed, using only those cases that proceeded to prosecution ($n = 345$).
Using the same explanatory factors, the logistic regression results in Table 5 were similar to those of the original decertification model. Specifically, offenders with a greater number of prior referrals were less likely to be decertified, while those charged with robbery, playing a non-primary role, not using a gun,[9] and using a public defender were

[9] Similar to the first decertification model, the probability of decertification was estimated with NONFIRE set at 0 and 1, and similar results were observed, with the difference being 35 percentage points between the two groups. Those who did not use a firearm were much more likely to be decertified than those who used a firearm.

Table 5: Logistic Regression Estimates for the Determinants of Decertification (n = 345)

Variable	B (SE)	|Wald|	Exp(B)
AGE	-.242 (.153)	2.503	.785
GENDER	.198 (.403)	.243	1.219
RACE	-.107 (.417)	.066	.898
PRIORREF	-.285 (.098)	8.547**	.752
PRIORVIO	.112 (.195)	.330	1.119
ROBBERY	.668 (.301)	4.925*	1.951
OTHEROFF	.832 (.533)	2.440	2.298
ROLENON	1.800 (.859)	4.389*	6.051
ROLEUNK	.691 (.450)	2.356	1.995
FIRENON	1.484 (.364)	16.614***	4.409
FIREUNK	-.334 (.509)	.429	.716
PUBDEF	.766 (.251)	9.350**	2.152
DAUPHIN	-.171 (.597)	.082	.843
PHILLY	-.313 (.415)	.570	.731
Constant	2.894 (2.657)	1.187	18.074
Log-likelihood	398.319		
Model X^2	70.492***		
Cox & Snell R^2	.185		
Nagelkerke R^2	.249		

* $p < .05$
** $p < .01$
*** $p < .001$

more likely to be decertified. Moreover, the effects of these variables were relatively stable in both models that examined decertification. This second decertification model also had rather weak explanatory power, as only between 18.5% and 24.9% of the "variance" was explained.

Hypothesis 5: Conviction

The logistic regression estimates for the predictors of conviction are presented in Table 6. The original bivariate association between decertification and conviction was significant and positive ($r = .18$; $p < .001$). In examining the full model, the positive effect of decertification remained significant ($b = .75$; $p < .01$), after accounting for the effect of other explanatory factors. In other words, decertified youth had a greater likelihood of conviction than similar non-decertified youth.

As previously discussed, the unstandardized regression coefficients produced from the multivariate analysis can be used to make separate predictions of the probability of certain events occurring. Using the logistic regression estimates in Table 6, the probability of conviction for decertified and non-decertified youth was estimated using Equation 1 from Chapter 5. All of the explanatory variables were set at their mean, except for decertification. The purpose here was to determine the probability of conviction when decertification equals 1 (i.e., decertified offenders) and when decertification equals 0 (i.e., non-decertified offenders). The results revealed that the probability of conviction for decertified youth was .68, while the probability of conviction for non-decertified youth was .50. Stated differently, the estimated probability of conviction for decertified youth was 18 percentage points higher than the probability for non-decertified youth, while controlling for the other variables in the model.

Aside from the effect of decertification on conviction, several other explanatory factors were significant in the full model. Males were significantly more likely to be convicted than females ($b = .81$; $p < .05$). Also, nonwhites were significantly less likely to be convicted than whites ($b = -.97$; $p < .05$). Finally, youth from Dauphin County had a greater likelihood of being convicted than those from Allegheny County ($b = 2.44$; $p < .01$), but there was no significant difference in the log odds of conviction between Philadelphia and Allegheny County youth ($b = .45$; $p = .15$).

A few other coefficients in Table 6 are worth noting. The number of prior referrals almost reached the traditional level of statistical significance, with an increased number of prior referrals resulting in a greater chance of conviction ($b = .12$; $p < .10$). Similarly, those

Table 6: Logistic Regression Estimates for the Determinants of Conviction (n = 423)

Variable	B	SE	|Wald|	Exp(B)
DECERT	.752	.240	9.784**	2.122
AGE	-.076	.132	.330	.927
GENDER	.812	.351	5.340*	2.252
RACE	-.966	.375	6.618*	.381
PRIORREF	.121	.067	3.208	1.128
PRIORVIO	-.046	.151	.094	.955
ROBBERY	.411	.243	2.847	1.508
OTHEROFF	-.287	.464	.382	.751
ROLENON	.837	.725	1.332	2.309
ROLEUNK	-.367	.347	1.119	.693
FIRENON	.032	.313	.011	1.033
FIREUNK	.367	.397	.856	1.444
PUBDEF	-.083	.217	.148	.920
DAUPHIN	2.438	.798	9.338**	11.453
PHILLY	.448	.312	2.066	1.565
Constant	.630	2.293	.075	1.877
Log-likelihood	525.858			
Model Chi-Square	55.311***			
Cox & Snell R^2	.123			
Nagelkerke R^2	.164			

* p < .05
** p < .01
*** p < .001

charged with robbery had a greater likelihood of being convicted, as compared to those charged with aggravated assault (b = .41; p < .10), but there was no difference in conviction between other violent offenders and those charged with aggravated assault (b = -.29; p = .54). Finally, the pseudo r-squares from this model indicate that between

12.3% and 16.4% of the "variance" in the log odds of conviction is explained by the explanatory variables, suggesting a rather limited amount of explanatory power.

Similar to the decertification model presented previously, Table 7 summarizes a second conviction model, including only those cases that were not withdrawn or dismissed at the initial preliminary hearing (n = 345). Because some variables had extremely high standard errors, they were excluded from the analysis. The high standard errors were due to some categories having zero cells. According to Mernard (2002), "When [the odds] are 0 or 1 for an entire group of cases, as defined by the value of a categorical independent variable, the result will be a very high estimated standard error for the coefficient associated with that category" (p. 78). For this reason, the county variables were excluded from the analysis.

The findings for this statistical model were similar to the one in which all cases were included, with two notable exceptions. The number of prior referrals did not quite reach statistical significance in the model in Table 6, however, it does in Table 7. The positive and significant coefficient indicates that as the number of prior referrals increases, the likelihood of conviction also increases ($p = .23$; $p < .05$). More importantly, though, the significant decertification effect disappeared when examining only those cases that proceeded beyond the preliminary hearing stage ($b = -.13$; $p = .62$). In other words, when examining the full sample, decertified youth had a significantly higher likelihood of conviction, but once the cases that were initially withdrawn and dismissed were removed from the analysis, there was no difference in the likelihood of conviction between decertified and non-decertified youth.

Table 8 presents the predictors of conviction, based on decertification status (i.e., separate models for juvenile and adult court cases). Using Equation 3 from Chapter 5, it can be determined whether the explanatory factors have different effects on the dependent variable, based on the type of court in which the case was processed. Due to some categories having zero cells, it should be recognized that the following models exclude the role and county variables from the analyses.

Older offenders in juvenile court were significantly less likely to be convicted than younger offenders ($b = -.523$; $p < .05$). On the other

Table 7: Logistic Regression Estimates for the Determinants of Conviction (n = 345)

Variable	B (SE)	|Wald|	Exp(B)
DECERT	-.133 (.270)	.240	.876
AGE	-.058 (.156)	.139	.943
GENDER	.990 (.393)	6.367*	2.692
RACE	-1.500 (.506)	8.800**	.223
PRIORREF	.234 (.095)	6.123*	1.264
PRIORVIO	-.308 (.187)	2.705	.735
ROBBERY	.537 (.292)	3.388	1.711
OTHEROFF	-.361 (.524)	.474	.697
ROLENON	.559 (.694)	.650	1.750
ROLEUNK	1.009 (.542)	3.466	2.743
FIRENON	.123 (.359)	.118	1.131
FIREUNK	-.542 (.599)	.819	.582
PUBDEF	.362 (.257)	1.983	1.437
Constant	1.456 (2.692)	.293	4.290
Log-likelihood	393.199		
Model Chi-Square	40.241***		
Cox & Snell R^2	.110		
Nagelkerke R^2	.154		

* p < .05
** p < .01
*** p < .001

Table 8: Split Model for the Determinants of Conviction (n = 423)

Variable	B (SE)	|Wald|	Exp(B)	|Z-test|
	Non-Decertified (n = 278)			
AGE	.094 (.161)	.344	1.099	
GENDER	1.246 (.479)	6.775**	3.475	
RACE	-.316 (.460)	.474	.729	
PRIORREF	.086 (.069)	1.557	1.090	
PRIORVIO	.116 (.165)	.498	1.123	
ROBBERY	.097 (.284)	.118	1.102	
OTHEROFF	.092 (.572)	.026	1.097	
NONFIRE	-.253 (.381)	.442	.776	
FIREUNK	.179 (.334)	.287	1.196	
PUBDEF	-.496 (.262)	3.601	.609	
Constant	-2.507 (2.807)	.798	.082	
-2 LL	359.418			
Model X^2	25.914**			
Cox & Snell R^2	.089			
Nagelkerke R^2	.119			

(Continued...)

Table 8 (continued)

Variable	B (SE)	|Wald|	Exp(B)	|Z-test|
	Decertified (n = 145)			
AGE	-.523 (.256)	4.163*	.593	2.04*
GENDER	.164 (.615)	.072	1.179	1.38
RACE	-1.151 (.681)	2.854	.316	1.02
PRIORREF	.099 (.195)	.255	1.104	.06
PRIORVIO	-.172 (.345)	.249	.842	.75
ROBBERY	1.171 (.502)	5.436*	3.225	1.86
OTHEROFF	-.910 (.861)	1.117	.403	1.00
NONFIRE	.584 (.560)	1.086	1.793	1.24
FIREUNK	-.183 (.543)	.114	.832	.57
PUBDEF	.659 (.405)	2.652	1.933	2.39*
Constant	9.170 (4.322)	4.501*	9603.284	
Log-likelihood	157.274			
Model X^2	25.411**			
Cox & Snell R^2	.161			
Nagelkerke R^2	.224			

*p < .05
**p < .01
***p < .001

hand, the age coefficient in adult court was positive and insignificant. The z-test (z = 2.04) revealed a significant interaction effect, as age played a stronger role and had a negative effect in juvenile court. Older offenders were significantly less likely to get convicted in juvenile court, as compared to older offenders in adult court, where age had no effect on the likelihood of conviction.

In addition, in adult court, attorney-type just missed statistical significance, as those who used a public defender were less likely to be convicted than were youth who did not use a public defender (b = -.50; p = .06). Regarding offenders in juvenile court, the positive coefficient suggests that youth who used a public defender were more likely to be convicted, but again statistical significance was not quite achieved ($b = .659$; $p = .10$). However, a significant interaction was found ($z = 2.39$), meaning attorney type had a significantly different effect in juvenile versus adult court. Youth who used a public defender in adult court were less likely to be convicted, while similar youth who used a public defender in juvenile court were more likely to be convicted.

The effect of gender was positive and significant in adult court, as non-decertified males were more likely to be convicted than non-decertified females. The coefficient for gender also was positive, but insignificant, for decertified offenders. The z-test ($z = 1.38$) revealed no significant interaction between gender and court of jurisdiction regarding conviction, meaning gender had a somewhat similar positive effect, regardless of court of jurisdiction.

Finally, of those in juvenile court, offenders who committed robbery were significantly more likely to be convicted than those who committed aggravated assault ($b = 1.17$; $p < .05$). The robbery coefficient in adult court was positive and insignificant. Again, the z-test did not reveal an interaction at the traditional significance level, but it still appears strong enough to be worth noting ($z = 1.86$; $p < .10$). The finding suggests that decertified youth charged with robbery had a greater likelihood of being convicted than those charged with aggravated assault, but in adult court, offense type had little impact on the likelihood of conviction.

Hypothesis 6: Target Conviction

In order to examine the potential effect of decertification and other explanatory factors on conviction on a target offense, only convicted offenders were included in the analysis ($n = 235$). Table 9 provides the logistic regression estimates for the determinants of target conviction. In the bivariate correlations, the relationship between decertification and target conviction was negative and approaching significance ($r = -.11$; $p < .10$). When accounting for the effect of other explanatory factors in the full model, the coefficient was still negative, but highly insignificant ($b = -.33$; $p = .47$).

To better illustrate this finding, using the results from the logistic regression model and Equation 1, the probability of target conviction

Table 9: Logistic Regression Estimates for the Determinants of Target Conviction (n = 235)

Variable	B (SE)	Wald	Exp(B)
DECERT	-.327 (.456)	.514	.721
AGE	-.058 (.241)	.057	.944
GENDER	.581 (.600)	.940	1.788
RACE	.511 (.524)	.951	1.667
PRIORREF	-.004 (.106)	.001	.996
PRIORVIO	-.085 (.280)	.093	.918
ROBBERY	.510 (.440)	1.345	1.665
OTHEROFF	-.820 (.743)	1.218	.440
ROLENON	-.555 (.710)	.610	.574
ROLEUNK	.111 (.710)	.024	1.117
NONFIRE	-.208 (.543)	.146	.813
FIREUNK	-.252 (.814)	.096	.778
PUBDEF	-.268 (.401)	.447	.765
DAUPHIN	1.382 (.853)	2.621	3.981
PHILLY	.929 (.547)	2.889	2.532
Constant	1.146 (4.139)	.077	3.144
Log-likelihood	193.088		
Model X^2	24.556		
Cox & Snell R^2	.099		
Nagelkerke R^2	.164		

* $p < .05$
** $p < .01$
*** $p < .001$

was estimated. For a "typical" decertified and convicted youth, the probability of being convicted on a target offense was .83, while the probability for a similar non-decertified youth was .87, a difference of only 4 percentage points.

While none of the other factors in the full model were statistically significant, two appear worth mentioning. The positive coefficients suggest that youth from both Dauphin ($b = 1.38$; $p = .11$) and Philadelphia ($b = .93$; $p < .10$) Counties were more likely to be convicted on a target offense than youth from Allegheny County, but again, because statistical significance was not reached, a county effect on target conviction cannot be fully established. The insignificant coefficients produced in the model are reflected in the model's limited explanatory power, as it only explains between 9.9% and 16.4% of the "variance" in the log odds of target conviction.

Table 10 presents the decertification-specific models for target conviction. Due to the role and county variables having extremely high standard errors as a result of zero cells, they were excluded from the analysis. In examining Table 10, only type of offense was significant in one model in predicting target conviction. For youth convicted in adult court, those charged with robbery had a significantly higher likelihood of conviction on a target offense, as compared to those charged with aggravated assault ($b = 2.17$; $p < .01$). There was no difference in the likelihood of target conviction between robbery and aggravated assault offenders in juvenile court, though it is interesting that the coefficient is negative. The z-test ($z = 3.14$) indicated that a robbery charge had a greater positive and significant effect on target conviction in adult court, while type of offense does not appear to effect the log odds of target conviction in juvenile court. Moreover, there were no significant differences in target conviction between those charged with other violent offenses and those charged with aggravated assault in either juvenile or adult court, as both coefficients are negative and insignificant ($z = .15$).

Hypothesis 7: Incarceration

Table 11 presents the logistic regression estimates for the determinants of incarceration, which considered only those offenders who were

Table 10: Split Model for the Determinants of Target Conviction (n = 235)

Variable	B (SE)	Wald	Exp(B)	Z-test
	Non-Decertified (n = 137)			
AGE	-.243 (.426)	.327	.784	
GENDER	-1.397 (1.386)	1.016	.247	
RACE	.965 (.853)	1.279	2.625	
PRIORREF	-.006 (.128)	.002	.994	
PRIORVIO	-.246 (.340)	.524	.782	
ROBBERY	2.166 (.747)	8.404**	8.720	
OTHEROFF	-.712 (.931)	.586	.491	
NONFIRE	-.393 (.766)	.264	.675	
FIREUNK	.634 (.786)	.649	1.885	
PUBDEF	-1.002 (.628)	2.548	.367	
Constant	6.393 (7.912)	.653	597.686	
Log-likelihood	87.123			
Model X^2	23.182*			
Cox & Snell R^2	.156			
Nagelkerke R^2	.282			

(Continued...)

Table 10 (continued)

Variable	B (SE)	Wald	Exp(B)	Z-test
	Decertified (n = 98)			
AGE	-.024 (.332)	.005	.976	.41
GENDER	1.370 (.758)	3.269	3.935	1.75
RACE	.255 (.689)	.137	1.291	.65
PRIORREF	-.226 (.281)	.649	.798	.71
PRIORVIO	.709 (.554)	1.640	2.032	1.47
ROBBERY	-.970 (.662)	2.147	.379	3.14***
OTHEROFF	-.985 (1.507)	.427	.373	.15
NONFIRE	-1.219 (.713)	2.920	.296	.79
FIREUNK	-.876 (.847)	1.069	.417	1.31
PUBDEF	.316 (.566)	.311	1.371	1.56
Constant	1.435 (5.396)	.071	4.198	
Log-likelihood	94.113			
Model X^2	10.263			
Cox & Snell R^2	.099			
Nagelkerke R^2	.152			

* p < .05
** p < .01
*** p < .001

Table 11: Logistic Regression Estimates for the Determinants of Incarceration (n = 235)

Variable	B (SE)	|Wald|	Exp(B)
DECERT	-.685 (.429)	2.544	.504
AGE	-.108 (.236)	.209	.898
GENDER	.271 (.639)	.180	1.312
RACE	.933 (.541)	2.973	2.541
PRIORREF	.367 (.167)	4.800*	1.443
PRIORVIO	-.005 (.334)	.000	.995
ROBBERY	.595 (.436)	1.862	1.813
OTHEROFF	1.107 (1.136)	.951	3.026
ROLENON	1.759 (.919)	3.662	5.807
ROLEUNK	.508 (.696)	.534	1.662
NONFIRE	-.933 (.521)	3.200	.394
FIREUNK	.198 (.838)	.056	1.219
PUBDEF	-.331 (.391)	.717	.718
DAUPHIN	-.612 (.751)	.663	.542
PHILLY	-.227 (.583)	.151	.797
Constant	1.922 (4.089)	.221	6.832
Log-likelihood	196.285		
Model X^2	57.054***		
Cox & Snell R^2	.216		
Nagelkerke R^2	.327		

* $p < .05$
** $p < .01$
*** $p < .001$

either adjudicated delinquent in juvenile court or convicted in adult court (n = 235). In the bivariate correlations, decertified youth had a significantly lower likelihood of incarceration among convicted offenders than non-decertified youth ($r = .26$; $p < .001$). However, after controlling for other factors, the significant effect disappeared (b = -.685; p = .11). In other words, there was no significant difference in the likelihood of incarceration between decertified and non-decertified convicted offenders, after taking into account the other explanatory variables.

In estimating the probabilities of incarceration, using Equation 1, the probability for decertified and convicted offenders was .77, while the estimated probability for convicted but non-decertified offenders was .87, a difference of ten percentage points. This difference suggests a somewhat greater chance for incarceration in the adult system, but again the difference was statistically insignificant.

In the full model, only one factor actually was statistically significant. Specifically, the more prior referrals a youth had, the greater was the likelihood of incarceration (b = .367; p < .05). There were, however, several factors worth noting that did not quite reach statistical significance. The positive race coefficient suggests that nonwhites had a higher chance of incarceration than whites (b = .933; p < .10). Surprisingly, youth who did not play a primary role in the offense had a higher chance of incarceration than youth who played a primary role (b = 1.759; p < .10). There was no significant difference in likelihood of incarceration between youth whose weapon type was unknown and those who used a firearm, suggesting that they were similar in terms of likelihood of incarceration. In contrast, those who did not use a firearm appeared less likely to be incarcerated than those who did use a firearm (b = .933; p < .10). Finally, in examining the full incarceration model, between 21.6% and 32.7% of the "variance" in the log odds of incarceration was explained by the independent and control variables.

Table 12 presents the split model, showing the predictors of incarceration for decertified and non-decertified youth. Role of the offender was excluded from the analysis due to zero cells and the resultant high standard errors. Of youth convicted in adult court, those who used a public defender had a lower likelihood of incarceration than those who did not use a public defender, but the coefficient did not quite reach statistical significance (b = -.460; p < .10). The effect of using a public defender also was insignificant in juvenile court, but the coefficient was in the opposite direction. The z-test (z = 2.10) did indicate a significant interaction, as the effect of attorney type on the

Table 12: Split Model for the Determinants of Incarceration (n = 235)

Variable	B (SE)	|Wald|	Exp(B)	|Z-test|
	Non-Decertified (n = 137)			
AGE	.090 (.167)	.291	1.094	
GENDER	1.053 (.511)	4.240*	2.866	
RACE	.156 (.472)	.110	1.169	
PRIORREF	.173 (.074)	5.438*	1.188	
PRIORVIO	.031 (.169)	.034	1.032	
ROBBERY	.183 (.291)	.394	1.200	
OTHEROFF	.213 (.578)	.136	1.237	
NONFIRE	-.141 (.416)	.115	.869	
FIREUNK	.379 (.341)	1.239	1.461	
PUBDEF	-.460 (.272)	2.865	.631	
DAUPHIN	1.582 (.686)	5.318*	4.866	
PHILLY	.846 (.418)	4.101*	2.331	
Constant	-3.982 (2.961)	1.809	.019	
Log-likelihood	345.001			
Model X^2	34.020**			
Cox & Snell R^2	.115			
Nagelkerke R^2	.155			

(Continued...)

Table 12 (continued)

Variable	B (SE)	|Wald|	Exp(B)	|Z-test|
	Decertified (n = 98)			
AGE	-.487 (.244)	3.999*	.614	1.95
GENDER	.336 (.655)	.263	1.399	.86
RACE	.215 (.627)	.118	1.240	.08
PRIORREF	.405 (.193)	4.414*	1.499	1.12
PRIORVIO	-.297 (.337)	.780	.743	.87
ROBBERY	1.222 (.470)	6.756**	3.395	1.88
OTHEROFF	.028 (.899)	.001	1.028	.17
NONFIRE	-.408 (.531)	.590	.665	.40
FIREUNK	.162 (.546)	.088	1.176	.34
PUBDEF	.550 (.398)	1.915	1.734	2.10*
DAUPHIN	.386 (.956)	.163	1.470	1.02
PHILLY	-.808 (.526)	2.362	.446	2.46*
Constant	6.680 (4.066)	2.699	796.247	
Log-likelihood	166.869			
Model X^2	31.647			
Cox & Snell R^2	.196			
Nagelkerke R^2	.263			

* p < .05
** p < .01
*** p < .001

log odds of incarceration depended on the court of jurisdiction. Convicted offenders in adult court who used a public defender were less likely to be incarcerated, while convicted offenders in juvenile court who used a public defender were more likely to be incarcerated.

Non-decertified and convicted youth in both Dauphin County (b = 1.582; p < .05) and Philadelphia (b = .846; p < .05) had a significantly higher likelihood of incarceration than similar youth in Allegheny County. In contrast, county type did not appear to impact on the likelihood of incarceration in juvenile court. The z-tests did reveal one interaction effect based on county and court of jurisdiction. Convicted, adult court youth from Philadelphia were significantly more likely to be incarcerated than comparable offenders from Allegheny County, but a negative, insignificant effect was observed in juvenile court ($z = 2.46$).

Although not providing a significant interaction, another interesting finding concerns the effect of age at referral. For youth in juvenile court, older offenders had a significantly lower likelihood of incarceration than younger offenders ($b = -.487$; $p < .05$). However, there was no age effect in adult court. The z-test ($z = 1.95$) all but reached significance and indicated that older offenders had a lower likelihood of incarceration in juvenile court, as compared to similar older youth in adult court, where no age effect was found.

Somewhat similarly, those charged with robbery and convicted in juvenile court were significantly more likely to be incarcerated than those charged with aggravated assault ($b = 1.222$; $p < .01$). On the other hand, being charged with robbery was insignificant in the model for those convicted in adult court. The z-test ($z = 1.88$) again approached significance and suggests that a robbery charge in juvenile court (as compared to an aggravated assault charge) had a greater positive effect on incarceration than the same charge on otherwise similar offenders in adult court. In contrast, there was no significant difference in the likelihood of incarceration in either juvenile or adult court for those charged with "other" violent offenses and those charged with aggravated assault.

Hypothesis 8: Incarceration Length

Table 13 presents the determinants of the natural log of incarceration length. The model is based on only those offenders who were convicted and incarcerated ($n = 181$). At the bivariate level, decertified youth served significantly shorter periods of incarceration than non-decertified youth. When considering other explanatory factors, the negative effect of decertification remained ($b = -1.14$; $p < .001$). Put differently, incarcerated offenders in adult court were given significantly longer sentences than similar incarcerated youth in juvenile court.

Table 13: OLS Regression Estimates for the Determinants of the Natural Log of Incarceration Length (n = 181)

Variable	B (SE)	Beta	|T|
DECERT	-1.137 (.129)	-.549	8.797***
AGE	-.112 (.071)	-.090	1.584
GENDER	.255 (.236)	.062	1.084
RACE	.717 (.201)	.223	3.560***
PRIORREF	.014 (.030)	.035	.453
PRIORVIO	-.043 (.075)	-.043	.571
ROBBERY	-.059 (.126)	-.029	.467
OTHEROFF	.214 (.242)	.052	.885
ROLENON	.260 (.262)	.060	.991
ROLEUNK	.429 (.195)	.200	2.197*
NONFIRE	.119 (.174)	.048	.682
FIREUNK	-.296 (.216)	-.122	1.369
PUBDEF	-.330 (.114)	-.167	2.880**
DAUPHIN	1.022 (.256)	.277	3.985***
PHILLY	.483 (.196)	.212	2.467*
Constant	4.162 (1.241)		3.353**
F	12.005***		
R-square	.522		

* p < .05
** p < .01
*** p < .001

Using Equation 2, the natural log of incarceration length was estimated for both decertified and non-decertified offenders, again setting all other explanatory factors at their means. For decertified offenders, the estimated natural log of incarceration length was 2.41 (or 11.13 months), while the estimated natural log for non-decertified offenders was 3.55 (or 34.70 months). When transformed back to months, the predicted incarceration length for non-decertified offenders was three times that of decertified offenders, illustrating that those processed and incarcerated in adult court were given much lengthier sentences than comparable offenders processed in juvenile court.

Five other explanatory factors also were significant in the model. Incarcerated nonwhites were sentenced to longer periods of confinement than incarcerated whites ($b = .72$; $p < .001$). Youth whose role was unknown were sentenced to longer periods of incarceration than those who played a primary role ($b = .43$; $p < .05$). There was, however, no significant difference in incarceration length between non-primary role youth and those who played a primary role, suggesting they were sentenced to similar periods of incarceration. Also, those who used a public defender were sentenced to significantly shorter incarceration time than those who did not use a public defender ($b = -.33$; $p < .01$). Finally, incarcerated youth in both Dauphin County ($b = 1.02$; $p < .001$) and Philadelphia ($b = .48$; $p < .05$) were sentenced to longer confinement than incarcerated youth in Allegheny County. In looking at the explanatory power of the full model, a rather impressive 52.2% of the variance in the natural log of incarceration length was explained.

Due to the sample size in the model in Table 13 being restricted to the 181 offenders who were incarcerated, Table 14 presents a second full model, also examining the predictors of "incarceration length." This multinomial logistic regression model included all of those offenders who were convicted ($n = 235$), with incarceration length being recoded into three categories: probation or other non-incarceration sentence; "county-length" sentences, with less than a minimum of 2 years; and "state-length" sentences, with a minimum of 2 years or more. State-length sentences were used as the reference group. Because the dependent variable now is measured as three categories, multinomial logistic regression was chosen as the appropriate statistical technique.

The coefficient for decertification was positive and significant for those in both the probation ($b = 3.09$; $p < .001$) and county sentence groups ($b = 3.27$; $p < .05$). This indicates that decertified offenders were more likely to receive either no sentence of incarceration or a county-length sentence, as opposed to a state-length sentence. In other

Table 14: Logistic Regression Estimates for the Determinants of Incarceration Type (n = 235)

Variable	B (SE)	|Wald|	Exp(B)
	Probation		
DECERT	3.093 (.674)	21.073***	22.044
AGE	.257 (.302)	.725	1.293
GENDER	-.237 (.929)	.065	.789
RACE	-2.239 (.830)	7.287**	.107
PRIORREF	-.389 (.183)	4.515*	.678
PRIORVIO	.119 (.368)	.104	1.126
ROBBERY	-.619 (.527)	1.378	.539
OTHEROFF	-1.390 (1.305)	1.135	.249
ROLENON	-2.194 (1.516)	2.095	.111
ROLEUNK	-1.494 (.877)	2.901	.224
NONFIRE	.903 (.718)	1.582	2.468
FIREUNK	.662 (1.015)	.425	1.938
PUBDEF	1.028 (.481)	4.568*	2.795
DAUPHIN	.031 (1.030)	.001	1.031
PHILLY	-.249 (.840)	.088	.780
Constant	-2.644 (5.350)	.244	

* $p < .05$
** $p < .01$
*** $p < .001$

(Continued...)

Table 14 (continued)

Variable	B (SE)	|Wald|	Exp(B)
	County Sentence		
DECERT	3.274 (.598)	29.947***	26.421
AGE	.331 (.251)	1.740	1.393
GENDER	-.434 (.832)	.272	.648
RACE	-1.843 (.764)	5.810*	.158
PRIORREF	-.051 (.101)	.260	.950
PRIORVIO	.155 (.245)	.398	1.167
ROBBERY	.086 (.428)	.040	1.089
OTHEROFF	-.284 (.915)	.097	.752
ROLENON	-.772 (1.324)	.340	.462
ROLEUNK	-1.474 (.737)	3.999*	.229
NONFIRE	-.126 (.643)	.038	.882
FIREUNK	1.199 (.812)	2.181	3.315
PUBDEF	1.094 (.393)	7.737**	2.987
DAUPHIN	-1.061 (.923)	1.322	.346
PHILLY	-.746 (.721)	1.068	.474
Constant	-3.731 (4.513)	.683	
Log-likelihood	359.128		
Model X^2	140.992***		
Cox & Snell R^2	.451		
Nagelkerke R^2	.512		

* $p < .05$
** $p < .01$
*** $p < .001$

words, offenders in adult court were more likely to receive a state-length sentence or longer incarceration time than offenders in juvenile court, which is consistent with the previous model that included only incarcerated offenders.

Several other factors also were significant in the multinomial model. Nonwhites were less likely to receive either no sentence of incarceration (b = -2.24; p < .01) or a county-length sentence b = -1.84; p < .05), as opposed to a state sentence. Stated differently, nonwhites were more likely to receive a state-length sentence or longer confinement time, which also is consistent with the previous model presented in Table 13.

The number of prior referrals also was significant, but only in the "Probation" model. Those with an increased number of prior referrals were significantly less likely to receive non-incarceration than a state-length sentence (b = -.39; p < .05). However, the coefficient for prior referrals in the "County Sentence" model was negative and insignificant, suggesting that prior referrals had little impact on distinguishing county-length versus state-length sentences.

Youth whose role was unknown in the offense were significantly less likely to receive a county-length sentence than a state-length sentence, as compared to those who played a primary role (b = -1.47; p < .05). The coefficient for this variable was negative and approaching signficance in the "Probation" model. In other words, those whose role was unknown were more likely to receive a state-length sentence, again confirming the results of Table 13. The coefficient for non-primary role was negative and insignificant for both the probation and county sentence groups, indicating that convicted youth who played either a primary or non-primary role in the offense were treated similarly in type of sentence received.

Finally, attorney-type was positive and significant in both groups. Those who used a public defender were more likely to receive either no incarceration (b = 1.03; p < .05) or a county-length sentence (1.09; p < .01), as opposed to a state sentence. Stated differently, those who used a public defender were less likely to receive a state-length sentence or shorter confinement time than youth who did not use a public defender, which also is consistent with the prior full model. Moreover, the pseudo r-squares were similar to that of the original model, as between 45.1% and 51.2% of the "variance" in the dependent variable is explained by this model.

Table 15 presents the decertification-specific models, for the natural log of incarceration length, using the 181 incarcerated offenders in the sample. The small subsample sizes for the two models should be

Table 15: Split Model for the Determinants of the Natural Log of Incarceration Length (n = 181)

Variable	B (SE)	Beta	|T|	|Z-test|
	Non-Decertified (n = 118)			
AGE	-.165 (.097)	-.144	1.700	
GENDER	.351 (.359)	.087	.979	
RACE	.868 (.288)	.273	3.020**	
PRIORREF	.054 (.038)	.172	1.444	
PRIORVIO	-.116 (.102)	-.139	1.147	
ROBBERY	-.077 (.164)	-.043	.473	
OTHEROFF	.346 (.319)	.098	1.083	
ROLENON	1.222 (.613)	.178	1.992*	
ROLEUNK	.602 (.284)	.315	2.118*	
NONFIRE	.151 (.294)	.058	.512	
FIREUNK	-.467 (.303)	-.224	1.540	
PUBDEF	-.341 (.161)	-.188	2.124*	
DAUPHIN	1.080 (.382)	.323	2.829**	
PHILLY	.866 (.318)	.393	2.726**	
Constant	4.442 (1.797)		2.471*	
F	3.514***			
R-square	.323			

* p < .05
** p < .01
*** p < .001

(Continued...)

Table 15 (continued)

Variable	B (SE)	Beta	|T|	|Z-test|
		Decertified (n = 63)		
AGE	.116 (.099)	.153	1.173	2.03*
GENDER	-.078 (.269)	-.037	.290	.96
RACE	.787 (.268)	.479	2.937**	.21
PRIORREF	-.035 (.065)	-.096	.540	1.18
PRIORVIO	-.031 (.126)	-.046	.244	.52
ROBBERY	.061 (.181)	.048	.340	.56
OTHEROFF	.213 (.357)	.079	.596	.28
ROLENON	-.349 (.236)	-.202	1.484	2.39*
ROLEUNK	.295 (.236)	.232	1.248	.83
NONFIRE	.332 (.186)	.265	1.780	.52
FIREUNK	-.195 (.268)	-.124	.726	.67
PUBDEF	-.269 (.151)	-.227	1.781	.33
DAUPHIN	1.055 (.310)	.496	3.397**	.05
PHILLY	-.005 (.216)	-.004	.021	2.27*
Constant	-.179 (1.643)		.109	
F	2.083*			
R-square	.378			

* p < .05
** p < .01
*** p < .001

noted in interpreting the results. The negative coefficient for age in the non-decertified model suggests that older youth in adult court received shorter confinement than younger offenders, but statistical significance was not reached. The age coefficient in juvenile court, in contrast, was positive and insignificant. There was a significant interaction between age and court of jurisdiction (z = 2.03), as older youth in adult court were sentenced to shorter periods of incarceration, while older youth in juvenile court experienced longer periods of incarceration.

The role youth played in the offense also interacted with court of jurisdiction. Interestingly, youth in adult court who did not play a primary role were confined for a longer period of time than youth who played a primary role ($b = 1.22$; $p < .05$). The effect of not playing a primary role for youth in juvenile court was negative and insignificant. There was a significant interaction ($z = 2.39$), as non-primary role youth were sentenced to longer confinement time in adult court, as compared to those in juvenile court not playing a primary.

Youth whose role was unknown in the offense also was significant in adult court, as they received longer periods of incarceration than youth who played a primary role ($b = .60$; $p < .05$), meaning they were treated somewhat similarly to non-primary role offenders. The coefficient for unknown role was positive, but insignificant, for those decertified to juvenile court. However, the z-test ($z = .83$) did not indicate a significant interaction between the two courts, indicating that that the positive effect was not significantly different between juvenile and adult court.

County of jurisdiction also had significant effects in the models. Dauphin County youth were sentenced to longer periods of incarceration than Allegheny County youth, in both juvenile ($b = 1.06$; $b < .01$) and adult court ($b = 1.08$; $p < .01$). Youth processed in Philadelphia's adult court also were given longer confinement time than youth processed in Allegheny County ($b = .89$; $p < .01$), suggesting that in adult court, Allegheny County provided shorter incarceration time than both Dauphin and Philadelphia. However, in juvenile court, the coefficient for Philadelphia was negative and highly insignificant, suggesting that in juvenile court, Dauphin County provided longer incarceration time than both Philadelphia and Allegheny Counties. One final significant interaction was found, as Philadelphia youth were given longer confinement time in adult court as compared to Allegheny County youth, but Philadelphia youth in juvenile court experienced similar confinement times as Allegheny youth ($z = 2.27$).

Hypothesis 9: Case Processing Time

Table 16 presents the determinants of the natural log of case processing time. At the bivariate level, there was no significant difference in the natural log of case processing time between decertified and non-decertified offenders. This insignificant relationship remained when accounting for other explanatory factors ($b = .165$; $p = .217$). In other words, when it comes to swiftness of punishment, both groups of offenders were similar in the amount of time taken to have their cases processed, from arrest to final disposition.

The natural log of case processing time for decertified and non-decertified offenders also was estimated with all other explanatory factors set at their mean. Using Equation 2, the predicted natural log of case processing time for decertified offenders was 4.957 (or 142.17 days), while the predicted natural log for non-decertified offenders was 4.792 (or 120.54 days). The difference in the predicted natural log was minor (0.165), and this small difference was reflected when transformed back to days (21.63).

The model did, however, reveal other significant factors in explaining the natural log of case processing time. Males experienced significantly longer case processing time than females ($b = .628$; $p < .01$). Those who used a public defender experienced significantly shorter case processing time than those who used other representation ($b = -.614$; $p < .001$). Youth processed in both Dauphin County ($b = 1.346$; $p < .001$) and Philadelphia ($b = .968$; $p < .001$) experienced longer case processing time than youth in Allegheny County.

Finally, although not reaching statistical significance, the positive coefficient for prior violent referrals suggests that as they increased, total case processing time also went up ($b = .141$; $p < .10$). This model explained a rather limited 22% of the variation in the natural log of case processing time, implying that other unmeasured factors were influencing the time for these cases to be processed.

Table 17 presents the decertification specific models, in which several explanatory factors were significant, but no significant interactions were discovered. Concerning gender, non-decertified males experienced significantly longer case processing time than non-decertified females ($b = .743$; $p < .01$). When examining the effect of

Table 16: OLS Regression Estimates for the Determinants of the Natural Log of Case Processing Time (n = 423)

Variable	B (SE)	Beta	|T|
DECERT	.165 (.133)	.059	1.235
AGE	.027 (.074)	.017	.369
GENDER	.628 (.190)	.159	3.307**
RACE	-.102 (.195)	-.025	.524
PRIORREF	-.016 (.037)	-.027	.425
PRIORVIO	.141 (.083)	.103	1.691
ROBBERY	-.022 (.138)	-.008	.162
OTHEROFF	.311 (.265)	.055	1.175
ROLENON	.392 (.340)	.054	1.152
ROLEUNK	-.165 (.201)	-.056	.822
NONFIRE	.006 (.173)	.002	.038
FIREUNK	.282 (.230)	.083	1.226
PUBDEF	-.614 (.121)	-.230	5.056***
DAUPHIN	1.346 (.288)	.229	4.671***
PHILLY	.968 (.174)	.319	5.552***
Constant	3.317 (1.280)		2.592*
F	7.647***		
R-square	.220		

* p < .05
** p < .01
*** p < .001

Table 17: Split Model for the Determinants of the Natural Log of Case Processing Time (n = 423)

Variable	B (SE)	Beta	|T|	|Z-test|
	Non-Decertified (n = 278)			
AGE	.061 (.102)	.033	.599	
GENDER	.743 (.269)	.166	2.756**	
RACE	-.171 (.296)	-.033	-.578	
PRIORREF	.001 (.046)	.002	.030	
PRIORVIO	.203 (.107)	.137	1.895	
ROBBERY	-.004 (.183)	-.001	-.021	
OTHEROFF	.632 (.365)	.098	1.732	
ROLENON	.378 (.981)	.021	.386	
ROLEUNK	-.382 (.278)	-.117	-1.375	
NONFIRE	.027 (.252)	.007	.106	
FIREUNK	.517 (.310)	.137	1.667	
PUBDEF	-.731 (.169)	-.243	4.315***	
DAUPHIN	1.346 (.411)	.196	3.277**	
PHILLY	1.117 (.244)	.322	4.574***	
Constant	2.561 (1.791)		1.429	
F	6.638***			
R-square	.261			

* p < .05
** p < .01
*** p < .001

(Continued...)

Table 17 (continued)

Variable	B (SE)	Beta	|T|	|Z-test|
	Decertified (n = 145)			
AGE	-.046 (.093)	-.041	.501	.78
GENDER	.389 (.226)	.142	1.718	1.09
RACE	.330 (.228)	.139	1.445	1.34
PRIORREF	-.142 (.073)	-.246	1.954	1.65
PRIORVIO	.115 (.133)	.110	.865	.57
ROBBERY	-.037 (.181)	-.020	.205	.13
OTHEROFF	-.057 (.335)	-.015	.170	1.39
ROLENON	.075 (.289)	.023	.258	.30
ROLEUNK	.192 (.256)	.091	.750	1.51
NONFIRE	.124 (.202)	.066	.610	.30
FIREUNK	-.173 (.299)	-.070	.580	1.60
PUBDEF	-.365 (.152)	-.197	2.406*	1.61
DAUPHIN	1.235 (.343)	.323	3.598***	.20
PHILLY	.608 (.218)	.297	2.784**	1.56
Constant	4.850 (1.557)		3.115**	
F	2.524**			
R-square	.214			

* p < .05
** p < .01
*** p < .001

gender in juvenile court, the positive coefficient did not reach statistical significance (b = .389; p < .10). However, the z-test (z = 1.34) did not support an interaction effect between gender and type of court, suggesting that gender had a similar effect on case processing time in both juvenile and adult court.

Attorney type was significant in both decertification specific models. In juvenile and adult court, violent offenders who used a public defender had significantly shorter case processing times than those who did not use a public defender. The difference in coefficients and z-test ($z = 1.61$) suggest that the negative effect of attorney type was somewhat stronger in adult court than in juvenile court, but the z-score did not reach statistical significance.

Similar to the full model, youth in both Dauphin and Philadelphia Counties experienced longer case processing time than youth in Allegheny County, here in both juvenile and adult court. The z-tests did not reveal a significant interaction for either Dauphin ($z = .21$) or Philadelphia Counties ($z = 1.56$), when comparing across juvenile and adult courts, indicating that the county effects were consistent across the two courts.

Finally, the number of prior referrals was not significant in the full model, but almost had a significant and negative effect on the natural log of case processing time for decertified offenders ($b = -.142$; $p = .053$). In other words, as prior referrals increased for offenders in juvenile court, case processing time decreased. Prior referrals was positive, but insignificant, for offenders in adult court. The z-test suggested that the effect of prior record on case processing time was different in juvenile court than in adult court, but statistical significance was not quite reached ($z = 1.65$; $p < .10$).

Hypothesis 10: Post-dispositional Recidivism

The last three hypotheses focus on post-dispositional recidivism. Included in these models are four additional independent/control variables: conviction, incarceration length, the natural log of case processing time, and time at risk for recidivism. Each of the recidivism models includes only those youth who were "on the street" during the 8-year follow-up period ($n = 404$).

Table 18 presents the determinants of post-dispositional rearrest. At the bivariate level, decertified youth were significantly more likely to be rearrested than non-decertified youth ($r = .12$; $p < .05$). When controlling for the effect of other explanatory factors in the full model, the decertification effect became insignificant. Similar to the bivariate correlation, the positive coefficient suggests that while controlling for

Table 18: Logistic Regression Estimates for the Determinants of Post-dispositional Rearrest (n = 404)

Variable	B (SE)	|Wald|	Exp(B)
DECERT	.51 (.285)	3.202	1.667
AGE	-.411 (.148)	7.665**	.663
GENDER	.788 (.361)	4.765*	2.199
RACE	-.203 (.379)	.286	.817
PRIORREF	.312 (.096)	10.564**	1.367
PRIORVIO	-.091 (.185)	.241	.913
ROBBERY	.003 (.278)	.000	1.003
OTHEROFF	-.373 (.533)	.489	.689
ROLENON	-1.343 (.666)	4.066*	.261
ROLEUNK	.211 (.422)	.250	1.235
NONFIRE	-.721 (.345)	4.355*	.486
FIREUNK	-.560 (.471)	1.412	.571
PUBDEF	.580 (.250)	5.378*	1.787
DAUPHIN	-.884 (.603)	2.151	.413
PHILLY	-.878 (.382)	5.278*	.415
CONVICT	.075 (.322)	.054	1.078
LNPROCES	.110 (.152)	.526	1.116
INLENGTH	-.036 (.022)	2.741	.965
RISKTIME	.000 (.021)	.000	1.000
Constant	6.794 (3.481)	3.809	892.609
Log-likelihood	450.08		
Model X^2	94.04***		
Cox & Snell R^2	.208		
Nagelkerke R^2	.281		

* p < .05
** p < .01
*** p < .001

explanatory factors, offenders in juvenile court experienced a greater chance of being rearrested than offenders in adult court ($b = .51$; $p = .07$). However, the insignificant coefficient does not clearly establish a difference in rearrest between juvenile and adult court offenders.

Equation 1 again was used to further illustrate the effect of decertification. In holding all other explanatory factors at their mean, the estimated probability of post-dispositional rearrest for decertified offenders was .70. The estimated probability for non-decertified offenders was .58. The difference of 12 percentage points suggests that decertified youth were at least slightly more likely to be rearrested than non-decertified youth.

One of the significant factors in the full model was age. Older offenders were less likely to be rearrested than younger offenders ($b = -.41$; $p < .01$). Males also were significantly more likely to be rearrested than females ($b = .79$; $p < .05$). Only one of the prior record indicators was significant, as an increase in the number of prior referrals resulted in a higher likelihood of rearrest ($b = .31$; $p < .01$).

Offense involvement also appeared to have an on effect recidivism. Youth who did not play a primary role in the offense were significantly less likely to be rearrested than youth who played a primary role ($b = -1.34$; $p <$ 05). There was no significant difference in recidivism between youth whose role was unknown and those who played a primary role, suggesting that the two groups were similar in the likelihood of rearrest. In addition to the effect of role, firearm use also was significant, as youth who did not use a firearm were less likely to be rearrested than youth who used a firearm ($b = -.72$; $p < .05$). There was, however, no significant difference in rearrest between those whose firearm use was unknown and those who used a firearm, again providing evidence of these two groups having similar chances of rearrest.

Attorney type also appeared to be associated with recidivism. Youth who used a public defender had a significantly higher likelihood of rearrest, as compared to youth who did not use a public defender ($b = .58$; $p < .05$). In addition, county of jurisdiction was significant, as youth processed in Philadelphia were less likely to be rearrested than youth processed in Allegheny County ($b = -.88$; $p < .05$). No significant difference in rearrest existed between Dauphin and Allegheny County youth.

One other finding worth noting is the effect of incarceration length. Though the negative coefficient did not reach statistical significance, it suggests that the longer the youth was confined, the lower the chance of rearrest ($b = -.04$; $p < .10$). Overall, the model explained between 20.8% and 28.1% of the "variance" in the log odds of post-dispositional recidivism, meaning over 70% was unexplained.

In examining the decertification specific models in Table 19, role of the offender was excluded due to there being zero cells and high standard errors. Furthermore, no factor had a significant interaction with type of court. At least one explanatory factor, however, still is worth mentioning. Of youth processed in juvenile court, the negative coefficient for race suggests that nonwhite youth were less likely to be rearrested following final disposition than whites, but the coefficient just missed the traditional significance level ($b = -1.12$; $p < .10$). There was no race effect in adult court, as the coefficient was positive and highly insignificant, indicating that there was no difference in rearrest likelihood between whites and nonwhites. The z-test did suggest an interaction between race and court of jurisdiction, as nonwhite youth in juvenile court had a lower chance of being rearrested following final disposition, as compared to similar nonwhite youth in adult court, but statistical significance was not quite reached ($z = 1.73$; $p < .10$).

Two other factors also can be considered. Non-decertified older youth were significantly less likely to recidivate than non-decertified younger youth ($b = -.56$; $p < .01$). The age coefficient for decertified youth was negative but highly insignificant. The z-test, though, did not reveal a significant interaction between age and decertification status in predicting post-dispositional recidivism ($z = 1.56$).

Finally, only one of the prior referral indicators was significant in one of the split models. An increase in the number of prior referrals resulted in an increased likelihood of post-dispositional arrest for youth processed in adult court ($b = .33$; $p < .01$). The coefficient was positive, but insignificant, for decertified youth. The z-test ($z = .04$) found no significant interaction between the number of prior referrals and decertification status, indicating a similar effect of prior referrals for offenders processed in both courts. Furthermore, consistent with the full model, the number of prior referrals for violent offenses did not appear to significantly affect recidivism for either decertified or non-decertified youth.

Table 19: Split Model for the Determinants of Post-dispositional Rearrest

Variable	B (SE)	|Wald|	Exp(B)	|Z-test|
	Non-Decertified (n = 260)			
AGE	-.561 (.192)	8.499**	.571	
GENDER	.909 (.474)	3.677	2.483	
RACE	.300 (.519)	.335	1.350	
PRIORREF	.329 (.110)	8.984**	1.390	
PRIORVIO	-.039 (.217)	.032	.962	
ROBBERY	-.343 (.347)	.974	.710	
OTHEROFF	-.096 (.686)	.020	.908	
NONFIRE	-.579 (.465)	1.553	.560	
FIREUNK	-.288 (.400)	.520	.750	
PUBDEF	.508 (.321)	2.512	1.662	
DAUPHIN	-1.053 (.847)	1.544	.349	
PHILLY	-.593 (.477)	1.540	.553	
CONVICT	.226 (.471)	.231	1.254	
LNPROCES	-.002 (.180)	.000	.998	
INLENGTH	-.040 (.025)	2.681	.960	
RISKTIME	-.002 (.023)	.011	.998	
Constant	9.351 (4.246)	4.850*	11512.934	
Log-likelihhod	283.210			
Model X^2	74.205***			
Cox & Snell R^2	.248			
Nagelkerke R^2	.332			

* p < .05
** p < .01
*** p < .001

(Continued...)

Table 19 (continued)

Variable	B (SE)	|Wald|	Exp(B)	|Z-test|
	Decertified (n = 144)			
AGE	-.058 (.258)	.050	.944	1.56
GENDER	.868 (.588)	2.176	2.382	.05
RACE	-1.122 (.635)	3.120	.325	1.73
PRIORREF	.338 (.221)	2.332	1.402	.04
PRIORVIO	-.201 (.370)	.294	.818	.38
ROBBERY	.334 (.499)	.447	1.396	1.11
OTHEROFF	-.487 (.908)	.287	.615	.24
NONFIRE	-1.018 (.556)	3.348	.361	.61
FIREUNK	-.600 (.599)	1.003	.549	.43
PUBDEF	.644 (.435)	2.191	1.904	.25
DAUPHIN	-1.095 (.948)	1.333	.335	.03
PHILLY	-.457 (.560)	.667	.633	.18
CONVICT	.141 (.509)	.077	1.151	.12
LNPROCES	.372 (.329)	1.280	1.451	1.00
INLENGTH	-.024 (.042)	.310	.977	.33
RISKTIME	-.022 (.047)	.211	.979	.38
Constant	2.200 (6.887)	.102	9.022	
Log-likelihood	157.956			
Model X^2	22.462			
Cox & Snell R^2	.144			
Nagelkerke R^2	.202			

* $p < .05$
** $p < .01$
*** $p < .001$

Hypothesis 11: Post-dispositional Violent Recidivism

Table 20 presents the determinants of post-dispositional violent recidivism. Hypothesis 10 was based on rearrests for any offense, while Hypothesis 11 examined rearrests for murder or any of the violent offenses targeted by Pennsylvania's Act 33 statute. At the bivariate level, there was no significant difference between decertified and non-decertified offenders when examining post-dispositional violent rearrest. When controlling for the effect of other explanatory factors, the insignificant decertification effect remained ($b = -.11$; $p = .69$). In other words, there was virtually no difference in post-dispositional violent recidivism between decertified and non-decertified offenders, although the negative coefficient was in the opposite direction of the one contained in Table 18.

The small difference also can be observed when estimating the probabilities of post-dispositional violent recidivism. With all other variables set at their mean, the estimated probability for decertified youth was .27, while he estimated probability for non-decertified youth was .29, a difference of only 2 percentage points. This provides further evidence of there being no difference in violent recidivism between the two groups of offenders.

Other factors were significant in the full model. Older offenders were less likely to be rearrested for a violent offense following final disposition ($b = -.52$; $p < .01$). Males also were significantly more likely than females to be rearrested for a violent offense ($b = 1.39$; $p < .01$). Type of offense also impacted on recidivism, as those who committed "other" violent offenses were significantly less likely to be rearrested for a violent offense, as compared to those who committed aggravated assault ($b = -1.35$; $p < .05$). There was no significant difference in post-dispositional violent recidivism between those charged with robbery and those charged with aggravated assault, suggesting that they were rearrested at similar rates.

Role of the offender also was significant, as those who did not play a primary role were less likely to be rearrested for a violent offense than those who played a primary role ($b = -2.42$; $p < .05$). There was no significant difference, however, between those whose role was unknown and those who played a primary role. Also, attorney type was

Table 20: Logistic Regression Estimates for the Determinants of Post-dispositional Violent Rearrest (n = 404)

Variable	B (SE)	|Wald|	Exp(B)
DECERT	-.114 (.284)	.160	.892
AGE	-.522 (.153)	11.645**	.593
GENDER	1.394 (.446)	9.754**	4.032
RACE	.619 (.423)	2.144	1.857
PRIORREF	.135 (.077)	3.086	1.144
PRIORVIO	.058 (.168)	.119	1.060
ROBBERY	-.196 (.278)	.497	.822
OTHEROFF	-1.348 (.681)	3.918*	.260
ROLENON	-2.417 (1.117)	4.682*	.089
ROLEUNK	-.281 (.409)	.471	.755
NONFIRE	-.436 (.344)	1.610	.646
FIREUNK	.394 (.473)	.694	1.483
PUBDEF	.559 (.257)	4.731*	1.749
DAUPHIN	-.291 (.630)	.214	.747
PHILLY	-.353 (.358)	.973	.703
CONVICT	.351 (.329)	1.135	1.420
LNPROCES	.239 (.151)	2.501	1.270
INLENGTH	-.001 (.021)	.004	.999
RISKTIME	.042 (.021)	3.977*	1.043
Constant	1.500 (3.435)	.191	4.481
Log-likelihood	430.650		
Model X^2	79.877***		
Cox & Snell R^2	.179		
Nagelkerke R^2	.250		

* $p < .05$
** $p < .01$
*** $p < .001$

important in predicting post-dispositional violent recidivism. Those who used a public defender were significantly more likely to be rearrested for a violent offense than those who did not use a public defender ($b = .56$; $p < .05$). Finally, those who had a greater time at risk were significantly more likely to be rearrested for a violent offense ($b = .04$; $p < .05$). The full model was able to explain between 17.9% and 25.0% of the "variance" in the log odds of post-dispositional violent recidivism.

Table 21 then presents the split models for the determinants of post-dispositional violent recidivism. Due to zero cells and high standard errors, role of the offender and type of offense were excluded from the models. Only county of jurisdiction had a significant interaction with type of court. The positive coefficient for Dauphin County offenders in adult court shows they were more likely to be rearrested for a violent offense, as compared to Allegheny County adult court offenders, but the coefficient did not reach statistical significance ($b = .96$; $p = .25$). Furthermore, the negative coefficient for Dauphin County offenders in juvenile court indicates they were less likely to be rearrested for a violent offense, as compared to juvenile court offenders in Allegheny County, but again, statistical significance was not reached ($b = -2.05$; $p = .11$). The z-test ($z = 1.98$) did indicate, however, that Dauphin County offenders exhibited a significantly different likelihood of violent rearrest depending upon court of jurisdiction. There was no significant difference in post-dispositional violent recidivism between Philadelphia and Allegheny County youth in either juvenile or adult court.

A few other findings are worth noting from the split models. Older offenders in adult court were significantly less likely to recidivate than younger offenders in adult court ($b = -.51$; $p < .01$). The age coefficient also was negative in juvenile court, but insignificant, however no interaction existed between age and court of jurisdiction ($z = .31$). In addition, males were significantly more likely to be rearrested in juvenile court than females. The gender coefficient also was positive for adult court offenders, but statistically insignificant. As with age, no interaction effect was detected between gender and type of court ($z = 1.24$).

Table 21: Split Model for the Determinants of Post-dispositional Violent Rearrest

Variable	B (SE)	|Wald|	Exp(B)	|Z-test|
	Non-Decertified (n = 260)			
AGE	-.505 (.193)	6.869**	.604	
GENDER	.880 (.506)	3.019	2.410	
RACE	.377 (.559)	.455	1.457	
PRIORREF	.148 (.084)	3.138	1.160	
PRIORVIO	.014 (.196)	.005	1.014	
NONFIRE	-.308 (.433)	.507	.735	
FIREUNK	.275 (.428)	.413	1.317	
PUBDEF	.778 (.330)	5.570*	2.177	
DAUPHIN	.962 (.837)	1.321	2.617	
PHILLY	.061 (.429)	.020	1.063	
CONVICT	.321 (.465)	.476	1.378	
LNPROCES	.158 (.169)	.876	1.171	
INLENGTH	-.010 (.019)	.260	.990	
RISKTIME	.036 (.020)	3.299	1.037	
Constant	2.107 (3.958)	.284	8.227	
Log-likelihood	273.811			
Model X^2	51.859***			
Cox & Snell R^2	.181			
Nagelkerke R^2	.253			

* p < .05
** p < .01
*** p < .001

(Continued...)

Table 21 (continued)

Variable	B (SE)	|Wald|	Exp(B)	|Z-test|
	Decertified (n = 144)			
AGE	-.407 (.254)	2.576	.665	.31
GENDER	2.422 (1.137)	4.538*	11.264	1.24
RACE	.387 (.701)	.304	1.472	.01
PRIORREF	.233 (.190)	1.513	1.263	.41
PRIORVIO	-.084 (.330)	.065	.919	.26
NONFIRE	-.776 (.506)	2.350	.460	.70
FIREUNK	-.434 (.594)	.533	.648	.97
PUBDEF	.381 (.417)	.835	1.464	.75
DAUPHIN	-2.047 (.1264)	2.624	.129	1.98*
PHILLY	-.372 (.560)	.440	.690	.61
CONVICT	.707 (.520)	1.851	2.028	.55
LNPROCES	.251 (.423)	.351	1.285	.20
INLENGTH	-.050 (.068)	.528	.952	.57
RISKTIME	-.021 (.066)	.101	.979	.83
Constant	4.140 (8.858)	.218	62.782	
Log-likelihood	157.077			
Model X^2	27.594*			
Cox & Snell R^2	.174			
Nagelkerke R^2	.241			

* p < .05
** p < .01
*** p < .001

Finally, adult court youth who used a public defender were significantly more likely to be rearrested for a violent offense than adult court youth who did not use a public defender (b = .78; p < .05). The coefficient for attorney type also was positive for juvenile court offenders, but insignificant. Again, no interaction effect was found between attorney type and court of jurisdiction ($z = .75$).

Hypothesis 12: Time to Recidivism Following Final Disposition

Table 22 presents the Cox regression estimates for the determinants of time to recidivism. Hypothesis 12 not only considers whether or not offenders recidivated, but also factors that could have an effect on how quickly they reoffended during the follow-up period. To test this hypothesis, a Cox proportional hazards model was employed.[10] At the bivariate level, among those who were rearrested, decertified youth had a significantly longer time to rearrest than non-decertified youth ($r = .13$; $p < .05$). However, when controlling for the effect of other explanatory factors and considering "censored" cases in the Cox regression model, the positive coefficient for decertification suggests that decertified youth have an increased risk of rearrest across the follow-up period (i.e., decreased survival time) as compared to non-decertified youth, but statistical significance was not reached ($b = .22$; $p = .15$). Therefore, there was not enough evidence to establish a significant difference in time to rearrest between juvenile and adult court offenders.

The "relative risk" associated with decertification on time to rearrest can be determined by examining the antilog or exponentiated coefficient in Table 22. The coefficient indicates that the hazard rate of rearrest is 1.248 times greater for decertified youth, as compared to

---

[10] This model assumes that the proportional hazard rate is constant at any point in time during the follow-up period (Allison, 1984; Cox, 1972). This assumption was tested for decertified and non-decertified offenders. First, using the Kaplan Meier technique, a visual inspection indicated that the hazard rates appeared to be somewhat proportional. Second, in order to statistically test this assumption, a time-dependent covariate was developed, as hazard rates will not be proportional if there is a significant interaction between time (i.e., time to rearrest) and an explanatory factor (i.e., decertification). The insignificant findings of an interaction between time and decertification further indicated that the hazard rates were proportional at an acceptable level for decertified and non-decertified offenders.

Table 22: Cox Regression Estimates for the Determinants of Time to Rearrest (n = 404)

Variable	B (SE)	|Wald|	Exp(B)
DECERT	.222 (.153)	2.100	1.248
AGE	-.229 (.083)	7.529**	.796
GENDER	.580 (.238)	5.955*	1.785
RACE	-.236 (.219)	1.159	.790
PRIORREF	.185 (.041)	20.214***	1.203
PRIORVIO	-.115 (.100)	1.319	.891
ROBBERY	-.103 (.162)	.405	.902
OTHEROFF	-.109 (.323)	.114	.897
ROLENON	-.722 (.415)	3.021	.486
ROLEUNK	.236 (.221)	1.145	1.267
NONFIRE	-.514 (.189)	7.377**	.598
FIREUNK	-.395 (.265)	2.226	.674
PUBDEF	.272 (.145)	3.489	1.312
DAUPHIN	-.362 (.336)	1.158	.697
PHILLY	-.388 (.186)	4.347*	.678
CONVICT	.051 (.175)	.086	1.053
LNPROCES	.007 (.061)	.013	1.007
INLENGTH	-.010 (.005)	3.830*	.990
Log-likelihood	2597.604		
Model X^2	89.269***		

* p < .05
***p < .01
***p < .001

non-decertified youth. Put differently, the hazard rate for decertified offenders is approximately 25% more than the hazard rate for non-decertified offenders.

Other explanatory factors were significant in the full model. The negative and significant coefficient for age indicates that at any point in time during the follow-up period, as age at referral increased, there was a decreased risk of rearrest or increased survival time (b = -.23; p < .01). The exponentiated coefficient (.796) further indicates that a one-unit increase in age resulted in a decreased hazard rate of approximately 20%.

Gender also was significant in the model. Males had a higher risk of rearrest (i.e., decreased survival time) than females at any point in time during the follow-up period (b = .58; p < .05). In examining the exponentiated coefficient (1.785), males had a 79% higher hazard rate of rearrest than females.

The coefficient for prior referrals was positive and highly significant. At any point in time during the follow-up period, those with an greater number of prior referrals had a higher risk or rearrest (i.e., decreased survival time) than youth with fewer prior referrals (b = .19; p < .001). The exponentiated coefficient (1.203) indicates that for every one prior referral increase, the hazard rate for rearrest increased by approximately 20%.

Weapon type also had an effect on time to recidivism. Those who did not use a firearm had a significantly lower risk of rearrest (i.e., increased survival time) than youth who used a firearm (b = -.51; p < .01). Based on the exponentiated coefficient (.598), those who did not use a firearm had a hazard rate that was about 40% lower than the hazard rate for those who used a firearm. In other words, those who used a firearm were rearrested more quickly than those who did not use a firearm. In contrast, there was no statistically significant difference between those whose weapon type was unknown and those who used a firearm, suggesting they had somewhat similar times to being rearrested.

County of jurisdiction also was a significant predictor. At any given point in time during the follow-up period, Philadelphia youth had a lower risk of rearrest (i.e., increased survival time) than Allegheny County youth (b = -.39; p < .05). In fact, youth processed in Philadelphia had a hazard rate that was 32% lower than the hazard rate for Allegheny County youth. The coefficient for Dauphin County also was negative, but highly insignificant, suggesting that youth from Dauphin County had a similar risk of rearrest as Allegheny County youth. Therefore, in general, Philadelphia youth had the lowest risk of rearrest across the follow-up period among all three counties.

Finally, incarceration length significantly impacted on time to rearrest. An increase in incarceration length resulted in a lower risk of rearrest (i.e., increased survival time) at any point in time during the follow-up period ($b = -.01$; $p = .05$). For every one-month increase in confinement time, the hazard rate of rearrest decreased by 1%. Put differently, it appears that length of incarceration contributed to a delay in reoffending.

The split model is then presented in Table 23. Due to zero cells and high standard errors, role of the offender was excluded from the analysis. Though no explanatory factors significantly interacted with court of jurisdiction, four were close to reaching statistical significance. First, older offenders in adult court had a significantly lower risk of rearrest (i.e., increased survival time) than younger offenders at any point in time during the follow-up period ($b = -.36$; $p < .01$). For every year increase in age, the hazard rate of rearrest decreased by approximately 30%. The age coefficient in juvenile court also was negative, but highly insignificant. The z-test ($z = 1.81$; $p < .10$) at least suggests that age had a stronger negative effect in adult court than in juvenile court.

Second, the negative and significant coefficient for race among decertified youth indicates that nonwhite youth in juvenile court had a lower risk of rearrest (i.e., increased survival time) than similar white youth at any point in time during the follow-up period ($b = -.85$; $p < .05$). The exponentiated coefficient (.430) shows that nonwhites had a hazard rate of rearrest that was 57% lower than the hazard rate for whites. The race coefficient in adult court was positive and insignificant. The z-test all but reached significance and suggests that nonwhite youth had a lower risk of rearrest in juvenile court, as compared to similar nonwhite youth in adult court ($z = 1.93$; $p < .10$).

Third, a violent prior record seemed to play more of a role in juvenile court, as an increased number of prior referrals for violent offenses resulted in an almost significantly lower risk of rearrest (i.e., increased survival time) among decertified offenders at any point in time during the follow-up period ($b = -.41$; $p < .10$). The coefficient in adult court was positive and highly insignificant. In testing for an interaction effect, the z-test pointed to prior violent referrals having a stronger and negative effect in juvenile court than in adult court ($z = 1.66$; $p < .10$).

Table 23: Split Model for the Determinants of Time to Recidivism

Variable	B (SE)	|Wald|	Exp(B)	|Z-test|
	Non-Decertified (n = 260)			
AGE	-.355 (.111)	10.176**	.701	
GENDER	.643 (.298)	4.660*	1.901	
RACE	.092 (.332)	.076	1.096	
PRIORREF	.186 (.046)	16.173***	1.205	
PRIORVIO	.004 (.120)	.001	1.004	
ROBBERY	-.306 (.195)	2.453	.737	
OTHEROFF	.411 (.416)	.978	1.509	
NONFIRE	-.589 (.251)	5.495*	.555	
FIREUNK	-.117 (.263)	.197	.890	
PUBDEF	.254 (.194)	1.712	1.289	
DAUPHIN	-.581 (.473)	1.512	.559	
PHILLY	-.178 (.235)	.572	.837	
CONVICT	.062 (.263)	.055	1.064	
LNPROCES	-.037 (.077)	.236	.963	
INLENGTH	-.014 (.006)	5.220*	.986	
Log-likelihood	1406.244			
Model X^2	72.555***			

* p < .05
** p < .01
*** p < .001

(Continued...)

Table 23 (continued)

Variable	B (SE)	|Wald|	Exp(B)	|Z-test|
	Decertified (n = 144)			
AGE	-.043 (.132)	.108	.958	1.81
GENDER	.633 (.387)	2.675	1.883	.02
RACE	-.845 (.353)	5.709*	.430	1.93
PRIORREF	.291 (.108)	7.232**	1.338	.89
PRIORVIO	-.405 (.215)	3.557	.667	1.66
ROBBERY	.277 (.285)	.942	1.319	1.69
OTHEROFF	-.451 (.562)	.643	.637	1.23
NONFIRE	-.721 (.320)	5.074*	.486	.32
FIREUNK	-.286 (.308)	.866	.751	.42
PUBDEF	.280 (.223)	1.569	1.323	.09
DAUPHIN	-.088 (.490)	.032	.916	.98
PHILLY	-.237 (.287)	.679	.789	.16
CONVICT	.118 (.268)	.192	1.125	.15
LNPROCES	.195 (.130)	2.239	1.215	1.54
INLENGTH	.005 (.015)	.093	1.005	1.18
Log-likelihood	852.292			
Model X^2	27.897*			

* $p < .05$
** $p < .01$
*** $p < .001$

Finally, type of offense seemed important, as the negative coefficient in adult court suggests that those charged with robbery had a lower risk of rearrest (i.e., increased survival time) than those charged with aggravated assault, but statistical significance was not reached ($b = -.31$; $p = .12$). The robbery coefficient was positive and insignificant for juvenile court offenders. The z-test implied that being charged with robbery had different effect in adult court than juvenile court, but again significance was not reached ($z = 1.69$; $p < .10$).

SUMMARY

This chapter focused on three main areas. First, the determinants of decertification were examined. Second, the independent effect of decertification was examined on case outcomes. Finally the independent effect of decertification was examined on post-dispositional recidivism. In terms of the determinants of decertification, both legal and non-legal factors appeared to be important. Those with an extensive prior record, those who played a primary role in the offense, and those who used a firearm were less likely to be decertified to juvenile court. In addition, type of offense seem to effect the decertification decision, as those charged with robbery were more likely to be decertified than those who were charged with aggravated assault. Finally, attorney type was significant, as those who used a public defender were more likely to be decertified than those who did not use a public defender.

Decertification then was used as the central independent variable for subsequent multivariate analyses. Some outcomes reflected a significant decertification effect, while others did not. While controlling for other explanatory factors, when examining all offenders, decertified youth were significantly more likely to be convicted on any offense, but when including only those offenders whose cases proceeded past the preliminary hearing, decertification was no longer significant. Among those who were convicted and incarcerated, decertified youth were sentenced to significantly shorter confinement time. However, there was no significant difference between decertified and non-decertified offenders in terms of conviction on target offense, and likelihood of incarceration (among those convicted), and case processing time. Of those youth who were "on the street" during the follow-up period, there was no significant difference between the two groups of offenders on any of the recidivism measures (i.e., post-dispositional recidivism for any offense, for a violent offense, and time to recidivism).

Several comments also can be made regarding the effects of other explanatory factors. Age only had an additive effect in the recidivism models, as older youth were significantly less likely to be rearrested for any offense and for a violent offense. Older youth also had longer survival times than those who were younger.

Concerning gender, males were significantly more likely to be convicted than females, and they experienced longer case processing time. In examining recidivism, males were significantly more likely to be rearrested for any offense and for a violent offense, and they also had an increased risk of rearrest across the follow-up period, as compared to females.

Race also was significant in several models. Nonwhites were less likely to be convicted on any offense than whites, but among those convicted and incarcerated, nonwhites experienced significantly longer confinement time. There was no independent race effect on any of the recidivism measures.

A significant effect of prior referrals was observed on numerous dependent variables. A greater number of prior referrals was associated with a significantly higher likelihood of conviction (including only those who proceeded pass the preliminary hearing), and among those convicted, a higher likelihood of incarceration. Concerning the recidivism measures, those with a greater number of prior referrals were significantly more likely to be rearrested for any offense and also had shorter survival times during the follow-up period.

Type of offense only exhibited an additive effect in one case outcome model. Youth who were charged with "other" violent offenses had a significantly lower likelihood of rearrest than youth charged with aggravated assault.

The offense seriousness indicators were found to significantly affect several dependent variables. Youth who did not play a primary role had a lower likelihood of post-dispositional rearrest for any offense and for a violent offense, as compared to youth who played a primary role. In addition, convicted and incarcerated youth whose role was unknown experienced significantly longer incarceration time than youth who played a primary role.

Firearm use only was significant in the recidivism models. Of the youth who were on the street during the follow-up period, those who did not use a firearm were less likely to be rearrested for any offense, as compared to those who used a firearm. Also, those who did not use a firearm had a significantly lower risk of rearrest across the follow-up period than youth who used a firearm.

The type of attorney also had a significant effect on a few dependent variables. Of the youth who were convicted and incarcerated, those who used a public defender served shorter confinement time than youth who used other legal representation. Youth who used a public defender also had significantly shorter case processing times. In examining the recidivism models, of the youth who were on the street during the follow-up period, those who used a public defender had a significantly higher likelihood of rearrest for any offense and for a violent offense.

County of jurisdiction also significantly impacted on several outcomes. Dauphin County youth had a higher likelihood of conviction than Allegheny County youth, and of those convicted and incarcerated, Dauphin youth served longer incarceration time. Dauphin County youth also experienced significantly longer case processing time than Allegheny County youth. In contrast, there was no significant difference between Dauphin and Allegheny County youth in any of the recidivism models.

Being processed in Philadelphia also was significant in a few models. Similar to Dauphin County youth, convicted and incarcerated Philadelphia offenders experienced longer confinement time than similar youth from Allegheny County, and Philadelphia youth also experienced longer case processing time. The recidivism models indicated that offenders from Philadelphia had a significantly lower likelihood of rearrest for any offense and increased survival time during the follow-up period.

Regarding the case outcome variables that were used as explanatory factors in the recidivism models, only one had a significant additive effect. Of the youth who were on the street during the follow-up period, the longer the confinement time, the lower the risk of rearrest across the follow-up period. This finding suggests that lengthier incarceration was associated with longer survival time.

Decertification specific models also were developed for each of the case outcomes and recidivism measures to determine whether the explanatory factors had a different impact depending upon the court of jurisdiction. Within the eight pairs of decertification specific models,

11 significant interaction effects were detected ($z \geq 1.96$). Concerning age, there was no significant additive effect on conviction on any offense. However, age had a different impact on conviction in juvenile and adult court. Older youth in juvenile court had a significantly lower likelihood of conviction than similar youth in adult court. This finding may be due to older youth in juvenile court being closer to ages 18 and 21, which is the age at which the juvenile court no longer can retain jurisdiction over the youthful offender. However, no such age limit exists in the adult system. Furthermore, among those convicted, older youth in juvenile court had a lower likelihood of incarceration than similar aged youth in adult court.

Type of offense only had a significant interaction with court of jurisdiction when examining target conviction. There was no additive effect of robbery in the full model; however, when looking at the decertification specific models, youth convicted of robbery in adult court had a significantly higher likelihood of target conviction than similar youth in juvenile court. One explanation for this finding is that in juvenile court, there is less emphasis on the charge because the focus is on the treatment, while the adult system does not have a similar focus.[11]

The offense seriousness measures also significantly interacted with type of court in examining incarceration length. No significant additive effect was observed for role of the offender in the full model. However, the decertification specific models revealed that the convicted and incarcerated youth who did not play a primary role in the offense were given significantly longer confinement time in adult court than similar youth in the juvenile system. One explanation for this finding could be the lack of control for other factors that could account for this observed relationship (e.g., victim injury). It may be that youth who played a non-primary role were involved with offenses generating greater victim injury, which then may have impacted on incarceration length.

Type of attorney also significantly interacted with type of court, as youth who used a public defender were more likely to be convicted on any offense in juvenile court than in adult court. Of those convicted,

---

[11] This reason was provided by one of the interviewees during the qualitative data collection.

youth who used a public defender in juvenile court had a significantly higher likelihood of incarceration than similar convicted youth in adult court.

Last, county of jurisdiction also had a different effect on three dependent variables. In the full model, being processed in Philadelphia had no independent effect on incarceration. However, the decertification specific models revealed that as compared to convicted Allegheny County youth, convicted Philadelphia youth in adult court had a higher likelihood of incarceration than similar convicted Philadelphia youth in juvenile court. In addition, the full model indicated that convicted and incarcerated Philadelphia youth were given significantly longer confinement time than similar youth from Allegheny County. The split models then revealed that as compared to convicted and incarcerated Allegheny youth, Philadelphia youth in adult court served significantly longer periods of incarceration than similar Philadelphia youth in juvenile court. Therefore, not only were Philadelphia youth more likely to be incarcerated, but they also experienced longer incarceration time. Finally, as compared to Allegheny County youth, being processed in Dauphin County had a stronger negative effect on violent rearrest in juvenile court than in adult court.

CHAPTER 7

Qualitative Findings

In the last chapter, the quantitative results were reported based on 423 youth who were initially transferred to adult court (i.e., legislatively waived) in Pennsylvania during 1996. The current chapter focuses on the more recent views of criminal justice professionals from the three counties which the quantitative data were drawn: Allegheny, Dauphin, and Philadelphia. The purpose of this chapter is to both supplement the quantitative findings and provide a greater understanding of the decertification process and Act 33 in general.

During the qualitative interviews, the four prosecutors in Allegheny County indicated that the only condition under which they would grant an interview was if there was no county reference when reporting the results. Therefore, the current chapter does not identify the respondents by county, but instead identifies them only by profession.

In total, it was hoped that nine interviews could be conducted, but due to the circumstances stated above, only seven were achieved. All interviews took place between the June 2004 and February 2005, with the average interview lasting approximately 25 minutes. In general, those who were interviewed appeared very open with their responses, with several of them indicating their strong interest in the subsequent research findings. However, as mentioned earlier, the group of four prosecutors in Allegheny County was extremely reluctant in providing their perspectives about Act 33 and decertification, resulting in their responses providing more limited information compared to the other interviews.

FACTORS IMPACTING ON THE DECERTIFICATION DECISION

This section reveals the views of criminal justice professionals regarding factors they believe to impact on the decertification process, along with what they think affects a judge's decision to decertify a case. The three judges were consistent with their opinions, in that they believed no one individual factor has the strongest effect. Rather, decertification depends on the various individual circumstances of each case. Amenability to treatment in the juvenile system also seemed to be a key issue of concern for these judges.

> [Judge 1]: It depends upon the delinquency history of the individual; it depends upon the seriousness and sophistication of the crime, and to some degree, it depends upon the individual. For example, when I described to you the individual who was brandishing the knife at his brother, I mean, this is a young man who had some emotional problems; he was slow and he had been a victim of neglect by his family, and this is a person who... simply based on the charges, shouldn't have been charged under Act 33....He had never been in a delinquency placement; he needed nurturing; he needed support; he needed education; he needed counseling; and he was certainly amenable to treatment as a juvenile.

> [Judge 2]: As far as a decertification, it's really going to depend on the circumstances. It's going to depend on a whole array of factors....Yeah, it may be a robbery with a weapon, but how serious of a robbery is it? How not so serious is it? It still may be a felony, but there are felonies and there are felonies....Was the victim injured? How severe was the threat or the injury, if at all? What's the victim's position? What's the government's position?...Was it something out of the ordinary for this youngster, or has this just been building up over the years, you know, one crime after the other?...So you have to look at the child's prior history in the system. It's a balance type of thing; not just one factor.

> [Judge 3]: It depends on the background of the juvenile. Two similar people can get different outcomes. Those who commit murder or inflict serious injuries are less likely to get decertified. It depends on the defendant's role in the offense. I also consider the impact on the victims and community. The more serious the offense, the less chance I will decertify. Age also is very important. Even if juveniles are good candidates for decertification, I may not decertify them if there is not enough time for the juvenile court to rehabilitate them, due to the juvenile court only having jurisdiction until the age of 21. I also look at their prior record in juvenile court, because there may be a progression of offenses, which will lower my likelihood of granting decertification. [Finally,] I also look at the type of services previously provided by the juvenile court. If youth seem to have exhausted juvenile court services, then there's no need to keep trying. In those cases, I am likely to retain the case in adult court.

In comparison, prosecutors identified similar types of cases that are successful in getting decertified:

> [Prosecutor 1]: The cases that typically get decertified are those in which juveniles exhibit the greatest amount of danger. This includes the number of prior records, the sophistication of the offender and the offense, seriousness of the offense, and the age of the offender.

> [Prosecutor 2]: Cases that are decertified are cases where there's little record in the juvenile system or a minor type of past juvenile contacts, cases that the victims are not "gung ho" about an adult prosecution; maybe they're related to the juvenile.

Finally, defense attorneys appeared to be in agreement with the other criminal justice professionals on what key factors influence the decertification decision. They also identified victim injury as a key issue.

> [Defense Attorney 1]: I would say anything involving a [firearm] probably wouldn't be decertified. Anything with a serious [victim] injury would not be decertified.
>
> [Defense Attorney 2]: The type of cases that are decertified typically involve those who are younger (closer to 15 or 16), those with very little prior record, little culpability, and when the victim injury is not serious. Cases where the juvenile has some mental health or retardation issues are likely to get decertified. Weapon type is also important, as offenders who use guns are harder to get decertified, and males typically use guns; females often use cutting instruments. No factor stands alone, but is examined in combination with everything else.

Overall, there were similar responses across professions as to what factors impact on the decertification decision. Similar to the quantitative data, the qualitative interviews revealed that age, offense seriousness, and prior record seem to have the greatest effect. However, other factors also appear to play an important role, such as the psychological stability of the youth, the extent of victim injury, and the opinion of the victim, which were not accounted for in the quantitative analyses. Most of the interviews indicated that one or a limited number of factors cannot be considered alone in determining the decertification decision. In sum, judges will look at the entire circumstances of each individual case when making their determination of which cases to decertify and which cases to retain in the adult system.

WHY NOT REQUEST A DECERTIFICATION HEARING?

It was revealed during the qualitative interviews that not all Act 33 youth request decertification hearings. Therefore, this issue was explored further, by asking the criminal justice professionals for reasons why they believe some youth may not file for decertification. The general view of judges was that some youth think they can get a more favorable eventual outcome in adult court, and also have a greater chance for release on bail.

[Judge 1]: The overwhelming majority of cases in criminal court are guilty pleas, [through] plea bargaining. And when you plea bargain, everybody gives up something. So kids know that they can come to criminal court and enter in a plea. The plea usually results in reduced charges...Sentencing guidelines are in effect here, whereas they are not in effect in juvenile court. They can get bail; they can't get bail in juvenile court. And kids actually believe... that they might get a lighter sentence; they may get no sentence; they may get probation here, whereas in juvenile court, they might get placement....Now if they know they're going to go to the penitentiary, then they're chomping at the bit to be decertified. But if they know that they may get probation, then they're chomping at the bit not to get decertified; they want to stay in the adult system. They want to stay in the adult system because kids tend to be very short-sighted; they look at the "here and now" and not look at the long-term consequences. So if they can get bail and get out of jail, versus sitting in [a secure facility], that's what they look at.

[Judge 2]: Some kids come in and say, "Transfer. Send me to adult court. Cause if you send me to adult court, I can make bail." Whereas in juvenile court, "I've been detained now since I got arrested for this crime and you're going to place me at some juvenile placement facility somewhere out in the wilderness someplace." Whereas if you transfer this case to adult court, you have to set bail, and [they] can make the bail....There is also the "macho image" of going to the big house. It's a source of pride for some of these kids. "Now, I don't want to be with the kids anymore, I want to be up with the big guys." Sometimes the kid is making a very shrewd decision. Yeah, he's going to have a record, but he sees the sentencing guidelines, and it's 3-6 months, so the kid will do 3 months in county prison, whereas in juvenile [court,] they're going to send him away for 9-12 months at a facility out in Indiana, PA...miles from Harrisburg. So these kids, they're not dumb, so that is a factor as well.

> [Judge 3]: Some juveniles want a trial, thinking they have a better chance of acquittal....Older youth may not request a decertification hearing, along with those who committed serious offenses. Also, those with extensive prior records may not request a decertification hearing. At the advice of their attorney, they may view a hearing as useless.

The prosecutors also added that in addition to believing that sanctions may be lighter in adult court, youth consider their likelihood of winning the decertification hearing when deciding whether or not to file for decertification.

> [Prosecutor 1]: Most defense attorneys will request a [decertification] hearing. However, for those who do not request a hearing, the rationale may be that there are lower sanctions in adult court than in the juvenile court, which uses indeterminate sentencing. Also, some defense attorneys know there's no chance of winning their motion for decertification.

> [Prosecutor 2]: I think in some cases, defendants realize there's no way that it's going to be decertified. Maybe the kid's got a huge history, violent history in juvenile court [and] now you've got an Act 33 crime. Maybe it's just short of homicide, and they just think it's a case where the judge is going to do it, so why even fight it. Sometimes I think the decertification process can open up the psychological profile of the juvenile and sometimes that [is not] good. If I'm a lawyer and you're my client, I know you've got a bad history, the psychological is going to be bad if it comes back, why file decertification if it's going to be a losing cause?

Again, the views of the defense attorney were similar to those of the judges and prosecutors. However, they also mentioned other factors having to do with the youth's attorney and the mentality of the youth.

> [Defense Attorney 1]: When you think about it, you would think they would do more time in the adult system, especially

> in a direct file case. I think [some] attorneys might not know to file a decertification petition....In my office they do, but we don't handle all the decertification hearings. I think the mentality among some of our younger clients is that it's cool; they're tough; they're going to go to state prison. I think that they think they'll have an easier time, maybe, than they would if they went to the juvenile system and they had to complete the program. They can keep jurisdiction over you until you're 21, and that kind of thing.
>
> [Defense Attorney 2]: The age of the youth may be a factor. By the time of the decertification hearing, there may really be no point because they're too old, and the judge probably won't decertify. Also, those with an extensive prior record may know decertification won't be granted.

The views of the respondents were generally consistent across professions. Numerous factors were thought to impact on whether or not Act 33 youth request a decertification hearing, including age, prior record, offense seriousness, the mentality of the youth, and the belief that youth may receive less severe treatment (e.g., bail, lighter sentence, acquittal, etc.) in the adult system. It again appears that no individual factor stands out in this decision made by youth and defense counsel. Instead, it may be a combination of both objective and subjective factors, including some speculation by youth on how they will be treated in the adult system.

PROBLEMS IN THE DECERTIFICATION PROCESS

The next area of questioning focused on the perceptions of the criminal justice professionals about problems in the decertification process. The judges' responses varied, but they all did offer suggestions on how the process could be improved. Two central issues of concern were the lack of a uniform decertification system and the age limitation for juvenile court jurisdiction.

> [Judge 1]: If we develop a system where one criminal court judge hears all the Act 33 cases, there will be a system in

place where you will file your decertification motion within 10 days after the preliminary hearing, and you will present it in court; you will get a hearing date, and it will move forward quickly.

[Judge 2]: There's a lack of uniformity. You have different judges, looking at different circumstances, and making different decisions based on those circumstances, so you don't have any uniform decisions in the decertification area....There are no clear standards for decertification. What should a judge base it on? Most judges just base it on their review of all the factors...and it's just a matter of balancing those, but is there a more accurate test we ought to be applying here?

[Judge 3]: There should be an increase in age for juveniles who are amenable to treatment in the juvenile court. In deciding whether to decertify a case, I consider the amount of time youth would have under juvenile court jurisdiction and whether that time would be sufficient for adequate rehabilitation. I believe that in cases in which decertification may be appropriate, the age of juvenile court jurisdiction should be increased, and I would decertify more cases.

In contrast, the prosecutors' views were somewhat different than the judges. Although some concern was expressed regarding discretion built into the process, it appeared that the prosecutors did not see any serious problems with the way decertification is operating.

[Prosecutor 1]: One problem is the discretion that everyone has. It's good, but it also has negative aspects. It gets too cumbersome for victims because it draws out the process.

[Prosecutor 2]: I think it's setup well. I mean, you have to have some type of avenue for cases to get back to juvenile court. I guess one inherent problem might be... that certain judges aren't attuned to the decertification process, so if it's an adult case... [the judges] get a decertification petition dropped in their chambers [and] they may not know what to do with it.

> But other than that, I think it's setup well. I haven't seen any inherent problems here with the process of going through. There's the opportunity for juveniles to have their bite of the apple and get back to juvenile court.

The defense attorneys, however, were more critical of decertification practices and generally believed that changes need to be made.

> [Defense Attorney 1]: In this county, we don't have a particular judge that they go to, nor do I think that we should. When a case is brought into adult court, I think they should be randomly assigned to one of our judges....I think we've gotten away from really looking at the main issue as to what's going to protect society and what's going to protect this kid, in the long run.

> [Defense Attorney 2]: It's a lengthier process because of the adult system, as opposed to the juvenile court process. There is a real disconnect between the offense and punishment and rehabilitation, due to the lengthier process. In addition, Act 33 youth are locked in adult prison; it tells a 16 year old, "You're a criminal."

When examining respondents' views on possible problems with the decertification process, their perspectives seemed to differ based on profession. The judges believed that several changes could be made, such as increasing the age of juvenile court jurisdiction for "decertified appropriate" youth, decreasing the length of time between arrest and the decertification hearing, and having more uniformity in decertification decision-making. The prosecutors saw fewer problems with decertification operations, aside from lengthening the process for victims, and some judges not being fully informed. Finally, public defenders were critical of decertification procedures, generally believing that the entire process is no longer focused on the best interests of the child and lengthens the time it takes for a youth to receive treatment and punishment.

CERTAINTY OF PUNISHMENT

One goal of Act 33 was to increase the likelihood of punishment in adult court, or to increase accountability for youthful violent offenders. With this in mind, this section reveals the views of the criminal justice professionals on whether they believe that non-decertified (i.e., adult court) youth have a higher likelihood of conviction than decertified youth. They also provided their thoughts on the role of plea bargaining in the process. According to the judges, there is little or no difference in the likelihood of conviction between the two court systems.

> [Judge 1]: I think that most of the kids we keep in the adult system probably have an equal chance of conviction because of the district attorney. One thing you know about the criminal justice system, for the most part, is that the district attorney is not bringing charges he knows he can't prove beyond a reasonable doubt. You know, the [youth] is going to be convicted no matter where he is....So for your serious offenses, I think the treatment is going to be the same. The standard of proof in juvenile court is the same standard of proof. And increasingly, juvenile court proceedings are more and more formal because the ramifications are very serious of a delinquency adjudication.

> [Judge 2]: With youth in the adult system, there's a right to a trial by jury. In juvenile court, there's no right to a trial by jury. I think a judge is less likely to give in to an unusual defense theory, or take into consideration "Look at that kid. He's 17, but he looks 12," whereas a jury may get into the sympathy routine with a young kid. Sometimes they do, when you have kids who really look younger than their actual age, there's an "Oh, he's a little angel; I don't believe he did that"....And a jury compromises, whereas a judge may not. A judge may say, well, they've proven all the elements of first degree robbery, where a jury may get tied up and come back with a verdict of a lesser form of robbery, a felony 2 robbery, as opposed to a felony 1, which will knock the guidelines down considerably.... [Concerning plea bargaining,] I think it

> happens more in the adult system than it happens in the juvenile system because in the juvenile system, you're on that fast track. I'm not saying there's no plea bargaining, but it's just less frequently than in the adult system....There are challenges, there are weaknesses exposed in the cases because of those challenges, and there might be more pressure to plea bargain the case.

> [Judge 3]: There is no difference. It depends on the evidence. There is a lot of plea bargaining in both systems. Fifty percent of the decertified cases are plead out. Actually, many cases are plead at the decertification hearing.

One prosecutor did not provide a full answer to this issue. However, another's response was consistent with the judges. Furthermore, he also discussed his views on the potential differences between the two groups of offenders in terms of the likelihood of target conviction.

> [Prosecutor 1]: [We] don't know because we don't keep statistics. There are so many factors that go into whether a conviction results.

> [Prosecutor 2]: I don't see much difference in [conviction] really; I would think it's pretty similar. If anything, I would think there's a higher rate of conviction in juvenile court than adult court, just because the juries, you never know what they're going to do....[As for conviction on a target offense,] in juvenile court, you can plea to a lesser charge and get the same result. In juvenile court, you're focused on the disposition. In juvenile court, it isn't as important what the actual charge it. These Act 33 offenses are serious offenses....So, if they're in the adult system, we probably hold fast to our guns because they are the more serious offenses, the greater the guidelines will be for sentencing....We'll cut you a break on the time because you're a kid and it's your first time going through the adult system, but we're going to make a plea to the actual offense.

The views of the defense attorneys were somewhat similar to both the judges and prosecutors. The lack of a jury trial in the juvenile system, though, was a key point of emphasis.

> [Defense Attorney 1]: I don't know if [non-decertified offenders] would have more of a likelihood of conviction. I think it would be probably less, because we would be trying this case with a jury and for the most part, our past juvenile court judges have been ex-prosecutors or law enforcement, and I do believe that they're on the side of prosecution or what *they* believe to be in the best interest of the child, and they're going to make a finding of something in the area of delinquency... [The District Attorney] has been of the opinion that there should not be so many "deals." His philosophy, and he made it very clear when he took office, was that he didn't believe there should be so many plea bargains. He thought that cases should be resolved by juries and to his credit, he still resolves cases by negotiated plea agreements, but there's still an awful lot of cases that we are forced to take to trial because they won't agree to anything and I think, at least in [this county,] if the case involves a weapon, if the case involves a robbery, especially like a convenience store, something that's going to get some press, I think the prosecution [and] police will not have an interest in attempting to work it out.

> [Defense Attorney 2]: I don't necessarily believe that there's a higher likelihood of conviction in adult court, because in the juvenile court, there are no jury trials. There's a lot of pressure to plea in adult court, while there's no incentive in juvenile court. In juvenile court, a youth is adjudicated delinquent, whether it's plead or not. There's a chance of getting off in adult court because of a jury trial.

The quantitative results in Chapter 6 first indicated that decertified youth were significantly more likely to be convicted than non-decertified youth. Subsequently, when looking at those cases that made it past the preliminary hearing stage and at conviction on a target offense, there was no significant difference in the likelihood of conviction in juvenile and adult court. In this section, the judges also reported that there likely is little or no difference in conviction rates between the two courts. Although one prosecutor indicated there are many factors that determine whether youth will be convicted, the other's view was consistent with the judges and the quantitative results, as he believed that the likelihood of punishment was perhaps greater in juvenile court. However, in examining target conviction, his response suggested a greater likelihood of conviction in adult court, which was not supported by the quantitative findings. Finally, the defense attorneys asserted that although there are plea bargains taking place, more often in the adult system, the juvenile court likely has a higher likelihood of conviction than adult court. Both prosecutors and defense attorneys also agreed that the uncertainty of juries lowers the conviction rate in adult court.

SEVERITY OF PUNISHMENT

Another purpose of Act 33 was to increase the punishment of youthful violent offenders, because the juvenile court was not thought to be able to "crack down" hard enough on these youth. This section examines the respondents' views on punishment severity. First, the judges tended to believe that adult court sentences are harsher than those of the juvenile court.

> [Judge 1]: [With the] sentencing guidelines [in adult court,] we're going to look at prior record scores; we're going to look at offense gravity scores; we're going to look at the individual defendant.
>
> [Judge 2]: Because the initial charge that got you there in the first place is so darn serious, I'd have to say the sentences are harsher in the adult system on direct files than they would be on decertifications. A lot of times, if there's a gun involved, a mandatory kicks in. Sometimes they'll plea bargain around it, but if you're talking about weapons, a lot of times mandatory sentences kick in.

> [Judge 3]: [Adult court sentences] are longer by statute. There are mandatory minimums in adult court. If a juvenile is convicted in adult court, depending on the offense, a certain sentence is required by law.

Next, the prosecutors' views were similar to those of the judges, emphasizing that the adult court focuses on and provides harsher punishment than the juvenile court.

> [Prosecutor 1]: In juvenile court, the focus is on kids' needs; there is no guaranteed disposition. The juvenile court is based on rehabilitation.

> [Prosecutor 2]: I think it is harsher [in adult court,] just because when you're talking about those offenses, the sentencing guidelines are pretty much up there. It's not calling for probation for those types of serious offenses. They're going to prison; you're not going to some juvenile placement, school, camp, whatever the juvenile thing is. I think prison, by its nature, is going to be harsher....You have a 15-16 year old kid, going to Camp Hill, Huntington, Graterford, wherever; it's harsh.

Last, the defense attorneys' views again were consistent with both the judges and prosecutors.

> [Defense Attorney 1]: Probably [harsher in adult court], because I think the sentences that would be mandated by a serious aggravated assault with a weapon or a robbery or a home burglary, I think those cases carry years, and depending on the prior juvenile record, yeah they'd probably serve much more time than they would get in juvenile court in the end.

> [Defense Attorney 2]: The adult court is allowed to hand out lengthier sentences than the juvenile court.

The quantitative results previously indicated that youth processed and convicted in adult court were given significantly longer incarceration time than those processed and adjudicated delinquent in juvenile court. Overall, the views of all the criminal justice professionals were consistent with the quantitative findings. The most cited reason was that violent offenses, especially if a weapon is used during the commission of the offense, carry recommended or mandatory sentences that simply are not available in the juvenile court.

Swiftness of Case Processing

Another explored area of both the quantitative and qualitative portions of the study was the length of time it takes for cases to be processed. This section provides the views of the respondents regarding whether adult court (i.e., non-decertified) cases take longer to process than juvenile court (i.e., decertified) cases. Due to strict time limitations during one of the interviews, one criminal court judge could not be questioned in this area. However, the other two judges did address this issue.

> [Judge 2]: Much longer [in adult court.] It's off the fast track.

> [Judge 3]: If decertified by agreement of both the ADA and defense attorney, the case is processed much faster. I don't know about contested cases that are decertified to juvenile court.

Similarly, the prosecutors were in agreement that cases take longer to process in adult court than in juvenile court.

> [Prosecutor 1]: Yes, because the Juvenile Act requires a set amount of time for hearings. It's not uncommon for adult court cases to take longer than one year.

> [Prosecutor 2]: If it's staying in adult court, you have to get through an arraignment [and] you've got to have time for motions. Our trial docket's overloaded, so it's going to sit a while. In juvenile court, with the time restriction of the Juvenile Act, the cases move through there. No question about it. Adult court is a lot slower.

The defense attorneys also believed that in adult court, cases take longer to process.

> [Defense Attorney 1]: Just getting to trial, there can be 2 or 3 postponements [in adult court.] In juvenile court, obviously, they're going to get to court much quicker and the lag is between adjudication and disposition, but I think that there's a lot more time to get to court in the adult system.

> [Defense Attorney 2]: The adult system is a much lengthier process.

In sum, there were no differences across professions when asked about which court takes longer to process cases, with the adult court being consistently cited. The quantitative data, in contrast, indicated that there was no significant difference in case processing time between decertified and non-decertified youth. It should be remembered, however, that case processing time was measured quantitatively as the number of days from time of arrest until date of disposition, for both groups of youth. The respondents for the interviews seemed to consider case processing time from the date of the decertification hearing to final disposition for decertified youth, as some of these individuals mentioned the Juvenile Act as a central reason why juvenile court cases are expedited through the system, and that the Act would not be in effect until after decertification occurred. This suggests that similarity in case processing times found in the quantitative analysis was perhaps due to the initial processing of all cases in adult court.

EVIDENCE OF DETERRENCE

Another cited purpose of Act 33 was to provide specific deterrence to offenders who are transferred to adult court. Therefore, the criminal justice professionals were asked whether they believe Act 33 is effective in reducing recidivism. The judges generally reported the Act does not achieve this goal.

> [Judge 1]: I think the statistics have shown that there's greater recidivism for kids who are processed through the adult

> system than kids who are processed in the juvenile system. I think that has been established statistically.
>
> [Judge 2]: During the 5 years this kid's in the state penitentiary, he's not going to be getting into any more trouble....But when the kid gets out, have you really solved anything with this particular kid? Has he learned a lesson, or are they going to be right back into it? I don't think recidivism is reduced by the direct file system. I really don't. It's just a gut feeling, a perception.
>
> [Judge 3]: I have no idea. Many criminal justice laws are made based on ad hominems, not research. Too many issues are based on what sounds good, not on research. No one reads articles, because practitioners cannot access them.

The prosecutors were not exactly sure as to whether Act 33 achieves its goal of specific deterrence by reducing recidivism.

> [Prosecutor 1]: After Act 33, the severity of juvenile crime decreased, but it may not be due to Act 33. It could be due to other factors not known about.
>
> [Prosecutor 2]: Probably. Again, I have no data to back it up. First of all, you're locking that person up for a longer period of time, so they're not going to be back on the street as fast, so that in of itself, is going to keep the kid from screwing up again....When they get out, are they less likely to reoffend, I don't know. I would think having that type of incarceration might shock them a little more, but the juvenile system has some decent programming for kids too, whereas the adult system is not as geared into that, so I don't know.

Finally, the defense attorneys also believed that Act 33 was not effective in reducing recidivism among waived youth, but they were more critical than both the judges and prosecutors.

> [Defense Attorney 1]: My personal opinion is that it is not [reducing recidivism]. I don't know that anyone is going to be scared away from doing it because they're facing a harsher penalty. I think what it is doing is increasing recidivism because we are taking these young kids and putting them in state prison and hooking them up with other people who are far worse than they could ever be. I think we're harming them more by putting them up there....You take a 16 year old who does whatever horrible thing, it's still a 16 year old, and you take that kid, I don't care if he lived on the street and he's learn the ways of the streets, or been in gangs, you put him up there with some of these people in the state prisons we have, no matter how bad he was when he came in, there was still hope, and you take that hope right away when you send him up there for years and years and years.

> [Defense Attorney 2]: I believe that Act 33 doesn't deter because juveniles don't know about the law. Last year, there was a big increase in Act 33 cases, so the message isn't getting out about the law. The harsher sentences don't work; the concentration should be on improving schools, instead of focusing on harsher penalties.

Overall, there did not appear to be much disagreement among the criminal justice professionals about Act 33 providing specific deterrence among transferred offenders. The judges generally believed that although the law can prevent crime through the incapacitation of transferred youth, once released from secure custody, these youth recidivate, in spite of being processed in the adult system. One judge also noted that many of our criminal justice polices are not based on sound research, but emotion. The prosecutors also questioned the effectiveness of Act 33 in reducing recidivism. Again, once released from confinement, they were unsure of whether youth processed in adult court were "rehabilitated" to the level they could have been if processed in juvenile court. The defense attorneys also believed that Act 33 was ineffective, stating that locking up youth in adult facilities increases the likelihood of recidivism. They further suggested that increased sanctions should not be the response of society, but instead there should be a preventive approach.

The views of the justice system professionals were consistent with findings from past research and, to a lesser extent, the quantitative results from this study of no significant differences in recidivism between decertified and non-decertified offenders. In terms of post-dispositional recidivism for any offense, for a violent offense, and for time to recidivism, current and past quantitative and qualitative research has failed to establish a beneficial deterrent effect from transfer to adult court.

OVERALL EFFECTIVENESS OF ACT 33

The next area of questioning focused on the views of the respondents on whether they believe that Act 33 achieves the goals of increased incapacitation, accountability, and greater public safety. Again, due to time limitations, this issue was not addressed by one of the judges, but was considered by the other two. In general, they were unsure of whether these goals were being met.

> [Judge 2]: As far as incapacitation, you can assure you're going to take a bite out of this kid, so to speak, for the time that he's incarcerated. The community is assured that during that time, he's not going to commit anymore crime. But in the long run, have you made the community safer once this kid gets out of jail? I'm not sure that you have. I think the recidivism rate is high enough to be a continuing concern.

> [Judge 3]: The public perception is that they see more youth in the adult system. However, they've been conditioned to believe it.

On the other hand, the prosecutors had more positive views toward Act 33 when thinking about these goals.

> [Prosecutor 1]: [Act 33] helped. We don't see as much gang violence. There may be a "wake-up" call for Act 33 kids,

regardless of whether they're decertified or not. Also, society seems appreciative of the tough law.

[Prosecutor 2]: I think it's very effective for offender accountability. To treat somebody different, just because they're 17, as compared to an 18 year old, doesn't make sense. These are serious crimes, and they are held accountable for it. From a public safety perspective, I think it's good too. It's taking these serious offenders off the streets, making sure that they're held accountable. You never know what a judge is going to do in a given case in the juvenile system, so even a serious offense in the juvenile system, the "wrong" judge could give them something that doesn't help him, doesn't punish him, so I think accountability is greatly increased by the act, I think. Public safety's increased. I'd like to think it cuts down on recidivism; I don't know that yet, but I think it's a good Act.

Last, the defense attorneys did not have as positive of a view toward the law achieving accountability and public safety.

[Defense Attorney 1]: I guess it's effective in that you're holding them accountable. Is it more accountable than they would be in juvenile court? I don't think so. As for public safety, obviously again, you're keeping the kid off the street for that period of time, but you're not creating anymore public safety that you would if they were off the street in juvenile court.

[Defense Attorney 2]: It's not effective because the law labels them as criminals. It teaches juveniles how to be good inmates. The focus should be on treating them in the juvenile court. Many kids in the juvenile court become productive and successful.

There was general disagreement among the criminal justice professionals about Act 33 achieving greater offender accountability and increased public safety. The judges acknowledged that although the public is "safer" while transferred offenders are confined, long-term public safety may not be increased. The prosecutors, however, had a more favorable view. According to them, the Act holds offenders accountable for their violent behavior and the public is much safer, because they will be "off the street." Defense attorneys also acknowledged that the Act, in some respect, holds offenders accountable and protects society, but then argued that the same goals are accomplished in the juvenile system. One defense attorney further expressed that because Act 33 offenders learn how to be "better criminals," the public may be less safe, as compared to if the youth were processed in the juvenile system, where the focus is on treatment.

FUTURE OF ACT 33

This section focuses on whether respondents believed Act 33 should stay in place, considering many offenders are either decertified or have their cases dismissed. The responses varied according to profession, and interestingly enough, there was some disagreement among the judges.

> [Judge 1]: A lot of Act 33 cases are not really valid cases. I mean, I have seen, in the criminal justice system, the police have the most discretion. Police can decide how someone will be charged [and] what they're going to be charged with. I have seen abuses...Since Act 33, they did build the penitentiary, Pine Grove, specifically for young offenders. And they don't have enough juveniles to fill the beds. They thought they would get this large wave of juvenile convictions and they were going to fill that prison, but it's a testimony to how weak and ineffective and unnecessary Act 33 was. They don't have enough juveniles to fill it....I think it was an unnecessary piece of legislation.

> [Judge 2]: Yeah, I see a reason to keep it in place, because obviously, some kids deserve decertification and some kids do not. Some circumstances deserve decertification and some circumstances do not. And so I think we need it in place.

> [Judge 3]: Yes. There are many kids, based on offense severity and prior record, who have no place in the juvenile system. You must think of this from a public safety point of view.

In comparison, the prosecutors consistently believed that Act 33 was a good law and should remain in effect.

> [Prosecutor 1]: Act 33 is a reflection of modern times. Kids are growing up faster. Even if most kids are decertified, it's still useful. It's good for kids who are retained.

> [Prosecutor 2]: The good thing about the Act is that there is the decertification process. It's not absolute that everyone who's a certain age and commits a certain crime has to go to adult court. They can still get back to juvenile court. The burden is on them...but that outlet is there. If you're decertifying everyone, then the Act shouldn't be in place, but we're not doing that here. I think we have one of the higher transfer rates in the Commonwealth, even outside of Act 33. We don't screw around too much with these kids. I don't know if it's helping the crime rate a lot, but we're at least holding them accountable.

Defense attorneys, though, were more critical of Act 33 than the prosecutors and two of the judges. They generally believed that Act 33 was ineffective and unnecessary.

> [Defense Attorney 1]: We don't have a lot of cases decertified here, so that's not an issue.[12]
> [Defense Attorney 2]: There was pressure 10 years ago to produce a law like Act 33. However, we now see what a failure it is. Society isn't safer by locking up kids as adults.

---

[12] The respondent was answering the question of, "If many offenders are decertified, is there a reason to keep Act 33 in place?" The respondent's view expressed in the next section more clearly captured her opinion of whether Act 33 should remain in place.

Overall, the views about Act 33 remaining an active law differed, based on profession. The general view of the judges was that Act 33 should continue because some offenders were not appropriate for juvenile court, based on their crimes. However, one judge did not hold this view and believed that Act 33 was abused and not effective overall. Prosecutors, however, were in agreement that the law should remain in effect because it holds youth accountable, and the Act is fair in that youth have the decertification option available for its use. The defense attorneys were clear in that they believed that Act 33 was not achieving its goals and should no longer be in existence.

LEGISLATIVE WAIVER VERSUS JUDICIAL WAIVER

Finally, the respondents were asked about the strengths and weaknesses of legislative waiver associated with Act 33, as compared to discretionary judicial waiver. Similar to some other areas of questioning, opinions appeared to vary based on the profession of the respondent. Judges tended to favor the previously relied upon judicial waiver mechanism.

> [Judge 1]: I think that it was a much more efficient system when the district attorney would make the decision whether or not to file a motion for certification; the district attorney had the burden of proof. In many counties in our state...juveniles don't have the access to attorneys that they should have. So under Act 33, the entire burden is on the juvenile to establish amenability. And the entire burden is on the juvenile to have competent, effective counsel to raise these issues, and to raise them in a timely fashion....I believe that Act 33 was unnecessary because...the people who are not being decertified were the same ones we were certifying in the first place.

> [Judge 2]: Under the [judicial] transfer system, you're accomplishing the decertification process all in one. In other words, you're making a determination right in one setting whether or not the youngster ought to go to adult court, as opposed to an automatic file in adult court....So it seems to be that the economical way is the transfer system, because you

> have a judge looking at the whole package who makes that initial decision....In terms of prosecutorial discretion, the prosecutor doesn't have to make that tough decision of whether they're going to ask for transfer or not. It's a direct file; you're there. Now the prosecutor can decide whether or not to fight a decertification, so it's an easier decision. As far as the youngster, it's a more traumatic decision. The youngster is automatically thrown into the adult court system. The youngster may say, "I want to stay here," but I sort of think most of them will fight to get back in the juvenile system.

> [Judge 3]: There [still] is judicial discretion under Act 33. The focus changed from the juvenile to public safety. The burden changed; it shifted from the state to the juvenile. There may be no difference in people who get decertified or retained, as compared to judicial waiver.

The prosecutors, on the other hand, had a much more favorable view toward legislative waiver and Act 33, as opposed to judicial waiver.

> [Prosecutor 1]: There's an initial message, whether or not the case is decertified. It's a community message that certain behavior will not be tolerated. The burden is on the juvenile to prove otherwise, while with judicial waiver, the burden is on the state. The passing of Act 33 brought about a different mindset for accountability and restorative justice. Also a different perspective of juvenile court judges, where it only used to be about the "best interests of the child." Kids should be happy when they're decertified. Act 33 brings a strength to the juvenile system.

> [Prosecutor 2]: I think the strength [of Act 33] is that it's immediate; it happens right after the offense. Another strength is that it takes the [juvenile court] judicial officer, who may or may not have an agenda, might think that kids shouldn't be in adult court, it takes them out of the equation.

> Although with decertification you can still get back there, I think it's important that the juveniles who are committing these types of crimes are held accountable from the outset....One weakness is that despite fitting the criteria, [some cases] still shouldn't be adult cases; there's not a whole lot, but there are some. Again, maybe the kid's never done anything wrong before and does something stupid that happens to be one of these types of offenses. And in those cases, you're stuck with going through the process to get it back to juvenile court. But overall, it's a good Act.

The defense attorneys again had a contrary view to that of the prosecutors, favoring judicial waivers more than Act 33 legislative waivers.

> [Defense Attorney 1]: My personal belief is that there really aren't any strengths [of Act 33]....If you've got any faith in your juvenile court system to begin with, then the judge has the capacity to send the case [to adult court]. If the kid's beyond help, if the case is that egregious, the kid's got so much of a record, then it's going to go up anyway [to adult court]. I think the taking of discretion away from the [juvenile court] judges and mandating that it goes to adult court to begin with, and at least for that period of time, that young child is held in an adult prison, the damage is already done....So my personal opinion is it's not worthwhile; it's not beneficial; it's not doing good for anyone; and for the people of the Commonwealth, I think we're creating monsters in these children that don't need to be, and we're warehousing them for a period of time, which is [an] enormous cost to the taxpayer.

> [Defense Attorney 2]: One weakness is that there is not enough discretion used [in Act 33 cases]....The Commonwealth should think about these things at the beginning; not all of these cases belong in the adult system. Another weakness is that the criminal court judge doesn't consider all the evidence that would be presented at trial. He's

> basically missing the defense when deciding on decertification. The judge looks at, "If this kid was guilty, what would be in the best interest of the public?" We should have a trial first, and then determine the court to send the kid [for sentencing]; it also would be cheaper.

There were varying beliefs about the strengths and weaknesses of legislative wavier and judicial waiver. The judges acknowledged some advantages of judicial waiver, and also stated that continuing discretion and decertification in the new system leads to similar results as in the old system. Their strongest comments indicated there may be no difference between the youth who are being retained in adult court under Act 33 and the youth who would have been transferred via judicial waiver. The prosecutors seemed to favor Act 33 over judicial waiver and maintained that the law holds offenders more accountable for their actions. They also expressed that the law no longer left discretion to juvenile court judges, who may shy away from "cracking down" and transferring violent offenders to adult court. Finally, the public defenders believed Act 33 sends the message that society has little faith in its juvenile court, and they also asserted that juvenile court judges should determine which cases get sent to adult court. It also was expressed that Act 33 doesn't weed out enough cases that do not belong in adult court, which would not be a concern if these cases originated in juvenile court.

SUMMARY

Several observations can be made regarding the responses of the criminal justice professionals reported and discussed in this chapter. When it comes to certain topics, there appeared to be agreement among judges, prosecutors, and defense attorneys. For instance, they all agreed that prior record, offense seriousness, age, and victim injury are important in the decertification decision, which is generally consistent with the quantitative findings. They also tended to believe that decertified youth have a higher likelihood of conviction than non-decertified youth, which also is consistent with the quantitative results. In addition, they reported that sanctions are harsher in adult court, and that adult court cases take longer to process. Last, they questioned whether Act 33 reduces recidivism for transferred offenders once they are released from secure custody.

The main areas of disagreement concerned the overall effectiveness of Act 33 and whether the law should continue to be in existence. Two judges were supportive of Act 33, because they believed that certain youth should not be processed in juvenile court. They did, however, acknowledge that the best part of the legislation was that the decertification process was a viable option for youth to pursue. The other judge was opposed to Act 33, believing it to be ineffective and removing too much discretion from juvenile court judges.

The prosecutors, overall, were very supportive of Act 33. They favored the law over discretionary judicial waiver and stated that even if the law does not reduce recidivism among transferred offenders, it holds them accountable for their actions and increases public safety. The also reported that the law is needed because the violent offenders who are targeted should not have their cases originating in the juvenile court.

The defense attorneys, as a whole, were the most opposed to the Act. They believed that Act 33 not only is ineffective, but it also increases recidivism, due to youth initially being placed and processed with adult offenders. They did not think society is any safer as a result of the law, and stated that the decision to transfer a case to adult court should be left to the discretion of juvenile court judges. Finally, the defense attorneys indicated that instead of society reacting inappropriately by automatically transferring more youth to adult court, efforts should be focused on juvenile court treatment and preventing initial violent behavior from taking place (e.g., by improving the quality of schools).

CHAPTER 8

Discussion

As a result of the youth violence surge that spanned from the mid 1980s to the mid 1990s, virtually all states "cracked down" on juvenile crime, and the most popular (yet controversial) societal response was facilitating the transfer of juvenile offenders to adult court (Torbet et al., 1996). Most contemporary transfer studies have examined the overall effectiveness of this practice by comparing youth who were judicially waived to adult court with youth who were retained in the juvenile system. The current study also sought to examine the effectiveness of juvenile transfer, but the focus was on Pennsylvania's legislative waiver law (Act 33), which automatically transfers youth to adult court based on the offender's age and alleged offense.

Those who support juvenile transfer generally assert that waiver policies target the most serious and violent offenders and provide harsher punishment than is available in juvenile court. These same individuals also tend to believe that society would be safer if violent youth were sent to adult court and removed for longer periods of time, preventing them the opportunity for engaging in further criminal behavior. The current study considered these issues, along with the effect of Act 33 on official recidivism. The general findings indicated that violent youth processed in adult court are treated more harshly at sentencing, in terms of incarceration length, but overall, there appeared to be few other beneficial outcomes.

FACTORS PREDICTING DECERTIFICATION

In the decertification models, several factors were found to have a significant effect on the decision to send an initially waived case back to juvenile court. First, the more prior referrals a youth possessed, the lower was the likelihood of decertification. In addition, offense seriousness seemed important, as youth who played a non-primary role and those who did not use a firearm were more likely to be decertified than offenders who played a primary role or used a firearm. These findings are somewhat contrary to early transfer studies, many of which were descriptive in nature and found property offenders to constitute a majority of waived youth (Bishop & Frazier, 1991; Bishop et al., 1989; Bortner, 1986; Champion 1989; Eigen, 1981a, 1981b; Gillespie & Norman, 1984; Lee, 1994). The results are more consistent, though, with the limited research that previously examined the characteristics of decertified juveniles (Singer, 1996; Snyder et al., 2000) and more recent transfer studies that focused on serious and violent offenders (Clarke, 1996; Clement, 1997; Fagan et al., 1987; Fagan and Deschenes, 1990; Fritsch, 1996; Houghtalin & Mays, 1991; Kinder et al., 1995; Myers, 2003b; Podkopacz & Feld, 1996; Poulos and Orchowsky, 1994).

In the current research, legal variables (e.g., offense seriousness and prior record) were the strongest predictors of decertification. The use of a firearm during the offense is particularly noteworthy, as further analysis indicated that the estimated probability of decertification for youth who used a firearm during the offense was over 30 percentage points lower than for those who did not use a firearm. The effects of these same legal variables also were expressed by the criminal justice professionals, as they all indicated that the more serious the offense (e.g., using a firearm) and the greater the prior record, the lower the likelihood of decertification to juvenile court.

One possible reason for these findings is that youth who used a firearm or had a greater prior record could be viewed as being no longer amenable to juvenile court treatment. In general, if judges perceive youth cannot benefit from being returned to juvenile court, they appear less likely to decertify those cases and end up keeping them in adult court. In this sense, Pennsylvania's Act 33 statute is achieving its goal of processing the more serious and violent youthful offenders in adult court.

On the other hand, another important point to consider is that Act 33 was implemented in part to reduce the discretion of juvenile court judges in deciding which cases to transfer to adult court. Juvenile court judges generally considered a wide variety of factors in previously making this decision in violent offender cases (e.g., age, prior record, offense seriousness, and amenability to treatment). Act 33 was intended to remove a great deal of this discretion, meaning age and offense, alone, determines which cases automatically were transferred to adult court. However, as a result of the decertification process, criminal court judges typically exercise the same discretion in the decertification decision that was used by juvenile court judges in the past to make the transfer decision. All of the criminal justice professionals stated that there are a variety of factors, in addition to age and offense seriousness, that impact on judges in making the decertification decision. In fact, one judge stated that similar judicial discretion continues to exist as a result of Act 33; only the court and who has the burden of proof have changed. Moreover, the unexplained variation in the quantitative decertification models suggests the influence of factors beyond those included in the models.

Another issue to consider is that most of the prior research in this area examined the predictors of juvenile transfer via judicial waiver. In other words, the juvenile court was the original court of jurisdiction, and the factors that impact on juvenile court judges in transferring cases were assessed. As mentioned earlier, offense seriousness and prior record were the strongest predictors of whether or not a juvenile judge transferred a case to adult court, meaning the less serious and frequent offenders were retained in juvenile court. The current study found that more serious and frequent offenders were tried and sentenced in adult court (although many were dismissed at the preliminary hearing stage), while less serious offenders with lower prior records were more likely to be decertified to juvenile court. This suggests that the cases that currently are being denied decertification (i.e., retained in adult court) are similar to those cases that were being judicially waived to adult court prior to Act 33. This observation also was made by several criminal justice professionals who claimed that with the decertification process, there is little or no difference between the non-decertified cases under Act 33 and previously transferred cases under judicial waiver.

PUNISHMENT CERTAINTY

In addition to Act 33 having a goal of "cracking down" on violent youthful offenders, it is also expected to provide general deterrence to potential juvenile offenders and specific deterrence to youth who already were punished under the statute. One element of deterrence theory is certainty of punishment (Beccaria, 1963). In order to provide greater deterrent effects, youth processed in adult court under Act 33 should have a higher certainty of punishment (i.e., conviction) than similar youth processed in juvenile court. The quantitative results indicated, however, that when examining all youth in the dataset, decertified youth had a significantly higher likelihood of conviction than non-decertified youth. When considering only those cases that proceeded past the preliminary hearing stage, there was no significant difference in the likelihood of conviction between the two groups of offenders. Finally, when assessing conviction on a target offense, there also was no significant difference between decertified and non-decertified youth. These quantitative findings corresponded fairly well with the results of the qualitative interviews, particularly with regard to conviction on any offense.

Early descriptive studies suggested that transferred youth had a high rate of conviction in adult court (Bishop & Frazier, 1991; Bishop et al., 1989; Champion, 1989; Gillespie and Norman, 1984; Houghtalin & Mays, 1991; Thomas & Bilchik). However, due to there being no comparison groups employed, it was not possible to determine whether these conviction rates were different than those of comparable offenders in juvenile court. Nevertheless, when looking at comparison studies focused on violent youthful offenders, the findings from the current research are contrary to most studies that examined the effect of transfer on conviction and found that youth in adult court have a higher likelihood of conviction (or punishment certainty) than similar youth in juvenile court (Eigen, 1981a, 1981b; Fagan, 1995; Myers, 2001, 2003a). One study did suggest that violent offenders in both court systems have virtually identical conviction rates (Rudman et al., 1995).

As mentioned above, the first conviction model presented in Table 6 included all offenders and provided evidence of a higher likelihood of conviction in juvenile court. One explanation for this finding is that the adult court, rather than the juvenile court, is now providing a screening function that eliminates "weaker" cases from further processing. After cases dismissed at the preliminary hearing stage were excluded from subsequent analyses, the findings pointed to similarities between the two courts, in both conviction on any offense and conviction on a target offense (among those convicted). In other words, after the adult criminal court dismissed the weaker cases, the remaining cases resulted in similar conviction rates in both courts.

Regardless of whether all cases are examined or only those making it past the preliminary hearing stage, the quantitative findings indicate Act 33 is not achieving its goal of a higher certainty of punishment in adult court, in terms of conviction likelihood. Furthermore, several of the criminal justice professionals also asserted there is little or no difference in likelihood of conviction between juvenile and adult court for serious and violent offenders. The main reason provided was that in adult court, the likelihood of conviction decreases due to the uncertainty of juries.

Another explanation for the similarity between the two courts on target conviction involves the role of plea bargaining in the process. Most of the criminal justice professionals indicated there is an increased pressure to plead cases in adult court, again due to the uncertainty of juries and the backlog of the court docket, which will lower the likelihood of conviction on target offenses. The respondents also stated that because the goal of the juvenile court is to provide treatment to youth, there is less pressure to adjudicate youth on the original Act 33 offense, because offenders likely will receive the same disposition regardless of the charge. Therefore, between plea bargaining in the adult system and limited pressure to convict on a target offense in the juvenile system, there ends up being little difference between the court systems on target conviction likelihood.

Whether looking at conviction on any offense or on a target offense, it seems clear that youth legislatively waived and processed in adult court have either a lower or similar chance of conviction than comparable youth decertified to juvenile court. If deterrence remains a goal of Act 33, it appears that the element of increased punishment certainty is not present. According to Beccaria (1963), certainty of punishment is the most important element of the theory, as those who believe they will be punished will be more likely to refrain from committing criminal acts.

PUNISHMENT SEVERITY

The second element of deterrence theory emphasizes that the punishment should be severe enough to outweigh the benefits derived from the illegal act (Beccaria, 1963). Policymakers essentially interpret this as meaning society's laws should provide harsh legal punishments for many types of crimes, which is a goal of most "get tough" laws, including Act 33. Based on harsher punishments being a goal, it would be expected that youth processed in adult court are given harsher sentences than similar youth processed in juvenile court. The two measures of punishment severity utilized in the current study were incarceration and incarceration length.

The quantitative findings indicated that among those convicted, there was no significant difference between decertified and non-decertified offenders in the likelihood incarceration. This finding is not consistent with the prior research using comparison groups (Eigen, 1981a, 1981b; Fagan, 1995; Myers, 2001, 2003a; Podkopacz and Feld, 1996; Rudman et al., 1986), which found that transferred offenders in adult court have a higher likelihood of incarceration than comparable non-transferred offenders in juvenile court. In the current study, the estimated probabilities did suggest the probability of incarceration for decertified and convicted youth was 10 percentage points lower than for convicted, non-decertified youth. However, while controlling for other factors, this difference did not reach statistical significance.

On the other hand, when examining incarceration length among the smaller number of incarcerated youth, a different result emerged, as adult court offenders were sentenced to significantly longer confinement time than similar juvenile court offenders. These findings are consistent with most research using comparison groups and assessing the incarceration length of transferred and non-transferred offenders (Eigen, 1981a, 1981b; Fritsch et al., 1996; Myers, 2001, 2003a; Podkopacz and Feld, 1996; Rudman et al., 1986). However, exceptions do exist (Fagan, 1995). In general, it appears that in terms of length of confinement among incarcerated offenders, Act 33 is achieving its goal of greater punishment severity. This finding also was supported by the criminal justice professionals, as they all indicated that adult court offenders receive longer sentences than similar youth in juvenile court. The main explanation for this finding is that in adult court, lengthier sentences are enabled and sometimes mandated, especially if a gun was involved, whereas in juvenile court, indeterminate sentencing is used and Pennsylvania juvenile courts only have jurisdiction over offenders until age 21.

Some may appreciate, more than others, that youth who are processed and incarcerated by adult courts are given harsh sentences. For example, interviewed prosecutors and judges expressed that because youth in adult court are confined for longer periods of time, they are not able to commit additional crimes. Put differently, Act 33 and the resulting confinement time produces lengthier incapacitation, whereby youth cannot recidivate during the time they are in secure custody. Therefore, from a public safety point of view, many would perceive society to be safer because some of these youth are incarcerated for several years or more.

Although adult court offenders who are incarcerated are often sentenced to extended confinement time, it must be remembered that many youth who are legislatively waived either have their cases dismissed or otherwise do not end up receiving a prison sentence. Moreover, another goal of Act 33 is deterrence of future criminal behavior. It has been established in this study that there is not a higher likelihood of conviction (or certainty of punishment) in adult court. Differences in the likelihood of conviction on a target offense and incarceration also were statistically insignificant. Therefore, the question becomes whether extended confinement time though adult court processing is enough to deter future criminal behavior. This issue will be explored further following the discussion of whether Act 33 meets the final element of deterrence theory.

PUNISHMENT SWIFTNESS

The last theoretical element of deterrence is swiftness of punishment. Becarria (1963) stated that in order for deterrence to occur, the punishment must occur quickly following the act, allowing a mental connection to be made between the act and the punishment. Again, if Act 33 is meant to provide deterrence, it should be expected that youth processed in adult court would have their cases processed in a timely manner. The quantitative findings indicated no significant difference in case processing time between decertified and non-decertified offenders.

This is contrary to all prior research that has examined this issue and found adult court processing to take much longer than comparable juvenile court processing (Fagan, 1995; Myers, 2001, 2003a; Rudman et al., 1986).

The reason for this finding is likely due to the way case processing time was measured in the current study, as well as the type of offenders included. Case processing time was measured as the date of arrest until final disposition for all offenders, which seems to lengthen the entire process for Act 33 youth who eventually were decertified to juvenile court. It must be remembered that prior studies in this area typically examined youth who were judicially waived to adult court by a juvenile court judge, and compared them to similar youth processed in juvenile court. Because the initial court of jurisdiction in those cases was the juvenile court, the juvenile cases were processed more quickly. However, for all offenders in the current study, the initial court of jurisdiction was the adult criminal court, which resulted in similar case processing time for decertified and non-decertified youth. All of the criminal justice professionals, in contrast, were clear in their belief that juvenile court cases are processed more quickly than adult court cases, due to Pennsylvania's Juvenile Act restricting the length of time for cases to be processed.

To further illustrate the similarity between the two court systems in this study, the difference in the estimated length of case processing was 21.63 days. Typical decertified youth took an estimated 142.17 days (nearly 5 months) and typical non-decertified youth took 120.54 days (roughly 4 months). A few observations can be made regarding this finding. First, when compared to past research (Fagan, 1995; Myers, 2001, 2003a; Rudman et al., 1986), it can be seen that Act 33 lengthens the time it takes to have juvenile cases processed for those youth who are decertified to juvenile court. These youth most likely would have been retained in juvenile court by a juvenile court judge under discretionary judicial waiver. Therefore, the amount of time it takes for decertified youth to have their cases processed is increased through legislative waiver, as compared to the time it would have taken if these cases originated in juvenile court.

Case processing time also is possibly increased for youth who are denied decertification. Had their cases originated in juvenile court, the decision to judicially waive the case to adult court would have come fairly quickly, due to the time restrictions imposed under Pennsylvania's Juvenile Act. However, due to Act 33 cases originating in adult court, the criminal justice system is not as restricted to certain time frames, as compared to those imposed on the juvenile court. Although cases dismissed at the preliminary hearing stage lower processing times for Act 33 cases in adult court, which also contributes to the findings of this study concerning case processing time, those that proceed for prosecution generally take many months to resolve.

In addition, because there does not appear to be swiftness of punishment (or treatment) in either court system under Act 33, the last element of deterrence theory is not met. One public defender also noted that because of Act 33, there is a large gap in time between the offense and punishment and rehabilitation. Due to there being no increase in certainty or swiftness of punishment from Act 33, the question again becomes whether the possibility of greater incarceration length, alone, is the only benefit of processing violent youth in adult court. This issue is addressed further below.

NO EVIDENCE OF SPECIFIC DETERRENCE

As mentioned before, deterrence theory states that in order for people to be deterred from committing crime, punishment should be based on the principles of certainty, severity, and swiftness (Becarria, 1963). The current research only provides support for Act 33 adult court processing in the area of more severe punishment via incarceration length. Therefore, it should be no surprise that in this study, of those offenders who were released during the post-dispositional follow-up period, there was no significant difference between decertified and non-decertified offenders in terms of recidivism for any offense, for a violent offense, or for time to recidivism.

This finding is somewhat contrary to prior research that found greater recidivism on the part of transferred youth, but these studies either used short follow-up periods not exceeding two years (Bishop et al., 1996; Myers, 2001, 2003b; Podkopacz & Feld, 1996) or examined cases that pre-dated the youth violence surge that began in the mid 1980s (Fagan, 1995). In past research that used an extended follow-up period of approximately seven years and examined offenders who were part of the youth violence increase, no difference in recidivism was detected between transferred and non-transferred offenders (Winner et al., 1997). Furthermore, the current research is the first to compare the recidivism of decertified and non-decertified youth processed under legislative waiver. Finally, most of the criminal justice professionals also questioned whether Act 33 deters future offending. They typically stated that it reduces or eliminates reoffending while the inmates are in custody, but were unsure of whether adult court sanctions have any long term deterrent effects once youth are released from secure custody.

It then appears that Act 33 is not achieving its goal of greater specific deterrence. As mentioned earlier, part of the reason for Act 33 being implemented was that the juvenile court was viewed as not being able to properly handle violent youthful offenders. The results of the current research show that in the long run, aside from the limited incapacitation effect achieved, there is no benefit to legislatively waiving these youth to adult court, because they tend to get rearrested at similar rates than their violent counterparts in juvenile court. Moreover, the current incapacitative effect produced through legislative waiver seemingly could (and was) achieved through traditional judicial waiver.

In addition to Act 33 not providing specific deterrence, labeling theory's deviance amplification hypothesis also was not supported. This hypothesis suggests that as a result of being labeled (e.g., being processed in adult court as a "criminal"), more deviance will occur than if the label never was applied (Paternoster and Iovanni, 1989). For this hypothesis to be supported, the results would have showed non-decertified youth recidivating at a significantly higher rate than decertified youth, while controlling for the other factors.

One possible reason for the finding of no significant differences in post-dispositional recidivism, violent recidivism, or time to recidivism may be that youth who are decertified tend to be younger offenders, while youth who remain in adult court tend to be older offenders. If examining recidivism over the long term, while acknowledging shorter incarceration times in juvenile court, many decertified youth will be released (perhaps with little or no supervision or aftercare) and will encounter their crime-prone years during late adolescence and young adulthood, while non-decertified youth are more often exiting those crime-prone years (Blumstein, 1995; Myers, 2001). Therefore, juvenile court offenders would be expected to commit more crime, perhaps offsetting the adverse labeling effect experienced by adult court youth, and allowing the two groups to eventually have similar rates of re-offending in the long run.

A second possible reason for the recidivism findings may be that even though decertified youth are eventually processed in juvenile court, under Act 33 they initially are processed in adult court. The initial label of "adult court criminal" may be strong enough to offset any subsequent actions by the juvenile court for decertified youth. Therefore, because all offenders (both decertified and non-decertified) are given this "criminal" label (and corresponding official criminal history), it may result in their behaviors being similarly amplified according to processes identified by modern labeling theorists (Paternoster and Iovanni, 1989).

Finally, it should be noted that under legislative waiver, the adult court is now receiving and often quickly dismissing "weaker" cases, which likely represent lower-risk youth with less chance of reoffending. These cases previously tended to stay in juvenile court and probably contributed to previous findings of lower recidivism among juvenile court offenders. The adult court also is receiving and keeping high-risk serious and violent offenders who often receive lengthy sentences of incarceration and subsequent parole supervision. Under the current system, the juvenile court appears to be receiving the "middle-risk" cases, which do receive significant attention in terms of conviction and incarceration in juvenile court. However, due to more limited juvenile resources and age/jurisdiction considerations, at-risk decertified offenders may not receive as lengthy of placement and aftercare services as they should, resulting in recidivism at similar or greater levels than non-decertified youth.

Overall, the results from this study suggest that Act 33 does not provide a greater specific deterrent for youth processed in adult court, and it may produce unanticipated deviance amplification effects even for decertified youth. The statute then appears to have no beneficial effects beyond those that could be achieved through traditional judicial waiver. Therefore, policymakers should consider alternatives to this type of law, which will be explored in the next section.

POLICY IMPLICATIONS

In general, the quantitative and qualitative findings from this study suggest that the way Act 33 currently operates is ineffective in increasing offender accountability, reducing recidivism, and increasing public safety. It appears, therefore, that various alternatives should be explored to address this apparent weakness. First, alternatives to the current statute can be considered. Second, prevention programs can be examined that can help prevent youth from entering the justice system and lessen the need to react to serious and violent offending that already has been established.

Alternatives to Legislative Waiver

One possible alternative to the current method, which was expressed by one of the judges, is to increase the maximum age for which the juvenile court can retain jurisdiction over adjudicated delinquents. Currently in Pennsylvania, the juvenile court can retain jurisdiction over youthful offenders until age 21. All of the criminal justice professionals stated that older offenders currently tend to have their decertification petitions denied. If the maximum age of jurisdiction was increased for juvenile court, lengthier treatment could be provided, and criminal court judges may be more likely to decertify cases. As expressed by one of the judges interviewed, there are many "decertified appropriate" youth who may be able to benefit from juvenile court treatment, if there was enough time for proper treatment to take place. However, moving in this direction would not only require an increase in the maximum age for juvenile court jurisdiction, but also a shift in resources to allow for lengthier treatment and supervision.

Another option, which seems more controversial, is to repeal the Act 33 statute all together. First, both quantitative and qualitative results strongly suggest the factors that predict decertification under Act 33 are the same factors that predict transfer under judicial waiver. If juvenile and criminal court judges consider the same factors under both systems of transfer, it seems to make more sense for cases to originate in juvenile court, where greater knowledge of the offender exists, cases can be processed more quickly, and there is a shorter time to punishment and treatment, while still preserving the ability to judicially waive the relatively small number of "most deserving" cases to adult court.

Second, the results from the current study and the findings from prior research suggest that when cases originate in juvenile court, non-transferred youth exhibit significantly lower recidivism than comparable transferred youth, at least in the short term. For cases originating in adult court, there was no significant difference in long-term official recidivism between decertified and non-decertified youth. Therefore, it could be that the legislative waiver method of transfer actually increases the likelihood of recidivism for decertified youth, as compared to what it would have been if they were retained in juvenile court by a juvenile court judge.

Prevention Programs

Aside from changes to the Act 33 statute, other policy implications center on attempting to prevent (or at least delay) the initial onset of delinquent and criminal behavior. Many contemporary prevention programs are focused on the family, community, or school. In general, these programs have goals of improving relationships within families, providing positive activities for youth in the community, and helping students increase their investment and success in school (Sherman, Farrington, Welsh, and MacKenzie, 2002; Wasserman and Miller, 1999). Many of these programs also are based on sound theory and research, and they have been found to be effective in preventing serious and violent juvenile offending.

Several limitations, however, have been uncovered regarding these programs. The main criticism has been that the environments of juveniles consist of many components, encompassing the individual, family, community, and school (Wasserman and Miller, 1999). When programs too narrowly focus on one area, they often are shown empirically to be ineffective in preventing delinquent behavior, because they only are targeting one of many risk factors. As a result, more comprehensive programs have been developed that target a wider variety of risk factors and integrate prevention and intervention efforts with justice system sanctions.

These "comprehensive strategy" programs seek to address the issue of serious and violent offending by juveniles on several dimensions (Howell, 2003). There are two main components of this approach. First, prevention and early intervention programs should be used to assess and target risk factors involving the juvenile, family, school, and community. Again, the goal is to focus on the many areas that ultimately have an influence on subsequent behavior, instead of focusing on just one.

The second component emphasizes graduated sanctions, coupled with appropriate rehabilitation programs (Howell, 2003). In order for these comprehensive strategy programs to work properly, youth do need to be held accountable for their behavior. Therefore, youth who commit acts of delinquency should have sanctions imposed against them. In general, the more serious the offense committed, the greater the sanction, utilizing a graduated system of intermediate punishments and juvenile correctional facilities. However, simply punishing youth is not enough. Providing rehabilitation programs, in addition to punishments, that address specific offender needs has been found to be the most effective approach to reducing or preventing recidivism (Howell, 2003; Sherman et al., 2002). There also should be stronger aftercare programs provided for when youth are released from their sanctions. By having this aftercare in place, positive behavior can be reinforced that was learned in the controlled and structured environment, allowing the youth to apply learned principles when returned to the community.

DIRECTIONS FOR FUTURE RESEARCH

The current study added in several ways to the existing literature surrounding the topic of juvenile transfer to adult court. First, the process and predictors of decertification were examined, which has been an under-researched area of inquiry. Second, while most previous studies compared judicially waived youth to a similar group of offenders retained in juvenile court, the current study examined youth who all initially were waived to adult court. Third, this study provided a comprehensive examination of Act 33, in terms of the certainty, severity, and swiftness of punishment, along with the future criminal offending of youth initially waived under this statute. Finally, through qualitative interviews, views on issues related to Act 33 were revealed by justice system professionals directly involved with the law and the decertification process.

Perhaps the only way to fully establish the effectiveness of juvenile transfer would be to utilize a true experiment, where youthful offenders are randomly assigned to either juvenile or adult court. However, due to political and perhaps ethical concerns, this option does not seem viable. Therefore, in the absence of a randomized experiment, more quasi-experimental and multi-method (i.e., quantitative and qualitative) designs should be employed. Furthermore, unmeasured explanatory factors (e.g., victim injury, offender demeanor and cooperation with authorities) should be explored, statistically controlled, and further assessed in both quantitative and more lengthy and in-depth qualitative research (e.g., extensive courtroom observations, interviews with numerous and diverse justice system professionals). This would allow for greater understanding and stronger conclusions to be made about the impact of court of jurisdiction and other factors on the relevant dependent variables.

Future research also should further explore the area of decertification. A large majority of past studies focused on transfer via judicial waiver. However, few studies have considered legislatively waived youth and compared them based on decertification status. Evidence of the need for further research can be seen in many of the quantitative and qualitative findings, which were sometimes contrary to prior research on the topic of juvenile transfer. In light of the past literature and current transfer policies, there is a great deal of understanding that get to be gained about the effectiveness of juvenile transfer and the decertification process.

Finally, researchers should examine case outcomes and recidivism across transfer mechanisms. In other words, future research should compare legislatively waived offenders (both decertified and non-decertified) with those processed under judicial waiver (both transferred and not transferred offenders). The method by which youth are transferred to adult court may have an effect on important outcomes; put differently, it may not be "transfer" itself, but rather how it is done. Support for this may be found in the current quantitative findings. Prior research on juvenile transfer has been fairly consistent in establishing significant differences between transferred and non-transferred offenders on certain dependent variables. However, when comparing decertified and non-decertified youth, many of those differences were not present. Again, there appears to be a need to compare outcomes and other aspects of the various transfer mechanisms in order to more fully understand the efficacy of waiver policies and practices.

References

Akers, R. L. (2000). *Criminological theories: Introduction, evaluation, and application* (3rd ed.). Los Angeles, CA: Roxbury Publishing Company.

Allison, P. D. (1984). *Event history analysis: Regression for longitudinal event data.* Newbury Park, CA: Sage Publications, Inc.

Barnes, C. W., & Franz, R. S. (1989). Questionably adult: Determinants and effects of the juvenile waiver decision. *Justice Quarterly, 6*(1), 117-135.

Beccaria, C. (1963). *On crimes and punishments.* Indianapolis, IN: Bobbs-Merrill. (Original work published in 1764.)

Becker, H. S. (1963). *Outsiders: Studies in the sociology of deviance.* London. Free Press of Glencoe.

Berk, R. A., Campbell, A., Klap, R., & Western, B. (1992). The deterrent effect of arrest in incidents of domestic violence: A bayesian analysis of four field experiments. *American Sociological Review, 57*, 698-708.

Bernard, T. J. (1992). *The cycle of juvenile justice.* New York: Oxford University Press.

Bishop, D., & Frazier, C. (2000). Consequences of transfer. In J. Fagan, & F. E. Zimring (Eds.), *The changing borders of juvenile justice: Transfer of adolescents to the criminal court* (pp. 227-276). Chicago, IL: The University of Chicago Press.

Bishop, D. M. (2000). Juvenile offenders in the adult criminal justice system. In M. Tonry (Ed.), *Crime and justice: A review of research* (Vol. 27pp. 81-167). Chicago, IL: University of Chicago Press.

Bishop, D. M., & Frazier, C. E. (1991). Transfer of juveniles to criminal court: A case study and analysis of prosecutorial waiver. *Notre Dame Journal of Law, Ethics & Public Policy, 5*, 281-302.

Bishop, D. M., Frazier, C. E., & Henretta, J. C. (1989). Prosecutor waiver: Case study of a questionable reform. *Crime & Delinquency, 35*, 179-201.

Bishop, D. M., Frazier, C. E., Lanza-Kaduce, L., & Winner, L. (1996). The transfer of juveniles to criminal court: Does it make a difference? *Crime & Delinquency, 42*(2), 171-191.

Blumstein, A. (1995). Youth violence, guns, and the illicit-drug industry. *The Journal of Criminal Law and Criminology, 86*(1), 10-36.

Bortner, M. A. (1986). Traditional rhetoric, organizational realities: Remand of juveniles to adult court. *Crime and Delinquency, 32*(1), 53-73.

Brame, R., Paternoster, R., Mazerolle, P., & Piquero, A. (1998). Testing for the equality of maximum likelihood regression coefficients between two independent equations. *Journal of Quantitative Criminology, 14,* 245-261.

Brennan, P. A., & Mednick, S. A. (1994). Learning theory approach to the deterrence of criminal recidivism. *Journal of Abnormal Psychology, 103*(3), 430-440 .

Brown, W. K., Miller, T. P., & Jenkins, R. L. (1987). The favorable effect of juvenile court adjudication of dleinquent youth on the first contact with the juvenile justice system. *Juvenile and Family Court Journal, 38*(3), 21-26.

Brown, W. K., Miller, T. P., Jenkins, R. L., & Rhodes, W. A. (1989). The effect of early juvenile court adjudication on adult outcome. *International Journal of Offender Therapy and Comparative Criminology, 33*(3), 177-183.

Brown, W. K., Miller, T. P., Jenkins, R. L., & Rhodes, W. A. (1991). The human costs of "giving the kid another chance". *International Journal of Offender Therapy and Comparative Criminology, 25*(4), 296-302.

Champion, D. J. (1989). Teenage felons and waiver hearings: Some recent trends, 1980-1988. *Crime and Delinquency, 35*(4), 577-585.

Clarke, E. E. (1996). *A case for reinventing juvenile transfer: The record of transfer of juvenile offenders to criminal court in Cook County, Illinois.* Chicago, IL: Children and Family Justice Center (Northwestern University School of Law).

Clement, M. J. (1997). A five-year study of juvenile waiver and adult sentences: Implications for policy. *Criminal Justice Policy Review, 8*(2-3), 201-219.

Cook, P. J., & Laub, J. H. (1998). The unprecedented epidemic in youth violence. In M. Tonry, & M. H. Moore (Eds.), *Crime and justice: A review of research* (Vol. 24pp. 27-64). Chicago: University of Chicago Press.

Creswell, J. W. (1994). *Research design: Qualitative & quantitative approaches*. Thousand Oaks, CA: Sage Publications.

DeFrances, C. J., & Strom, K. J. (1997). *Juveniles prosecuted in state criminal courts*. (Report No. NCJ-164265). Washington, DC: Bureau of Justice Statistics/Office of Juvenile Justice and Delinquency Prevention.

DeJong, C., & Jackson, K. C. (1998). Putting race into context: Race, juvenile justice processing, and urbanization. *Justice Quarterly, 15*(3), 487-504.

Deng, X. (1997). The deterrent effects of initial sanctions on first-time apprehended shoplifters. *International Journal of Offender Therapy and Comparative Criminology, 41*, 284-297.

Dilulio, J. J. (1995). The coming of the super-predators. *Weekly Standard, 1*, 23-28.

Dilulio, J. J. (1996). They're coming: Florida's youth crime bomb. *Impact,* 25-27.

Dunford, F., Huizinga, D., & Elliot, D. S. (1990). The role of arrest in domestic assault: The Omaha police experiment. *Criminology, 28*, 183-206.

Eigen, J. P. (1981a). The determinants and impact of jurisdictional transfer in Philadelphia. In J. C. Hall, D. M. Hamparian, J. M. Pettibone, & J. L. White (Eds.), *Major issues in the juvenile justice information and training: Readings in public policy* (pp. 333-350). Columbus, OH: Academy for Contemporary Problem.

Eigen, J. P. (1981b). Punishing youth homicide offenders in Philadelphia. *The Journal of Criminal Law and Criminology, 72*(3), 1072-1093.

Empey, L. T., Stafford, M. C., & Hay, C. H. (1999). *American delinquency: Its meaning and construction* (4th ed.). Belmont, CA: Wadsworth Publishing Company.

Fagan, J. (1990). Social and legal policy dimensions of violent juvenile crime. *Criminal Justice and Behavior, 17*(1), 93-133.

Fagan, J. (1995). Separating the men from the boys: The comparative advantage of juvneile versus criminal court sanctions on recidivism among adolescent felony offenders. In J. C. Howell, B. Krisberg, J. D. Hawkings, & J. J. Wilson (Eds.), *A sourcebook: Serious, violent, & chronic juvenile offenders* (pp. 238-260). Thousand Oaks, CA: Sage Publications, Inc.

Fagan, J., & Deschenes, E. P. (1990). Determinants of judicial waiver decisions for violent juvenile offenders. *The Journal of Criminal Law and Criminology, 81*(2), 314-347.

Fagan, J., Forst, M., & Vivona, T. S. (1987). Racial determinants of the judicial transfer decision: Prosecuting violent youth in criminal court. *Crime and Delinquency, 33*(2), 259-286.

Farrington, D. P. (1998). Predictors, causes, and correlates of male youth violence. In M. Tonry, & M. H. Moore (Eds.), *Crime and jusice: A review of research* (Vol. 24pp. 421-475). Chicago: University of Chicago Press.

Farrington, D. P., Osborn, S. G., & West, D. J. (1978). The persistence of labelling effects. *British Journal of Criminology, 18*(3), 277-284.

Farrington, D. P. (1986). Age and crime. In M. Tonry, & N. Morris (Eds), *Crime and justice An annual review of research* (Vol. 7pp. 189-250). Chicago, IL: The University of Chicago Press.

Feld, B. C. (1998). Juvenile and criminal justice systems' responses to youth violence. In M. Tonry, & M. H. Moore (Eds.), *Crime and justice: A review of research* (Vol. 24pp. 189-261). Chicago: University of Chicago Press.

Feld, B. C. (2000). Legislative exclusion of offenses from juvenile court jurisdiction: A history and critique. In J. Fagan, & F. E. Zimring (Eds.), *The changing borders of juvenile justice: Transfer of adolescents to the criminal court* (pp. 83-144). Chicago, IL: The University of Chicago Press.

Feld, B. C. (1995). The social context of juvenile justice administration: Racial disparities in an urban juvenile court. In K. K. Leonard, C. E. Pope, & W. H. Feyerherm (Eds.), *Minorities in juvenile justice* (pp. 66-97). Thousand Oaks, CA: Sage Publications.

Frazier, C. E., & Bishop, D. M. (1995). Reflection of race effects in juvenile justice. In K. K. Leonard, C. E. Pope, & W. H. Feyerherm (Eds.), *Minorities in juvenile justice* (pp. 16-46). Thousand Oaks, CA: Sage Publications, Inc.

Fritsch, E. J., Caeti, T. J., & Hemmens, C. (1996). Spare the needle but not the punishment: The incarceration of waived youth in Texas prisons. *Crime and Delinquency, 42*(4), 593-609.

Gillespie, L. K., & Norman, M. D. (1984). Does certification mean prison: Some preliminary findings from Utah. *Juvenile and Family Court Journal, 35*(13), 23-34.

Gottfredson, D. C., & Barton, W. H. (1993). Deinstitutionalization of juvenile offenders. *Criminology, 31*(4), 591-607.

Griffin, P., Torbet, P., & Szymanski, L. (1998). *Trying juveniles as adults in criminal court: An analysis of state transfer provisions.* (Report No. NCJ

172836). Washington, DC: Office of Juvenile Justice and Delinquency Prevention.

Houghtalin, M., & Mays, G. L. (1991). Criminal dispositions of New Mexico juveniles transferred to adult court. *Crime and Delinquency, 37*(3), 393-407.

Howell, J. C. (1996). Juvenile transfer to the criminal justice system: State of the art. *Law and Policy, 18*(1/2), 17-60.

Howell, J. C. (1997). *Juvenile justice and youth violence.* Thousand Oaks, CA: Sage Publications, Inc.

Howell, J. C. (2003). *Preventing & reducing juvenile delinquency: A comprehensive framework.* Thousand Oaks, CA: Sage Publications, Inc.

Jensen, E. J., & Metsger, L. K. (1994). A test of the deterrent effect of legislative waiver on violent juvenile crime. *Crime and Delinquency, 40*(1), 96-104.

Keiter, R. B. (1973). Criminal or delinquent? A study of juvenile cases transferred to the criminal court. *Crime and Delinquency, 19*, 528-538.

Kinder, K., Veneziano, C., Fichter, M., & Azuma, H. (1995). A comparison of the dispositions of juvenile offenders certified as adults with juvenile offenders not certified. *Juvenile and Family Court Journal, 46*, 37-42.

Klein, M. W. (1986). Labeling theory and delinquency policy: An experimental test. *Criminal Justice and Behavior, 13*(1), 47-79.

Klemke, L. W. (1978). Does apprehension for shoplifting amplify or terminate shoplifting activity? *Law & Society Review, 12*(3), 391-403.

Krisberg, B. (2005). *Juvenile justice: Redeeming our children.* Thousand Oaks, CA: Sage Publications, Inc.

Kurlychek, M. C., & Johnson, B. D. (2004). The juvenile penalty: A comparison of juvenile and young adult sentencing outcomes in criminal court. *Criminology, 42*(2), 485-517.

Kutner, M. H., Nachtsheim, C. J., Neter, J., & Li, W. (2005). *Applied linear statistical models* (5th ed.). New York, NY: McGraw-Hill/Irwin.

Lee, L. (1994). Factors determining waiver in a juvenile court. *Journal of Criminal Justice, 22*(4), 329-339.

Lemert, E. M. (1951). *Social pathology: A systematic approach to the theory of sociopathic behavior.* New York, NY: McGraw Hill.

Lemmon, J. H., Sontheimer, H., & Saylor, K. A. (1991). *A study of Pennsylvania juveniles transferred to criminal court in 1986.* Harrisburg, PA: The Pennsylvania Juvenile Court Judges' Commission.

Leonard, K. K., & Sontheimer, H. (1995). The role of race in juvenile justice in Pennsylvania. In K. K. Leonard, C. E. Pope, & W. H. Feyerherm (Eds.), *Minorities in juvenile justice* (pp. 98-127). Thousand Oaks, CA: Sage Publications, Inc.

Lewis-Beck, M. S. (1980). *Applied regression: An introduction.* Thousand Oaks, CA: Sage Publications, Inc.

Lipton, D., Martinson, R., & Wilks, J. (1975). *The effectiveness of correctional treatment: A survey of treatment evaluation studies.* New York, NY: Praeger Publishers.

Martinson, R. (1974). What works? Questions and answers about prison reform. *The Public Interest, 35*, 22-54.

Matsueda, R. L. (1992). Reflected appraisals, parental labeling, and delinquency: Specifying a symbolic interactionist theory. *American Journal of Sociology, 97*(6), 1577-1611.

Maxwell, J. A. (1996). *Qualitative research design: An interactive approach.* Thousand Oaks, CA: Sage Publications, Inc.

McGuire, M. D. (2002). Cumulative disadvantage as an explanation for observed disproportionality within the juvenile justice system: An empirical test. *Juvenile and Family Court Journal, 53*(1), 1-17.

Merlo, A. V., Benekos, P. J., & Cook, W. J. (1997). "Getting tough" with youth: Legislative waiver as crime control. *Juvenile and Family Court Journal, 48*(3), 1-15.

Menard, S. (2002). *Applied logistic regression analysis* (2nd ed.). Thousand Oaks, CA: Sage Publications, Inc.

Minor, K. I., Hartmann, D. J., & Terry, S. (1997). Predictors of juvenile court actions and recidivism. *Crime and Delinquency, 43*(3), 328-334.

Murray, C. A., & Cox, L. A. (1979). *Beyond probation: Juvenile correctiosn and the chronic delinquent.* Beverly Hills, CA: Sage Publications, Inc.

Myers, D. L. (2001). *Excluding violent youths from juvenile court: The effectiveness of legislative waiver.* New York, NY: LFB Scholarly Publishing LLC.

Myers, D. L. (2003a). Adult crime, adult time: Punishing violent youth in the adult criminal justice system. *Youth Violence and Juvenile Justice: An Interdisciplinary Journal, 1*(2), 173-197.

Myers, D. L. (2003b). The recidivsm of violent youths in juvenile and adult court: A consideration of selection bias. *Youth Violence and Juvenile Justice, 1*(1), 79-101.

Myers, D. L., & Kiehl, K. (2001). The predispositional status of violent youthful offenders: Is there a "custody gap" in adult criminal court? *Justice Research and Policy, 3*(1), 115-143.

Norusis, M. J. (1997). *SPSS professional statistics 7.5*. Chicago, IL: SPSS Inc.

Osbun, L. A., & Rode, P. A. (1984). Prosecuting juveniles as adults: The quest for "objective" decisions. *Criminology, 22*(2), 187-202.

Pate, A. M., & Hamilton, E. E. (1992). Formal and informal deterrents to domestic violence: The Dade County spouse assault experiment. *American Sociological Review, 57*, 691-697.

Paternoster, R., Brame, R., Mazerolle, P., & Piquero, A. (1998). Using the correct statistical test for the quality of regression coefficients. *Criminology, 36*(4), 859-866.

Paternoster, R., & Iovanni, L. (1989). The labeling perspective and delinquency: An elaboration of the theory and an assessment of the evidence. *Justice Quarterly, 6*(3), 359-394.

Paternoster, R., & Piquero, A. (1995). Reconceptualizing deterrence: An empirical test of personal vicarious experiences. *Journal of Research in Crime and Delinquency, 32*(3), 251-286.

Pennsylvania Juvenile Court Judges' Commission. (1996). *The Juvenile Act*. 42 Pa.C.S. Sec. 6301 et seq. Harrisburg, PA: Juvenile Court Judges' Commission.

Platt, A. (1969). *The child savers*. Chicago, IL: University of Chicago Press.

Podkopacz, M. R., & Feld, B. C. (1996). The end of the line: An empirical study of judicial waiver. *The Journal of Criminal Law and Criminology, 86*(2), 449-492.

Poulos, T. M., & Orchowsky, S. (1994). Serious juvenile offenders: Predicting the probability of transfer to criminal court. *Crime and Delinquency, 40*(1), 3-17.

Risler, E. A., Sweatman, T., & Nakerud, L. (1998). Evaluating the Georgia legislative waiver's effectiveness in deterring juvenile crime. *Research on Social Work Practice, 8*(6), 657-667.

Rudman, C., Hartstone, E., Fagan, J., & Moore, M. (1986). Violent youth in adult court: Process and punishment. *Crime and Delinquency, 32*(1), 75-96.

Schneider, A. L., & Ervin, L. (1990). Specific deterrence, rational choice, and decision heuristics: Applications in juvenile justice. *Social Science Quarterly, 71*(3), 585-601.

Shadish, W. R., Cook, T. D., & Campbell, D. T. (2002). *Experimental and quasi-experimental designs for generalized causal inference.* Boston, MA: Houghton Mifflin Company.

Sherman, L. W., & Berk, R. A. (1984). The specific deterrent effects of arrest for domestic assault. *American Sociological* Review, 49(2), 261-272.

Sherman, L. W., Farrington, D. P., Welsh, B. C., & MacKenzie, D. L. (Eds.). (2002). *Evidence-based crime prevention.* New York, NY: Routledge.

Sickmund, M., Snyder, H. N., & Poe-Yamagata, E. (1997). *Juvenile offenders and victims: 1997 update on violence.* (Report No. NCJ-165703). Washington, DC: Office of Juvenile Justice and Delinquency Prevention.

Siegel, L. J., Welsh, B. C., & Senna, J. J. (2003). *Juvenile delinquency: Theory, practice, and law* (8th ed.). Belmont, CA: Wadsworth/Thomas Learning.

Singer, S. I. (1996). *Recriminalizing delinquency: Violent juvenile crime and juvenile justice reform.* New York, NY: Cambridge University Press.

Singer, S. I., & McDowall, D. (1988). Criminalizing delinquency: The deterrent effects of the New York Juvenile Offender Law. *Law & Society Review, 22*(3), 521-535.

Smith, D. A., & Paternoster, R. (1990). Formal processing and future delinquency: Deviance amplification as selection artifact. *Law & Society Review, 24*(5), 1109-1131.

Smith, D. A., & Gartin, P. R. (1989). Specifying specific deterrence: The influence of arrest on future criminal activity. *American Sociological Review, 54*(1), 94-106.

Snyder, H. N., & Sickmund, M. (1999). *Juvenile offenders and victims: 1999 national report.* (Report No. NCJ 178257). Washington, DC: Office of Juvenile Justice and Delinquency Prevention.

Snyder, H. N., Sickmund, M., & Poe-Yamagata, E. (2000). *Juvenile transfers to criminal court in the 1990's: Lessons learned from four studies.* (Report No. NCJ-181301). Washington, DC: Office of Juvenile Justice and Delinquency Prevention.

Snyder, H. N. (1998). *Juvenile Arrests 1997.* (Report No. NCJ 173938). Washington, DC: Office of Juvenile Justice and Delinquency Prevention.

Snyder, H. N. (2002). *Juvenile arrests 2000.* (Report No. NCJ-191729). Washington, DC: Office of Juvenile Justice and Delinquency Prevention.

SPSS advanced statistics 7.5. (1997). Chicago, IL: SPSS Inc.

Sridharan, S., Greenfield, L., & Blakley, B. (2004). A study of prosecutorial certification practice in Virgina. *Criminology & Public Policy, 3*(4), 605-632.

Tanenhaus, D. S. (2000). The evolution of transfer out of the juvenile court. In J. Fagan , & F. E. Zimring (Eds.), *The changing borders of juvenile justice: Transfer of adolescents to the criminal court* (pp. 13-43). Chicago, IL: The University of Chicago Press.

Tannenbaum, F. (1938). *Crime and the community.* New York, NY. Columbia Press University.

Taylor, R. W., Fritsch, E. J., & Caeti, T. J. (2002). *Juvenile justice: Policies, programs, and practices.* Woodland Hills, CA: Glencoe/McGraw-Hill.

Thomas, C. W., & Bilchik, S. (1985). Prosecuting juveniles in criminal courts: A legal and empirical analysis. *The Journal of Criminal Law and Criminology, 76*(2), 439-479.

Thomas, C. W., & Bishop, D. M. (1984). The effect of formal sanctions on delinquency: A longitudinal comparison of labeling and deterrence theories. *The Journal of Criminal Law & Criminology, 75*(4), 1222-1245.

Torbet, P., Gable, R., Hurst, H. I., Montgomery, I., Szymanski, L., & Thomas, D. (1996). *State responses to serious and violent juvenile crime.* (Report No. NCJ-161565). Washington, DC: Office of Juvenile Justice and Delinquency Prevention.

Torbet, P., & Szymanski, L. (1998). *State legislative responses to violent juvenile crime: 1996-97 update.* (Report No. NCJ 172835). Washington, DC: Office of Juvenile Justice and Delinquency Prevention.

Triplett, R. (1993). The conflict perspective, symbolic interactionism, and the status characteristics hypothesis. *Justice Quarterly, 10*(4), 541-558.

Vito, G. F., & Wilson, D. G. (1985). *The American juvenile justice system* (Law and Criminal Justice Series No. 5). Beverly Hills, CA: Sage Publications.

Vold, G. B., Bernard, T. J., & Snipes, J. B. (1998). *Theoretical criminology* (4th ed.). New York, NY: Oxford University Press.

Ward, D. A., & Tittle, C. R. (1993). Deterrence or labeling: The effects of informal sanctions. *Deviant Behavior: An Interdisciplinary Journal, 14*(1), 43-64.

Wasserman, G. A., & Miller, L. S. (1999). The prevention of serious and violent juvenile offending. In R. Loeber , & D. P. Farrington (Eds.), *Serious & violent juvenile offenders: Risk factors and successful interventions* (pp. 197-247). Thousand Oaks, CA: Sage Publications, Inc.

Wellford, C. (1975). Labeling theory and criminology: An assessment. *Social Problems, 22*, 332-345.

Winner, L., Lanza-Kaduce, L., Bishop, D. M., & Frazier, C. E. (1997). The transfer of juveniles to criminal court: Reexamining recidivism over the long term. *Crime and Delinquency, 43*(4), 548-563.

Wooldredge, J. D. (1988). Differentiating the effects of juvenile court sentences on eliminating recidivism. *Journal of Research in Crime and Delinquency, 25*(3), 264-300.

Wordes, M., Bynum, T. S., & Corley, C. J. (1994). Locking up youth: The impact of race on detention decisions. *Journal of Research in Crime and Delinquency, 31*(2), 149-165.

Zimring, F. E. (1998). *American youth violence*. New York, NY: Oxford University Press, Inc.

Index